HOW THE LIGHT GETS IN

Also by Pat Schneider

POETRY

White River Junction
Long Way Home
Olive Street Transfer
The Patience of Ordinary Things
Another River: New and Selected Poems

NONFICTION

Writing Alone and with Others
The Writer as an Artist
In Our Own Voices: Writings by Women
 in Low-Income Housing (Ed.)

PLAYS

The Undertaking
After the Applebox
A Question of Place
Berries Red
Dream: The Musical

LIBRETTI

The Lament of Michal
Autumn Setting
My Holy Mountain (Oratorio)
I Have a Dream (Oratorio)

HOW THE LIGHT
GETS IN

Writing as a Spiritual Practice

PAT SCHNEIDER

OXFORD
UNIVERSITY PRESS

OXFORD

UNIVERSITY PRESS

Oxford University Press is a department of the
University of Oxford. It furthers the University's objective
of excellence in research, scholarship, and education
by publishing worldwide.

Oxford   New York

Auckland   Cape Town   Dar es Salaam   Hong Kong   Karachi
Kuala Lumpur   Madrid   Melbourne   Mexico City   Nairobi
New Delhi   Shanghai   Taipei   Toronto

With offices in

Argentina   Austria   Brazil   Chile   Czech Republic   France   Greece
Guatemala   Hungary   Italy   Japan   Poland   Portugal   Singapore
South Korea   Switzerland   Thailand   Turkey   Ukraine   Vietnam

Oxford is a registered trade mark of Oxford University Press
in the UK and certain other countries.

Published by Oxford University Press
198 Madison Avenue, New York, NY 10016
www.oup.com

Library of Congress Cataloging-in-Publication Data
Schneider, Pat, 1934–
How the light gets in : writing as a spiritual practice /
Pat Schneider.
pages   cm
ISBN 978-0-19-993396-9 (hardback)   ISBN 978-0-19-993398-3 (pbk.)
1. Creative writing—Religious aspects.   I. Title.
PN171.R45.S36 2013
801—dc23
2012044749

1 3 5 7 9 8 6 4 2

Printed in the United States of America
on acid-free paper

Ring the bells that still can ring
Forget your perfect offering
There is a crack in everything
That's how the light gets in.

Leonard Cohen,
"Anthem"

CONTENTS

POEM: THE FISH

POEM: THAT ONE

POEM: CONFESSION

POEM: BLESSING FOR A WRITER

PREFACE

JOURNAL ENTRY

(Undated, as I was beginning to write this book.)

This time I want to find my way, explore my way, take my time. I want more than I have ever asked of myself before. Maybe it requires a silence and a centering that I have not yet—in my whole life really—given myself.

I'm not after poems this time. I'm not out to teach, either. I want to go for the big one, the presence—the Presence—the mystery, the Beloved. I want to explore, go into the cave, go up against the wall, go all the way. And there's nothing that does not act as a door, if I open it. The shock of hearing that R.M., a beautiful young woman in one of my workshops, was stabbed fourteen times, is a doorway through which I come face to face with the unnamable. But so is the beauty of a carrot, cut by my own hands into rounds on my kitchen counter— rings within rings, a minor universe in orange.

When I was a child . . .

This time I want to go for the big one. Some people in Missouri wade into deep water, reach far back into underwater caves in the river banks, catch huge catfish in their bare hands, pull them out alive. Something wild, something hidden, human hands reaching for that wildness, touching it. What does it mean—our violence, our hunger, our need?

Where is the big one now, now that I am seventy and have survived four fractured vertebrae, a fractured coccyx, a fractured wrist, and a fractured hip? Now that I have survived being in the church and survived leaving the church, survived poverty and the privilege of education, now that I am an old woman with memories of love, aware of my own addictions and betrayals, now that I am myself a history written in blood and bone, broken and healed and broken again? Where is the Presence?

It is where it has always been: in the hard, inedible peach in the worn-out orchard of memory; in the white chicken feather caught in the wire fence, blowing in the wind of a long ago place and time; in the cluttered apartment where a young woman I have mentored and taught and fiercely protected offers the inside of her elbow to the needle that shoots heroin into her vein.

The Presence is in the lily, oh, yes. It is in the altar cloth and the crucifix, in the minaret and the yarmulke and the shawl, in the Hebrew/Aramaic/Greek/Latin/English Bible, in the sacred stories, pictographs, dances, and other rituals of native peoples, in the Holy Koran and in the sayings of the Buddha.

It is in the grave with my lost mother, my lost father. It is in the great hidden catfish, the crawdad, the dolphin, the comet, the grandmother, the grandfather, the stories we live and the stories we imagine. It is in the light that brushes a strand of hair on the head of my granddaughter, my grandson.

The Presence is mystery. It is breath. It breathes, and I feel its breath on my hand as I write the words: This time I want to go for the big one.

—P.S.

HOW THE LIGHT GETS IN

Introduction: What Has No Name

Beyond the name there lies what has no name.
—JORGE LUIS BORGES, tr. Richard Wilbur

Those colors which have no name... are the real foundation of everything.
—VINCENT VAN GOGH

I SIT WRITING THESE WORDS in an old library in Berkeley, California. Around me, Gothic windows let in California sunlight, and if I were to walk outside, the Golden Gate Bridge would be visible in the distance. Pacific School of Religion is a founding member of the Graduate Theological Union, a consortium of theological schools that share a common library for several Protestant, Catholic, Jewish, Moslem, Buddhist, and other centers of study, offering traditional histories of theology and also curricula that include Black studies, Gay and Lesbian studies, and women's studies in religion. It was here at age twenty-one that I came to study, and it is here at age seventy-one that I have come back to teach.

At twenty-one I came here in trouble. My family was broken, my mother mentally ill, my brother in prison. He and I had spent our early childhood in rural Missouri, then lived in an orphanage and in the slums of St. Louis. I loved him with all my heart; I had traveled to the west coast as soon as I graduated from college in Missouri to try to help him. But there was nothing I could do. Without my applying for it, I was given a full scholarship to Pacific School of Religion.

In this rich and diverse theological environment, I was in many ways healed and set free to become the person I am now. This year I have returned to teach the summer courses in creative writing that I have taught for more than twenty years on this campus that I love.

Recently, as I was thinking about two of the dominant themes of my life—spirituality and creative writing—it occurred to me that when I begin to write, I open myself and wait. And when I turn toward an inner spiritual awareness, I open myself and wait. That insight made me want to think more deeply about the relationship between creative writing and conscious spiritual practice. This book is the result. It is not a manual nor a "how-to"—it is an exploration.

The first stumbling block was language. Writing requires the use of words, and words always carry, or fail to carry, *particular* human experience. The words that I choose to use to name that which is ultimately unnamable come out of my own individual human experience.

Poets everywhere, I imagine—certainly Hebrew, Muslim and Christian poets—have written of the difficulty in trying to name deity. Writers of ancient Hebrew sacred texts used "YHVH" (pronounced most often as "Yahweh" or "Jehovah") but warned against saying the name out loud. Devout Jews use words that refer to the name, but are not the name: "Hashem" (*the name*) in speaking, and where ten or more are gathered for prayer, "Adonai." Joy Harjo, one of America's foremost Native American voices, writing about a character named Lila, says this:

> Some say God is a murderer for letting children and saints slip through his or her hands. Some call God a father of saints or a mother of demons. Lila had seen God, and could tell you God was neither male nor female and made of absolutely everything of beauty, of wordlessness.
>
> This unnameable thing of beauty is what shapes a flock of birds who know exactly when to turn together in flight in the winds used to make words. Everyone turns together though we may not see each other stacked in the invisible dimensions.[1]

Rabi'a al 'Adawiyya (712–801 C.E.), a Sufi saint sometimes called Rabia of Basra or Rabia al Basri, was born to a poor family in what is now Iraq. Her parents died of famine, and she was eventually sold into slavery. After she was freed, Rabi'a chose a solitary life of prayer, living much of her life in desert seclusion. Her fame as a Sufi holy woman spread, and people began to journey to her retreat, to ask advice, to study, to learn. Today she is greatly revered by devout Muslims and mystics throughout the world. She wrote this poem, in which "He" and "my Beloved" refer to the object of her mystical experience:

IT WORKS

Would you come if someone called you
by the wrong name?

I wept, because for years He did not enter my arms;
then one night I was told a
secret:

Perhaps the name you call God is
not really His, maybe it
is just an alias.

I thought about this, and came up with a pet name
for my Beloved I never mention
to others.

All I can say is—
it works![2]

The act of naming the divine is what ties Rabi'a's earthly life to her God. Like many people, both ancient and contemporary, I stumble when I try to name the presence I encounter at the heart of my own spiritual experience. For example, because my own mother suffered a form of untreated mental illness that harmed my brother and me, I cannot find comfort in the phrase "Mother God" or the word "Goddess." What is more, because my father abandoned us, the words "Father God" do not give me a feeling of trust.

I can, of course, intellectually set aside those deep associations, but feelings have a deeper hold on us than our mental constructs. Changing our minds does not always change our feelings. Other words, like "spirit," "mystery," and "pray" do work for me, but might not hold the same meaning for another person. When we humans dare to approach the deepest and most holy experiences of our lives, all language becomes metaphor. For now I will write using a word, lowercase, that means to me that-which-is-unnamable: *mystery*.

Each person's relationship with mystery is as unique as our relationships with those we love. Instinctively, we speak about the one we love in concrete terms, telling a story, allowing the listener to see and hear images. When we want to tell about falling in love, we tell it in concrete terms: *We met on a street corner, in the rain. We ran to a bistro where we stood under an awning. We talked about the weather, and we laughed as water ran off our hair, down our noses.* Similarly, speaking or writing about *mystery* requires concrete image and story.

In my own stories about spiritual experience, just as in the stories I received as a child, the truth, if there is truth, is seen "through a glass, darkly."[3] To me, this means that no matter how deeply or widely we study, there is always more to be seen, and no one sees all that there is to see. I do not believe there is or ever has been anyone who knows all there is to know. There is not and never has been a belief system that holds exclusive truth. There is no book that contains all of the truth. But there is spirit, there are wise men and wise women, there is story, art, theater, music, and dance. There is metaphor, there is holiness, there is mystery.

All of us live in relation to mystery, and becoming conscious of that relationship can be a beginning point for a spiritual practice—whether we experience mystery in nature, in ecstatic love, in the eyes of our children, our friends, the animals we love, or in more strange experiences of intuition, synchronicity, or prescience.

Writing can be a spiritual practice. To write about what is painful is to begin the work of healing. To write the red of a tomato before it is mixed into beans for chili is a form of praise. To write an image of a child caught in war is confession or petition or requiem. To write grief onto a page of lined paper until tears blur the ink is often the surest access to giving or receiving forgiveness. To write a comic scene is grace and beatitude. To write irony is to seek justice. To write admission of failure is humility. To be in an attitude of praise or thanksgiving, to rage against God, or to open one's inner self and listen, is prayer. To write tragedy and allow comedy to arise between the lines is miracle and revelation.

Throughout my life, as my spiritual experience and my theological understanding have developed, my experiences and understanding of writing have grown with me. Recently I have realized that they are deeply connected and together form the path my life has taken. Now I have entered my seventies. Age brings with it new awareness, new opportunity, new challenge. Writing is for me the surest way to find out where I am and to open the gate to where I might go next. It is time to pick up the central threads and see how they weave together. And so I have taken upon myself this task: to give voice to what has been growing within me, a conviction that writing itself can open into mystery.

SOMETIMES WRITING

Sometimes writing sits in you
like a wild animal. Maybe
you see its eyes.
Maybe you don't see it at all,
but the hair on the back of your neck
knows it is there
where the deepest shadows lie.
Often the shadows lie
about what's hiding in them.

The panther that has stalked you
since you were a child
is old now. No longer wild,
and tired of guarding the treasure
you yourself left behind—
blind and deaf, she will give it all to you
if you just let her go.

But how are you to know
whether the fox on the hill
in the cemetery carries your mother's name
or is the same fox you saw
crossing your back yard in the snow

unless you put your pen to paper
and use it to release the animal
that hides in the shadow of your hand?

—P.S.

CHAPTER **1**

There Is a Spirit

… a Spirit is manifest in the Laws of the Universe
—ALBERT EINSTEIN

EINSTEIN SAYS THERE IS "a Spirit manifest in the Laws of the Universe." By "the Laws" I assume he means everywhere—within us as well as out there where "the morning stars sing together," as an ancient poet said. If there is a Spirit, do the morning stars sing together inside us, too? And can we sing to the Spirit? Can we communicate with it? Does it communicate with us? Is it "manifest" only in universal "Laws," or does it meet us personally? Can we pray? Are we heard? Does it answer? Do we hear?

There is a tale of a rabbi who was famous for his great prayers. One day, after a particularly brilliant display of his public praying, an angel appeared and told him that he was doing fairly well, but a man in a nearby village was better at praying. The rabbi went in search of the man and found him to be an illiterate tradesman. The rabbi asked, "How did you pray on the last holy day?"

The man told him that he couldn't even read—he only knew the first ten letters of the alphabet—so he felt inadequate to pray. "So I said to God, 'All I have are these ten letters; take them and combine them however you want so that they smell good to you.'"[1]

To pray is to open oneself completely, intimately, into the Presence that is beyond our ability to name. And we have so few letters! And the ones we have are sometimes very confusing. The poet William Wordsworth said a newborn child comes "trailing clouds of glory." He did not say, but it is true, that a newborn comes also trailing clouds of genetic material and family history: clouds of tradition, ritual, prejudice, and resistance to difference or change. Growing to maturity requires an incredible balancing act if we are to live at peace with our own portion of letters among the many alphabets, the many understandings of mystery. Both writing and praying are acts of deep vulnerability. It is so easy for us to mistrust our own ten letters of the alphabet. But if we do not reach into inner *and* outer space—for morning stars sing together in both— we may miss the most exquisite relationship human life offers.

I began to learn my own "ten letters" from my mother, Lelah Ridgway, who had roots in rural American conservative fundamentalism. As an adult I learned more in urban liberal churches, in a brief but meaningful sojourn with the Quakers, and finally outside organized religious practice. Although my *understanding* of spirituality has changed throughout my life, the central *experience* has not changed: There has been for me a deep and a continual sense of presence, and there have been experiences of meeting, or encounter, with that presence. Because of my own place in time and the tradition out of which I come, I use the word "prayer" for that meeting of the human mind with what I am calling "the mystery." That, too, has a deep history. Caddo people call God/Spirit "The Great Mysterious" and Muscogee people "The Master of Breath." In the Hebrew tradition, Yahweh's self-identification as "I am" refuses any reduction to a name.

The word "prayer" evokes strong feelings for many people, depending on past experience—positive for some of us, negative for others. Any other word that I might choose—"contemplation," "meditation"—would come with its own set of varying reactions, and so I choose the word that I have used since childhood: *prayer*. Prayer is, for me, an intentional openness to the presence of mystery in my life. Sometimes it is labor, sometimes ecstatic surprise. Sometimes both.

* * *

When we write deeply—that is, *when we write what we know and do not know we know*—we encounter mystery. Similarly, when we pray deeply, we encounter mystery. In writing, that encounter is sometimes described as a creative spark, the sudden emergence of an image, word, or idea that the writer recognizes as full of meaning. It doesn't happen all the time.

Andrew Fetler, one of my MFA professors at the University of Massachusetts, was fond of saying that writing is "bull labor." Well, yes, it can be. On the other hand, there are those times when writing—*good* writing, powerful writing—comes up in us and out onto our pages as an artesian spring, flowing without effort. So it is with prayer, as well. Sometimes prayer begins with a petition on my part, gentle or desperate—even "labor." Stanley Moss, an American poet who has "argued with God" through a lifetime of writing, begins his poem "Psalm" with "God of paper and writing, God of first and last drafts..." and ends it with, "My Shepherd, I want, I want, I want."[2] The "wanting" can be desperate, as when Emily Dickinson wrote about losing those she most loved, "Twice have I stood a beggar/ Before the door of God."[3]

But there are times, both in pain and in pleasure, when communication seems to be initiated from outside myself. Those times come as surprise—often with an element of strangeness—a breaking-in of a profound and unexpected Presence.

Writing, too, has both of those dimensions. Often it begins as labor: the difficult act of getting my posterior onto my chair and my fingers around the pen or onto the keyboard. Then the difficult labor of *staying there*. But sometimes, too, writing breaks in, begins somewhere deeper than conscious thought. Either way, when writing or praying truly happens, I have a sense of hovering over a deep, dark interior of memory and imagination. Ira Progoff, in his *Intensive Journal Workshops,*[4] suggests a writing exercise where the writer imagines a well, sees the dark water in the well, and invites an image to rise to the surface. Then he asks the writer to write about the image, or what it suggests. He is talking, of course, about accessing the subconscious, the dwelling-place of memory and imagination.

In writing and in prayer we are essentially alone in the presence of mystery, regardless of whether we have companions around us. The inner journey is one we walk alone, as the old gospel song says: *You've got to walk that lonesome valley. You've got to walk it by yourself. Ain't nobody else can walk it for you, you've got to walk it by yourself.*

In her book, *The Last Report on the Miracles at Little No Horse,* Louise Erdrich tells the story of a woman who spends her life disguised as a priest, serving in a remote Ojibwe village. Near the end of her life, Father Damien (Agnes) practices her sermon by speaking aloud to a congregation of snakes that lives under the rock upon which she has built her church. She begins, "What is the question we spend our entire lives asking?" and answers, "Our question is this: Are we loved? I don't mean by one another." She closes her sermon to the snakes with these words: "I am like you, curious and small. Like you, I pause alertly and open my senses to try to read the air, the clouds, the sun's slant, the little movements of the animals, all in the hope I will learn the secret of whether I am loved."[5]

I want to be, in my writing and in my prayer, where Father Damien is at the end of her life: naked of assumption and honest in my questions, before the mystery I cannot know or even name.

*   *   *

Beginning to write is an intentional, particular, inner act; usually it seems like turning toward something unknown in my mind—an inward looking, listening. A clearer metaphor might be fishing. I go fishing in my mind. I put out bait, the bait of my own longing, my desire, and my hunger for connection, for a tug of something alive at the end of a line. Something that I may have to struggle with to pull in, but that will be wild and important to me, whether I keep it or let it go. In writing, my desire is for the flash of recognition, the image that I only partly glimpse, but recognize as a glimmer of something worth trying to capture in words on my page.

One day this week I felt sluggish and unable to write. I held my pen above my page, but I could not focus my attention. It strikes me that such moments are like casting or dangling a line with the wrong kind of bait. I wanted a successful bit of writing. Wrong bait.

I began three miserable attempts, and each was wooden, lifeless. I crossed each one out in turn, and then somehow became quieter in my mind—a deeper desiring, a less frantic desiring. It's like those times when you can't remember a name, and you try and try, and then more or less give up, and the name floats effortlessly into your mind. I think it has to do with cooperating with the unconscious rather than trying to beat it into submission. My pen was still poised above my page, but I quit trying. Suddenly I thought, *tonight, words are turtles.*

That may not seem very promising, but I love turtles. I grew up with them in the Ozark Mountains where a box turtle is a child's most common experience of wild animals. They are just the right size for a five-year-old to pick up and hold in both hands. *Tonight, words are turtles.* Experience has taught me to recognize the tiny jolt of joy that tells me a phrase or an image is worth pursuing. So I wrote quickly, with only one glitch:

> *Tonight, words are turtles*
> *sleeping under mud.*
> *Even when I poke them*
> *they will not wake up.*
> *Leave us alone,*
> *their silence says.*
> *When we decide to surface,*
> *we will tell you what we dreamed.*

The glitch was in the sixth line. I wrote "their silence says," and later changed it to "their closed shells say" to make it more concrete, more visual. However, I read it to one of my daughters, and she responded with, "I like 'silence' better." So perhaps there was no glitch at all.

Or there was. It doesn't matter. Either way, I like that little poem. It's an honest expression of where I was in that moment. Even the colloquial word "poke" I like, because it reinforces the voice that first said, "words are turtles," a voice closer to my early Ozark beginnings than to my later New England life. More important, after writing those words, I was able to go on writing about something else. I got to my writing by fishing. By again and again dropping the bait of my desire, waiting and listening.

* * *

When I consciously initiate prayer, my experience is very much like consciously beginning to write. I open a door in my mind, and on the energy of my desire, I reach out into mystery. Isn't this what we do when we fall in love—reach out with longing, with desire? Writing and prayer are both a form of love, and love takes courage.

Frequently what comes in response to my reaching out for writing is not a phrase—not words at all, but an image. Sometimes I refuse to accept the first image that comes to mind; I reject it and fish for something more familiar. Or, if I know well the monster that lives under the surface of my own mind's deep water, and can't bear it right then, I may reel in the line and go where the fish are more familiar, less frightening. Such refusal blocks my writing. Where the greatest dangers lie, the greatest artistry also lies. If I refuse the delicate image that beckons me to take it, I am left with only the frustrated static of attempting to write something out of nothing. Over time, with practice, I have come to know that difference. Stopping and starting again, sometimes several times, I am usually now able to recognize and take the first image that surprises me—no matter how inconsequential. It may lead me to another image, and another, writing as Gertrude Stein advises, "Begin and begin again," taking each beginning as a bread crumb on the forest path, until I find my way home. That's where we want to be— that place where effort ends and writing flows.

Sometimes we are not ready, are not able, to muster enough courage or enough honesty to accept the image or phrase that is given. For example, in writing my autobiographical book, *Wake Up Laughing,* I refused over and over again one image, refused it so deeply that I didn't even know I had seen it many times in my mind, until finally I began to write it. The image was a bed—the bed where I slept in the tenement apartment when I returned home from the orphanage at age thirteen. That bed was too painful, too shameful, too long held in secret, to write about. But when the entire book was written, something was missing, not an insignificant detail—more like the keystone in an arch. Instantly upon recognizing that something was missing, I knew what it was. I gathered my courage, wrote about the bed, put it where it belonged in the middle of the book, and the book was done.

Far more than praying on my knees in my childhood and youth, writing has demanded of me honesty, courage, listening, and waiting. Putting pen to paper has become my most essential spiritual practice, my most effective prayer. That is not to say that writing is my only prayer, or that all of my writing is prayer. But more and more, the two acts have merged. I reach writing through an act of waiting and listening: I make false starts; I get in my own way; I try again. Putting words onto paper—when it is done as an honest act of search or connection, rather than as an act of manipulation, performance, self-aggrandizement or self-protection—is a holy act. The desired communication may be with the self, with a known or unknown reader, or with something or someone beyond the self in the realm of what we might call "the spiritual." Or with all three.

When I achieve true waiting, true listening, something happens that I experience as a gift. Whether it comes from my own subconscious reservoir or from outside myself makes no difference to me. If I am a creature made in the image of God—and I do accept the teaching of ancient Hebrew prophets and poets that in fact I am so created, and the teaching of some theologians that *all* of creation, even the rock and the turnip, is an image of God—then the creature that I am partakes in the holiness of the creator. If I am made in the image of the creator, then I am myself a creator, and my acts of creating participate in mystery.

That's a pretty astounding thought. If it's true, how can I so often undervalue my own creativity, and the creativity of every person—even the creativity of the most humble of creatures? How the earthworm poops and feeds the zinnia; how the zinnia feeds the bee; how the bee feeds me! Mystery, everywhere!

The mystery into which I "go fishing," or into which I open a mental door when I write, is not alien or frightening, even though what comes up may be. I will say more about this later. For now, it is enough to say that like anyone who fishes, I am free to reel in the line and try again on another day.

*   *   *

A contemporary theologian, Catherine Keller, has drawn attention to the Hebrew word *Tehom*, "the deep," in Genesis 1:2. The entire verse reads, "The earth was without form and void, and darkness was upon the face of the deep; and the Spirit of God was moving over the face of the waters."[6]

Writing, when it is soul work, is creative, and if what I believe is true—that we are "made in the image of God"—then we, too, as creators, may brood upon the waters of our own "deep." The human mind is vast; its edges open out into the vastness of the mystery that is beyond the physical dimensions of the brain. Emily Dickinson says, "The Brain is just the weight of God."[7] Both the biblical text and Dickinson here invite me to think not about "union" with the mystery, but *meeting*. Relationship. And yet, that meeting is intensely intimate, often secret, and closer than any other relationship. Meister Eckardt says, "The eye with which I see God is the same eye with which [God] sees me."[8] Yet that "seeing" is not necessarily visual. As Joy Harjo says, "we may not see each other stacked in the invisible dimensions." Our inner seeing tends to be "through a glass, darkly," or in metaphor (Moses' burning bush, Flannery O'Connor's ragged figure behind a tree). Moses, the ancient text tells us, was put by God into a cleft of the rock and told, "You may see my back, but my face shall not be seen."[9] An anonymous English monk in the late fourteenth century, in awe before the presence of mystery, counseled spiritual pilgrims to accept—even dwell in—"The Cloud of Unknowing."[10]

To open a door in one's mind, whether in writing, in prayer, or in writing-as-prayer, is to invite an experience of "the deep." It is rather like standing on the edge of a cliff overlooking the ocean at night, a cliff from which I can hear the pounding surf below me, and see in the distance a multitude of stars. I am aware of danger, but I am also aware of my own freedom and my own good sense. Although I could do so, I will not back up, close down, and refuse to see or hear. Although I could do so, I will not step out and lose myself. I will not fall to my death. I will stand where I am, and allow the vast expanse to come to me through my eyes, through my ears, through wind moving the tiny hairs on my skin, through the pressure of the solid rock against the soles of my feet. I feel awe, I feel my own smallness, but I feel that I, too, belong. If I am open to the possibility, I sense that I am seen; I am known; I am held in the attention of the mystery.

I asked two friends from quite different Christian communities to read this chapter. One friend is an Episcopal priest. The other is a leader in the Seventh-Day Adventist Church. They were both stopped by my refusal here to step over the cliff, and asked about the spiritual experience of complete self-giving. "There is a kind of death, I think," my Episcopal friend said, "death of autonomous ego." And my Seventh-Day Adventist friend said, "Yes, but I love the story about having faith enough to jump, knowing that the wind will rise up to meet you."

These questions will haunt me through the writing of the chapters that lie ahead, and only near the very end will I understand what lies under them for me. Rumi famously said, "There are hundreds of ways to kneel and kiss the ground." I'm pretty certain there are more than "hundreds." I suspect there are as many variations on experience of mystery as there are human persons; in fact, each person throughout a lifetime has variations of experience, and given the magnitude of mystery, it is probable that even the most learned among us have "only the first ten letters of the alphabet."

TO BREAK SILENCE

To break silence
is to shatter the glass
invisible

wall

between the waters of dreams
and the waters of waking
in the blue and green denial
of connection.

To break silence
is to be on the far side
of the gate to the garden of origin

fallen

to consciousness,
angel and flaming sword
held against the possibility
of innocence.

To break silence
is to take upon oneself the burden
of one's name

called

nothing now derivative,
it is to turn, to face the Presence
in the primal wilderness
of creation.

—P.S.

CHAPTER 2

Prayer

... finally to unfold again
as if never before
is to be the prayer.
—MARK NEPO, Sufi poet

THE FIRST TIME I RETURNED to Pacific School of Religion (PSR), seven years after I had been a graduate student there, it was to write and direct their centennial play. My beloved theology professor, Dr. Hugh Vernon White, had lost his wife to Parkinson's disease. The lectures of this gentle, aging man had fallen on my ears like poetry, and I had wished he were the father I'd never had. When I returned to PSR, I invited him to my apartment for coffee and asked, "Dr. White, now that your wife has died, what can you tell me about death?" He bent over his cup, his white hair a gentle aura around his head, and thought about it. When he spoke, he spoke slowly. "Sometimes someone we love moves away from us even before they die, but they do not move out of the attention of God. God's love is his attention."

"God's love is God's attention." Maybe it is because the word "love" is overused, or maybe it is simply because I loved Dr. White so much, but his word, "attention," helped me to understand my own experience in prayer. I feel held in the attention—the *companionable* attention of mystery.

I am talking about an encounter with a mystery so profound we can have no name adequate to it. But it is personal. It is intimate. It is "closer than breathing, and nearer than hands and feet."[1]

And it is companionable. Even if I don't have "alphabet" enough to speak its name, it knows me by heart.

Perhaps the most stunning experience I have ever had in prayer will illustrate what I mean. When my husband, Peter, asked me to marry him, I was surprised. We had known one another only three months, both of us graduate students at Pacific School of Religion. I had been "proposed to" before, but this was different, and I wasn't sure why. I was thrown into what I can only describe as *fear and trembling*. It was 1957, long before "nice young people" lived together to test their relationship.

My distress was not caused by Peter, but by my family of origin. My mother was living in two small, furnished rooms where she had landed after traveling from Missouri to California to find my brother, Sam. She had been in San Francisco for several months, but she had never unpacked the boxes and suitcases that held everything she owned in the world. The orphanage that Sam had been in would not keep him after age seventeen; the director had advised our mother to sign for him to enter the army. He was already an alcoholic, in maximum security prison before he was twenty because he walked away from the army.

A few days after Peter proposed, I went to Dr. Robert Leslie, the professor of Pastoral Psychology at Pacific School of Religion. I wept so hard I could barely talk. Finally I choked out the words, "I will destroy Peter. My family is a mess. I lived in an orphanage when I was a kid; I had no father; my brother is in jail. I don't know how to be a wife and mother. I will destroy him."

Dr. Leslie listened quietly, and replied, "Pat, given where you have come from, and what you have been through, you are not weak. You are very strong."

He said more, but that's what I remember, and what at some level I knew to be true. Still, I couldn't decide, and so I prayed. Intensely, privately, I begged for an answer. Only twice before in my life I had prayed like this, once when I was a little child and once when I was nineteen, and each time in different ways, I finally broke through to what was for me a sudden, clear answer. But this time, nothing happened.

I was on full alert for some time, watching Peter. He held in his body and in his spirit a kind of silent patience that I found deeply reassuring. One evening he sat on the floor in a room crowded with students and listened as we all responded to a theological idea that Dr. White had presented. As the discussion wore on, Peter didn't say a word. Then, as we were drawing the questions to a close, he spoke. His voice was beautiful—rich and deep. More than that, his words were gentle, free of pretension, and wise. "Is it possible…," Peter said, and asked a question that seemed to sum up and resolve our discussion. After he spoke, we were all silent, as if there was nothing more to say. I was stunned by his insight and restraint.

I prayed, then, even more intensely. I begged for a specific answer: Shall I marry him, or not? No "feeling" would do. I needed absolute clarity, and I asked for it, over and over again. Suddenly in my mind, words addressed me as clearly as if a person next to me, older and wiser than I, had spoken them, kindly, but firmly. *I will bless you if you do, and I will bless you if you don't.*

The shock was intense. I had no doubt that the discussion was closed. I had my answer, but it was not at all what I had expected. All I was asking for was *Yes* or *No*. What I was given was freedom and responsibility.

* * *

Surprise is a major factor in distinguishing an answer to prayer from a projection of my own mental processes. When I can't believe I made up the answer myself, I have to look around to see where it came from. Maybe it does, in fact, come up from the swirl and complexity of the unconscious, the way writing surfaces. That's O.K. The mystery abides there, too.

I was talking with my longest-time friend, Evelyn May, about this, and she told me her story of a surprising answer. Ev is a person who has lived in dialogue with mystery. Like me, she has wrestled with it all the way from her fundamentalist beginnings. And she has wrestled mystery out to the edges of possibilities a bit more strange than I myself have entertained. But she has never wavered from her relationship to what she still calls comfortably "God." As her husband lay dying in his late thirties of juvenile diabetes, she begged God for a sign. Over and over, in various moods, some of them angry—"Just give me a *sign* that you are there. All I'm asking is a sign. You've given them so many times to other people—why won't you give me a sign? Why won't you? Why won't you?" Finally, she said, the answer came. *Because you don't need it.*

This is not a rational or a logical matter—it is experience. I—like Ev, like uncounted multitudes in uncounted persuasions—*experience* a response to intense prayer. I experience it as communication from a mystery beyond myself that holds me in loving and companionable attention. Not necessarily "warm and fuzzy" attention, but a sense of having been heard—seriously, and intimately.

Mary Beth Toomey, a friend whose Quaker practice I deeply respect, told me that in these experiences she feels, too, "the deep knowledge of safety—being beloved, no matter what."

Yes, that, too.

* * *

As it happened, I married a funny man. Once I asked him to build a bird feeding station attached to the house outside my study window. He did it, complete with feeder, suet holder, branch of a tree stuck in a flag-pole holder, and landing platform exactly at the height of my desk, only inches from the intended birds. Four days passed, and no birds. I bemoaned that fact, often. Suddenly one day Peter was lurking around my study, sitting in my easy chair, practically twiddling his thumbs—all very un-Peter-like behavior. Finally he asked in an innocent tone of voice, "Any birds yet?"

I glanced at the feeder. There was a small, garishly yellow bird. Peter had gone to Eugenie Stacey's yard, next door. He had stolen her stuffed toy canary from her dwarf maple tree, climbed a ladder, and attached it to my bird feeder. Unfortunately, its little wire feet couldn't cling to the metal roost, so it was hanging upside down on the feeder. *Never mind*, his grin said. I had my bird. (When it got dark, I sneaked it back into Mrs. Stacey's tree. The next morning I told her about it, in case I had put it on the wrong limb.)

Sometimes in writing and sometimes in turning my attention toward mystery, I have the feeling that I am being played with, or at least held in fond affection the way a parent teases and loves a child. I have written about leaving the church, and trying to find my father's people in the rocky hills of Missouri's Ozarks.[2] Those were earnest and serious matters. But what I discovered was a kind of delight, of surprise, of almost childlike humor at play in my life. Similarly, those answers that came to Evelyn and to me, after the shock wore off, are funny. Of course, I had to make up my own mind. Of course, Ev didn't need a "sign." She just needed to be reminded that she didn't need one.

It is, after all, ridiculous—comic—to think that this utterly finite little self that I am could be in personal relationship, even in dialogue, with an infinite Presence. But what if it is possible? Isn't it a little bit, deliciously, funny?

* * *

When I married as a young woman of twenty-three, I prayed as I had prayed all of my life—I knelt beside my bed, folded my hands, and prayed to God or to Jesus. Peter came from a German-American family that was very devout, but in a different Protestant tradition than my own. He had memorized a catechism as a child, and whatever his life of prayer at that time was, he kept it private, except for the ritual prayers that he led in church services as a pastor. As for individual prayer, Jesus said, "But when you pray, go into your room and shut the door and pray to your Father who is in secret."[3] Before long, I found it just entirely too "public" to kneel and pray beside a bed where my husband was already under the covers. But rituals are very hard to give up, and when I stopped kneeling, I lost a regular practice of personal prayer. My praying became those formal prayers in church, or moments on the run, cries for help, and occasional bursts of ecstatic gratitude. Mixed in with all that was some sense of loss and some grief.

Thinking about this, my mind turns to those traditions where prayer is required at certain times of the day. I think of Muslim men kneeling on their prayer mats in mosques and in public places, and nuns and monks in convents and monasteries praying the Liturgy of the Hours. And I remember that even in the busiest days, our four children and Peter and I bowed our heads before meals, sang, or held hands together in silence. That was part of my continuing prayer life—maybe the best part.

*   *   *

It takes courage to write honestly. I can say that now, at this moment, in this writing, because although it is fifty-two years since I was that young woman on her knees, to go back there intimately in my mind is to feel those feelings again—the desire to believe every word of scripture literally, and the confusion of something new happening to me that I didn't yet understand. It takes both honesty and courage to try to wrestle the truth of experience onto a page. But in writing it, we come to understand what we didn't understand before. Virginia Woolf, reading her own early diaries, commented, "My, how that young woman could write!" Writing can move us to compassion for our younger selves, struggling with the same questions we probably will raise later, but with so much more of life and its lessons behind us. I wrote above that my only prayer life as a young woman was in church and on the run, but when I shared that writing with workshop members and heard their responses, I recalled those sweet times at the table, singing or in silence with my family.

As it takes courage to write honestly, so also it takes courage to pray honestly. My neighbor, talking with me across the flowers that border our yards, asked what I am writing. I told her I was writing about writing and prayer. She responded that she doesn't pray— "all that asking for stuff turns me off."

Well, the answers that both Evelyn and I received may indicate that pleading prayers are not the favorite prayers of the mystery, either. The silence of Quakers, the candles of Catholics, the humorously irreverent poetry of Stanley Moss may be sweeter than Ev's and my insistence that we be *answered*. In fact, they are sweeter to me: "Some believe the gods come as swans,/ showers of gold, themselves, or not at all./ I think they come as bathers: lovers,/ whales fountaining,

hippopotami squatting in the mud."⁴ The very word, "pray," calls up
for many of us emotional experiences of family, church, synagogue,
temple, mosque, tradition, rebellion, apathy, and/or pain. Marian
Calabro, author of the stunning book *The Perilous Journey of the
Donner Party*, was visiting as I worked on this chapter. When I suggested that it takes honesty and courage to pray, she noted that the
sheer repetition of prayer helped several members of that entrapped
pioneer group, especially the children, to survive. "Prayer meant
memorization and repetition in my Catholic childhood," she added.
As I sat thinking, she added, "I understand what you are talking about
in writing—that kind of listening—but not in prayer."

I asked if she didn't sometimes experience the familiar words of
memorized prayer taking her to some inner awareness of Presence.

"Yes," she said, "although that experience came later in life."

An email conversation about it with one of my children got
this response:

> Interesting that you push her, and that she concedes. But you do
> have to acknowledge…that some people (me) have never expe-
> rienced prayer as such, producing what you describe. Yes, I have
> experienced inner awareness of presence. No, it has never hap-
> pened in a moment I would call prayer, certainly not when
> prayer was happening around me. It's not that I have found all
> prayer to be unpleasant, but I experienced it like you experience
> the silence between movements of a musical piece. Marking
> time, perfectly pleasantly, but that's it.…For your daughter, flesh
> of your flesh, raised at your table, prayer is—flavorless. Not
> hated, not painful, perfectly fine for other people.

Maureen Buchanan Jones, a poet and novelist, also grew up
Catholic. She said, "For me, praying is like reaching out to touch
something warm. I say a shortened form (most nights) of 'Hail,
Mary'—just to experience that connection—like reading *Good
Night, Moon* to a child. And the image in my mind is sixteen years
old and very real. It's to remind myself and 'Mary' that I
remember."

Needless perhaps to say, what I know about prayer comes simply out of my own experience, woven not only through my particular rural Midwestern, and then East Coast, American culture, but also through an ordinary, busy woman's life: marriage, four living children, more pets than I can count, several jobs, books written, life lived in some complicated relationships. Where was there time for prayer? Often it was only the moment of silence we kept before eating. Only the hurried turn of the mind toward petition or gratitude while the hands folded laundry or washed dishes.

* * *

Máire O'Donohoe was on her way back to Ireland from years of work in Africa when she joined my workshop at Pacific School of Religion in 1989. She was torn about whether her return to Ireland would include leaving the Ursuline order in which she was a nun. I had just left the Methodist Church even though it had saved me from poverty by giving me a full scholarship to college. We were both rocking in small boats on a very rough sea.

Over the next fifteen years I went every summer to Ireland, leading workshops that she and others sponsored, and Máire, who did not leave the order, became a teacher and counselor to me, although I could not move back into any organized church community. One rainy day we stood together in the ruins of a Protestant church in Catholic County Donegal, in the shadow of Errigal Mountain, and I wept the loss of the church that I had loved and served passionately for the entire first half of my life. She listened to me, and loved me in my wanderings, and for that time she simply became for me the face of the Presence.

On another day she took me into a beautiful, shadowy Catholic church. She went to the front where two banks of candles burned in the silence, and explained to me that she needed to light a couple of candles for people in pain. I thought of Mrs. Stacey, my aged next-door neighbor at home, how she had lost most of her eyesight to macular degeneration, how she walked carefully with her cane, heading uptown past my house, to attend Mass at St. Brigid's

Church. She was an Irish-American Catholic. It would matter to her to have a candle lit for her in a church in Ireland. I followed Máire, bought a candle, and lit it for Mrs. Stacey. And as in most of Máire's teaching, I learned without her saying a word that there are truly many ways to pray, and lighting a candle is one of them. That little candle still burns in my heart, although Mrs. Stacey died years ago, turning me toward blessing her each time I think of her Irish wit and her slow, faithful walks to Mass.

Sometime after that, I was in Japan to lead a workshop, and reconnected with a friend from college, Junko Uetani. She had suffered the death of her only child, a son, when he was struck by a car while jogging on a narrow Japanese highway; and shortly after, her husband died. She believed his death was primarily from sorrow over the loss of their son. Junko and I met before I was twenty during the single year I attended a Methodist missionary school. I had not seen her since. She was and still is a very committed evangelical Christian. When she took me to visit a beautiful Buddhist temple, we came to a large round container full of sand, and in the sand there were many little candles. Junko bowed deeply to me, and apologized, asking if I would be offended as a Christian if she lit a candle for her son. I had not told her that I no longer was comfortable calling myself by any religious tradition. I asked her if I, too, could light a candle. I lit two—one for her son, and one for myself. *It's me, it's me, it's me, O Lord,/ Standin' in the need of prayer.*

Rumi's lovely reminder that there are hundreds of ways to kneel and kiss the ground takes me to my own history in the faith of Junko, and to this beautiful poem by poet Yorifumi Yaguchi:

THE ONE I WANTED TO CALL

The one I wanted to call was
The God of
Abraham, Isaac, and Jacob,
Who had appeared to Moses
As "I am who I am,"

Who had existed in the human body
Of Jesus, the Nazarene.
How should I call him?
"Father"? "Mother"? or "Parent"?
I tried to find the Japanese word for Him

And looked around the vast field of words
But couldn't. Finally a desperate "oh, kamisama"
Fell out of my mouth, and then signs of
Hearkening gods among the grasses and woods
Came flying to me, twisting themselves around me.[5]

I still go down on my knees now and then, bowing my head in silence as I hold Peter's hand before we eat, lighting a candle on my desk, a mix of my own early tradition and a new awareness of mystery "among the grasses and woods…twisting themselves around me." Prayer now, as in the beginning, is turning my attention toward mystery.

My purpose is no longer to petition God, although there surely are moments when I do that—but rather, to participate in the mystery of our human connection to one another and to the mystery that holds us (I believe) in loving attention. Often, prayer for me is "like the silence between movements of a musical piece," as my daughter said.

Here is more of the poem excerpt by Mark Nepo that opens this chapter:

…Now
I understand: to blossom
is to pray, to wilt and shed
is to pray, to turn to mulch
is to pray, to stretch in the dark
is to pray, to break the surface
after great months of ice
is to pray, and to squeeze love
up the stalky center toward the sky

with only dreams of color
is to pray, and finally to
unfold again as if never before
is to be the prayer.[6]

By turning toward the mystery that holds me in loving attention, I myself become a prayer. No words are necessary unless they arise spontaneously. Although ritual and tradition are often beautiful ways of joining "the morning stars" as they "sing together," no particular form is necessary. And words, if they arise—heard only inwardly or spoken or written—don't have to be "holy" or "about God." I myself, when I turn my attention and "unfold again"—am the prayer.[7]

Both prayer and writing invite us to explore the full range of human awareness, out to the edges of what we have experienced and beyond, out to the edges of what we can intuit, and beyond. Both invite us to imagine, to be brave in what we imagine, and to keep the doors of all of our imaginings open. Allowing writing and prayer to overlap—writing as a spiritual practice—invites a dynamic relationship with mystery. A block in writing is like a lock on prayer. I will say more about writing blocks later. In an open, unfolding relationship with mystery, all the locks can open, and all the blocks can become stepping-stones to more than we have yet discovered, more than we have ever met.

ABOUT, AMONG OTHER THINGS, GOD

Come.
The primrose blooms in the garden.
The mourning dove calls in the sycamore tree.
Rain on the sill of the window,
sounds of every kind of weather
are sweet in this old house.
Come.

In the pantry, jars of beans,
lentils, sunflower seeds. Sesame. Jars
of preserves, small cans
of spices stand in rows.

It is here.

A woman stands in the doorway
and calls. Her apron bleached from washings
and from hanging in the sun. Behind her,
through the doorway, the house
is dark and cool, and the word
that she calls into the late afternoon,
into the shadows gathering under the lilacs,
into the long, long shadow of the sycamore tree
is come.
Come home.

—P.S.

CHAPTER 3

Ransom

There's Ransom in a Voice
—EMILY DICKINSON
Nothing can save you / except writing
—CHARLES BUKOWSKI
The life you save may be your own.
—FLANNERY O'CONNOR

THE CHILD WATCHES. The child learns. Blackberries hang heavy and ripe on thorny vines at the edge of the field. They seem to steam in the humid summer air. The child has a small bucket made from a tin can. She picks berries one by one and drops them into the can. She carefully examines each berry to make sure there are no triangular gray bugs on the ones she puts into her mouth.

She wants to be saved. She doesn't exactly know what that means, but she has heard about it, and she wants it.

* * *

I am afraid to write the story that is at the heart of this chapter. Fear is the best indicator I know that there is something alive in the dark woods of the mind. Fear tells me it is important. But it is appropriate to respect the boundaries of the psyche—sometimes we are just not ready to see what we will see, or feel what we will feel, if we write into our fear. So I get to the edge of this cliff, but I don't jump. I need to stand here on the edge of what I know.

When my granddaughter, Sarah, was three years old, she asked me to draw with her. I answered, "Oh, Sarah, I can't draw! I just make messes!"

She drew herself up with a long intake of breath, looked me straight in the eye across the table filled with crayons and paper and said firmly, "Grandma! When you draw, you *don't make messes!* You just squabble around!"

This is one of the best lessons in creating art I've ever encountered. So to write this chapter, which feels like a vulnerable act, I need first just to "squabble around."[1]

*   *   *

"The human heart can go to the lengths of God," Christopher Fry says. "Affairs are now soul size./ The enterprise/ Is exploration into God."[2]

Is it true? What does it mean? Is "going to the lengths of God" what some call "Enlightenment," or "Beatification" or "Salvation," or "Liberation" or "Redemption" or "Ransom"?

Even if it is true of "the human heart," is it truly possible that it can happen in the human heart as we write? Emily Dickinson writes, *Silence is all we dread. / There's Ransom in a Voice—*[3]

It was Suzanne Webber, a poet and fiction writer, who asked, "Are you going to write about salvation?" I was stunned by the question. How did she know? And how scary is that, that she should perceive where I have to go to write this book, even before I have named it to myself? Because silently, and immediately, after one silent, horrified *No*, I knew the answer: Yes. I am going to try to do that. But what can I say about the place where the spiritual experience of enlightenment or salvation intersects with the experience of writing?

First, it is important to say that the issue here is not the dimensions of mystery ("How great Thou art"), but the dimensions of the human heart. Any parent of more than one child knows the anxiety that precedes that second birth. *How can I possibly love this new child as much as I love the first? My heart is utterly full of love—there's no more room!* And the second baby arrives, and instantly, the heart stretches. Our capacity doubles, then perhaps triples, and for me, by the time our fourth child was on the way, I understood. The more we open ourselves to love, the larger our capacity for love becomes.

So it is in opening ourselves to mystery. If we stay knotted into our smallest measure of capacity, of course we cannot "go to the lengths of God." But if we dare to open ourselves, we unfold like the winged creature emerging from a chrysalis, or like the flower described in the poem near the end of the last chapter. We unfold into love.

What my Episcopal friend calls the "death of the autonomous ego," I would have called, in my youth, "born again" or being "saved." Strange. My own stance has moved away from "letting go" or "falling into" mystery; it has moved toward "meeting" or "relationship" with mystery. This is true of my writing life as well.

But I do want to think about "letting go," by whatever name we might call it. At this moment I am a writer, trying to write as a spiritual practice—trying to do the thing itself as I write about it. I am trying to write my way into understanding what it means to me now to be a spiritual pilgrim, and in order to do that I need to remember and understand my own journey toward and into what I am calling "mystery." Both as writer and as pilgrim, it's scary. I don't know who's going to read my words. As a writer do I "let go"? Do I back up and be safer? Do I stand here, feeling the wind and listening?

What fundamentalist Christians called, and still call, "salvation" is trapped in a doctrine I can no longer embrace. I say no to "hell." At least to hell somewhere other than here, here where some humans live in a hell of other humans' making. Or of their own. I say no to hell hereafter. But to love, yes. Ecstatic meeting, yes. Mystery, yes. Even to the possibility of being "saved," in some sense, by *a personal relationship* with what I call "mystery."

Yes, I'm going to write about salvation.

The writer of the book of Ecclesiastes begins his (her?) famous poem, "For every thing there is a season, and a time to every purpose under the heaven."[4] There is a time for refusing to fall. There are times when one must hold one's ground, wrestle with the angel, decide whether to follow a cruel command as Abraham at least tried to do when he was told to kill his own son, as soldiers must do when they are commanded to kill the enemy. There are times when most of us, depending on our orientation, have to confront our received religious tradition or confront some new challenge to that tradition—confront it face-to-face.

So also is there a time for letting go, for utter relinquishment of control, for free-fall. And that experience is ecstatic—or terrifying, or both at the same time—whether we come to it through writing or through ritual or through private or public spiritual experience. It is at the heart of creativity; it is at the heart of spirituality, and it takes as many forms as there are human persons.

What is required to be open to an experience of mystery? Perhaps nothing is required. No formula, no specific words to be said or acts to be performed. No baptism, no creed, no doctrine, no priest, no confession of faith, no adherence to tradition. Maybe it is as simple as so many religious leaders, saints, and mystics have said, as simple as that itinerant preacher, Jesus, believed it to be, back before the first words were written about him. He said we are loved. He called God "Abba." In Aramaic, his original language, *abba* is the intimate name for father/mother. There is no adequate word in English to equal its intimacy or depth of meaning. In English it might translate "Dad/Mom, or Mama/Daddy," but those do not do it justice.

A loving parent desires connection with the child but is wise enough to allow the child the freedom to try to stand alone. A loving parent is available to the child even when the child feels cut off or abandoned. A loving parent certainly does not punish children by condemning them to the fires of hell. In order to be loved, a child does not have to follow the parent's rules. If we are loved, as the mystics, saints, and poets in all the major religious traditions teach, then we are valued, sought, longed for, welcomed, and received no matter what path we take toward and into the moving, attentive presence of mystery.

What if "going to the lengths of God" is available to every person and to every sentient being—available on each being's own unique terms, in that being's language, in that being's recognizable forms, rhythms, locale, and capacity? Something happened to me when I was five years old that causes me to ask—what if, after all, even a five-year-old is capable of "going to the lengths of God" because the mystery at the heart of creation is everywhere, and is everywhere available? What if the mystery itself is dynamic, changing—a shape-shifter, as some American Indian cultures have taught, and as Calvin Luther Martin suggests we all are, in his book about living among the Eskimo, *The Way of the Human Being*?[5]

There is so much of mystery around us, among us, within us. The idea of shape-shifting embraces a much deeper spiritual relationship between all living things than is celebrated in most other systems of belief. We have been slow in my lifetime to deeply understand even those persons whose bodily shape and mental ability differ from our own. Poet Theresa Vincent's daughter, Patricia, was born blind, deaf, and profoundly palsied. Patricia, at eighteen years old as I write these words, has never spoken, weighs less than fifty pounds, and has always been cared for at home. In her poems, Theresa has opened my mind and heart to the rich possibilities of embodied spirit, of communication through touch, and of the healing possibilities of love through intense attention across barriers that most of us can hardly imagine. Here is the title poem of her collection:[6]

NOTHING HAS BEEN LOST

Believe the body.

Believe she knows
flesh,
bone,
mouth,
bowels.

Believe breath.
Believe silence.

Do not believe in redemption –
nothing has been lost.

*   *   *

Nothing has been lost, but much is hidden. What lies hidden in the dark? What treasure? And what are we to do with buried treasure? If in my writing I dig up treasure, might I not damage it? Or might it not tarnish in the bright light of day? Might someone convince me that it is, after all, only trash and not treasure at all?

The journey of the hero in search of emotional or psychological treasure is what many of the old myths and fairy tales are about—that's why they come complete with dragons, demons, witches, and wizards. Just as buried trauma, in time, surfaces as "flashbacks" or ripens to a readiness to be consciously processed, so does there come a time when it is no longer satisfying to leave one's secret treasure—whatever it may be—buried in the deepest cellar of the psyche. Often trauma and treasure are closely aligned, as in myth and fairy tale—the terrifying trauma guards the treasure, holds it, and hides it.

Whatever this writing becomes, in its beginning it is "writing as a spiritual practice." If I write as a spiritual practice, I must go into the cave of my own childhood. The "dragon" is my fear, guarding an experience that is one of the most meaningful in my life. Can I write it so simply and truthfully it will not be diminished? Do I have enough humility to present the experience of a child? Am I able and willing to be that child again, for the time it takes to tell the story? I am trying to get there.

*   *   *

As a young man, my mother's father was passionately religious. However, by the time she was a teenager, he had worn out his Bible trying to make sense of it. She said he wore out his floor, too, by pacing, wrestling with the Bible's contradictions. Finally his faith split and fell off him cleanly as the hull of a hazelnut, and all that was left was his passion, which he turned full throttle to Darwin and thundered that he'd rather see my mother in her grave than baptized.

She sneaked away one day with her dress-up clothes in a flour sack, changed clothes in some bushes, walked to a Methodist camp meeting and got baptized. She wanted with all her heart to be a nurse and entered a hospital program that gave free nurse's training in exchange for aide work in the wards. But at the end of three months, she was required to buy a uniform. Times were hard: her father had lost his store; they were living in a rural log cabin. They could not help her buy a uniform. She left the training program and joined a fundamentalist sect on a hilltop called Mount Zion.

Those religious people, the women with long hair and long skirts and long sleeves, kept their bodies covered in the simmering heat of southern Missouri Ozark afternoons, when even the grasshoppers slept under blades of tough grass along the sides of the gravel road that ran parallel to the creek. The men, too, wore long sleeves in the open-air tabernacle across the two-track dirt road from our house. I think the men at work could go bare-armed, but it is the women I remember clearly, their long hair and long dresses. It is a kindly memory. My mother's hair was long, too, wrapped in a braid all the way around her head like a crown of holiness.

They called themselves "Holiness people." They believed in what they called "a second work of grace: sanctification." Salvation was the first work—salvation from sin and from the fires of hell. Those who were saved could "backslide" into sin, but if you were sanctified, you were a saint and could no longer sin.[7]

When they married, my parents lived for a time in a house they rented within the community, where she had lived as a community member before she met him. I don't know how they met, or where; I do know that they were married by a justice of the peace, and that she insisted they change the spelling of their last

name when, through marriage, she gave up her name, Lelah Ridgway, and became Mrs. Cleve Vought. She divorced him five years
later, and he went back to "Vogt," the original spelling of his name.
The five sons of Harv and Elzina Vogt, my grandparents, were
hard-drinking men, one of them shot to death through a screen
door by his father-in-law. Life in the Holiness community must
have been very uncomfortable for my liquor-and-women-loving
father. It was the 1930s—the country was mired in the Great De-
pression; the banker in town hanged himself. Everyone else did
what he or she had to do to survive.

"He was good looking," she would tell me, and add quickly,
seeming embarrassed, "I had to marry him. Mama and Papa
couldn't support me."

"Oh, I loved him," she would say. "But love can die."

* * *

Writing about deep memory can bring up from the unconscious
seemingly random images and phrases that we have known all our
lives, like that line of Mama's. They float in and out of conscious
memory like flotsam and jetsam on the surface of the ocean that is
our unconscious life. Writing them—*slowing down* and allowing
the images to write themselves, without trying to analyze them—
can bring about an amazing experience of personal revelation.

I have written elsewhere[8] about Margaret Robison urging me
to write about my father, and my resistance. But I have not earlier
written the full story. It was a late evening; we had talked for hours,
and she had told me about her childhood. After she went home,
I sat on the couch in my darkened living room all night, thinking
about her childhood and trying to think about my own. Always the
turn to my own childhood was interrupted immediately by the
thought: *Don't think about that! That would hurt Mama!*

I became interested in the intensity of that message, and how
it absolutely came up every time I tried to set my own childhood
next to Margaret's in my mind. It was five o'clock in the morning
when words came. I didn't have paper or pen. I was sitting in the

dark. The words came slowly, indelibly, in the form of a nursery rhyme, almost like singing, but with no tune:

> Daddy was a bad man.
> He made Mama cry.
> I loved him, Mama said.
> But love can die.
>
> Daddy was a weak man.
> He told a lie.
> I loved him, Mama said,
> But love can die.
>
> You look like your daddy—
> Green, green of eye.
> I loved him, Mama said…

The silence of the final line that *did not* repeat itself was huge. I understood in that moment why the fragment of memory had floated in and out of consciousness for the more than forty years of my life. It was perhaps the deepest fear possible, to a child: that *love can die*. And if it can die for my father, can it not also die for me?

But why did it come as a nursery rhyme? Because nursery rhymes were almost a first language for me. I was not yet three years old when I could say thirty nursery rhymes by memory. It was planned that I would say them on the local radio station, but my mother stood me on the kitchen table and rehearsed me so much in the week preceding the arranged appearance that I suddenly stopped saying them and never would say them again.

The painter Ben Shahn has said, "Form is the shape of content." That is very important for writers to understand. When we are faithful to the *content* of what we are writing, when we slow down and write exactly what we remember without trying to say what it means, it will form itself, take its own form, make itself clear in image and in speech, rather than in intellectual argument or explanation. The *content* of the answer to my question needed the *form* of the nursery rhyme.

I was asking myself a question—where and what was my childhood? The answer had been there all along. A big part of it was the fear, *"but love can die."*

* * *

My parents had left the Holiness community when I was two years old, Sam was a newborn, and our father found a job in a cheese factory. I was four the day my father put his old car up on concrete blocks in the yard of our tiny rented house next door to the factory. The hot sun poured through the window, and my short, chubby legs felt almost too much heat on the seat cushions as I pretended to drive. He was singing as he worked; he could yodel an excellent imitation of Gene Autry. That day he was singing, "South of the border, down Mexico Way…" Now I know that he was happy. He was leaving.

He had received severance pay from the cheese factory as a reward for quitting instead of getting a second hernia operation that he needed. He divided the money with my mother and told her he was leaving for good.

He had left other times and had returned, asking for forgiveness. This time he had been gone longer when he wrote asking for the rest of the money to come home on, but she had already filed for divorce and returned to Mount Zion. Her divorce was a serious sin to the Holiness people. She may have been prohibited from joining, or she may have chosen not to join again, but she no longer participated in their worship. Her parents had joined a socialist colony in Louisiana where everyone's belongings were shared—owned—by the colony. Her parents were penniless—she had nowhere other than Mount Zion to go. With the money from the factory, she rented a farmhouse halfway down the hill at the edge of the community.

Only once did she take me to a church, and it was not to the Mount Zion tabernacle. We walked a long way on gravel roads and stopped to rest from the intense summer sun in the shade of dusty roadside trees. One was full of half-ripe persimmons. She teased me by having me taste one, and laughed at my puckered mouth and horrified expression. She loved to play and tease; it is not difficult for me to imagine why she had been drawn to my father's good looks and ready laugh.

At the little church we sat in a pew for awhile, and then she gave me something to play with and told me to stay where I was. She went up to the front and knelt at the altar rail. I could see that she was crying. Perhaps I appeared anxious, because some lady took me by the hand and led me out behind the church.

The little church stood in the woods; there was no pavement anywhere—just loose Ozark gravel. Behind the church there were no windows, and the space between the trees and the building was small. The woman took me to the first tree, and told me to sit down and wait there. Close to me under the tree was a little "sensitive plant." That's what Mama called them. She had shown me how, if you gently touched a delicate compound leaf, it would close up, fold up on itself as if by magic. I spent the time waiting for my mother concentrating intensely on the sensitive plant. How it felt everything, how it was green and alive, how it knew how to survive. How it took care of itself.

* * *

I have no memory of ever again attending church with my mother. She told me—not in a tone of hostility, but in a tone of the sadness and the confusion of an outsider—to stay away from the tabernacle that stood directly in front of our farm house, across the gravel road. I could play there when it was empty, but I was to stay away when people were there, and I obeyed. But it was as near to the front door of our house as our barn was near to the kitchen door. On summer evenings when the house was hot, we sat on our front porch eating warm cornbread crumbled into milk and listened to the singing from across the road. There was a roof on poles under great oak and sycamore trees, benches, a platform for the visiting evangelist and perhaps a quartet of singers, and benches for those who came to a revival meeting. Sawdust on the ground kept down the dust.

We watched the lightning bugs above Mama's peonies, and listened as heart-rending sweet music floated to us in four-part harmony from the open sides of the tabernacle—music that Garrison Keillor has called "the most sensual music in the world":

> *Just as I am, without one plea,*
> *But that Thy blood was shed for me,*
> *And that Thou bidd'st me come to Thee,*
> *O Lamb of God, I come! I come!*

Often she softly sang along. It was delicious, seductive, and since she successfully shielded me from all images of hell-fire, it was free from any touch of fear.

* * *

One of the great things about working with memory in writing is the way you get to be in two or more times at once. The far past, the near past, and the present brush against each other and even overlap. Madeleine L'Engle said, "I am still every age that I have been."[9] As I wrote the lines of the old hymn, they sang again in my mind—slow, tender, full of the inflection of Missouri country folk. I was a child swinging my legs below the edge of the porch in the twilight. At the same time I was this woman that I am now, looking back at the little girl and growing in understanding of the woman she has become. That work of going into silent, closed places of memory and writing through it again is sacred work, redemptive work. Under pain, if we go deeply enough, there is joy. Under confusion there is clarity. Under suffering there is grace. Not because pain, confusion, and suffering are unreal. Bodies of real children are burned by real bombs; homes and lives are lost in real tsunamis and hurricanes. But facing the hard realities of both our internal life and the life of the world can move us to an entirely different perspective, one that may include understanding, action, acceptance, or compassion.

At this moment, writing about the tabernacle gives me a portion of acceptance and compassion. I still love that sweet old song, although I have long ago given up what theologians call the substitutionary doctrine of atonement (Jesus's blood is substitution for our sins) that is its theological under-story. Yet as I write these words, it is a summer evening in the Ozarks, 1939. I am barefoot, and in some inarticulate way, bereft. My daddy has left us, and we have moved to a strange new place called Mount Zion where ladies wear long dresses and never cut their hair. I sit on the shadowy porch and consider the sweet song's invitation.

* * *

As a teenager, after she ran away to be baptized, Mama had passionately believed in salvation and sanctification. Although we never discussed it, I think she could not accept that to her friends at Mount Zion, her divorce made her a sinner in danger of the fires of hell. She had left my father, his drinking, his going to prostitutes, then crying and telling her about it, his bringing gonorrhea home. In that little farmhouse she gave me an intensive course in how to hate my father. She was a single mother with no income but the little bit she could make from selling canaries that she bred in an upstairs room devoted to them, and from walking up and down a gravel road selling chicken eggs to people who had chickens of their own. She bought a cow and a goat; she planted a large garden and canned enormous amounts of vegetables.

But she no longer had anything to do with the beliefs of those religious people. Until she died, she lived in the schism between a belief in salvation, which she accepted; a belief in sin, which troubled her; and a belief in hell, which she rejected. She no longer wore their long dresses or refused to cut her hair. She called their religion "the little stingin' kind."

And yet, she had friends among them. I don't doubt that they treated her kindly—that they earnestly tried to save her from her back-sliding, sinful life. I can only imagine her suffering, caught between a religion she could no longer embrace and a personal experience of God that must have been her only solace—an experience that now was judged inadequate by the very people who had led her to it. She continued to sing their music until the day she died. A lifetime later, one of the songs both my brother Sam and I remembered and sang together in the summer before he died at age sixty-three must have come from her days at Mount Zion, for it is not in common books of gospel songs. Even my friend Horace Boyer, who was for a time a gospel music expert for the Smithsonian Museum, could not locate it. But after a few years' passage brought us the Internet, one of my children found it in a video of a young man singing without accompaniment in a country church:

> *Often I've watched the clouds up in the sky;*
> *Often I've heard they were many miles high,*
> *And I said as they sailed out of sight far away,*
> *I'm going higher some day.*
> *I'm going higher, yes, higher some day.*
> *I'm going higher to stay*
> *Over the mountains, above the blue sky,*
> *Going where men neither suffer nor die,*
> *Loved ones to meet in that sweet bye and bye,*
> *I'm going higher some day.*[10]

* * *

We had been at Mount Zion for a full year when I turned five years old. I, too, was beginning to know by heart some of the words, some of the rich harmonies, the tender promises, the yearning: *Savior, like a shepherd lead us,/ Much we need thy tender care...*

One day I said, "Mama, I want to be saved."

I clearly remember the asking, and clearly remember her gently putting me off. I remember asking again and again—my hand on her cotton dress skirt, pulling on it, insisting, *I want to be saved.* She laughed about it years later—how she didn't know what to do with a child barely five years old who seemed so convicted of sin, so in need of salvation.

She did believe firmly in the possibility of love and welcome. And so, finally, one day she said, "All right. Come with me." She led me out to the two straggly peach trees that comprised the whole of our pathetic, worn-out orchard. Telling the story when I was grown, she still shook her head in disbelief. "You cried like a hardened sinner," she said.

I don't remember crying. I do remember that once I had cracked hickory nuts on a big rock, pounded them with a smaller rock, and picked the tiny, elusive, delicious white kernels out bit by bit. When my little brother, who was not yet three years old, ate my entire pile of kernels and wanted more, I fed him the white worms I found in the nuts instead. That wasn't nice, but I doubt that I cried because of that sin.

Maybe she told me to ask God to forgive me for my sins—that was part of the formula—but she never again talked to me in terms of sin, and so I don't know why I cried. What remains in me is that her voice was gentle and she told me to pray, and to offer to give my heart—was it to God or to Jesus? I'm not sure.

Writing this, I am both outside and inside the little girl. It is easy to lose the child because the woman who I am sees now, in this moment of writing, that the child has lost her daddy and is asking for a father God to claim her, love her, take the heart she offers him. Never before have I seen this. It is the writing that puts the connection before me.

I want to go back into the child, and the way to do that is through concrete image. The ground is hard; the rocks are uncomfortable. Mama and I find enough dirt to kneel on our bare knees without pain. I fold my hands into prayer position and I must have looked up, because even now, seventy years later, I know that there are two hard, little, immature peaches on that tree. Only two. And not many leaves.

I pray—to Jesus, I think. Maybe to God—to take my life. *I give you my life,* I say—and yes, I can feel it now inside me—I cry. I beg. I am "a beggar before the door of God."[11]

Suddenly, I am received. I am. It is true. I am loved, I am owned, I am delighted in. The peaches above me are beautiful—they are

no longer little green knots. They are a promise; they are a sign.
I belong to God. I am not alone. I don't have to be afraid any more.

Mama told me after I was grown that I came to her again and
again for days after that day, hugged her around her legs and said,
"Mama, aren't you glad?"

She didn't know what to make of it.

I knew. I was saved.

* * *

Emily Dickinson said, "Silence is all we Dread...," but trying to
break silence can be "dread-ful" also. The first time I tried to write
this experience was several years ago. It took the form of a poem—
tracing the outline, going as far as was safe at that time. In a revision after I wrote the first draft, I changed the two peaches to one
peach, for the sake of the poem.

PERSONAL ADDRESS

To you only I speak,
although you are forever
changing names, places
of residence, appearance,
affect. Reputation.

When I was a child
you hovered in the rafters
of the tabernacle, above
the visiting evangelist's head.
My mother said I should repent,
and so I did. Of what,
I have forgotten. I was
five years old. I do remember
how the tree, under which she knelt
and prayed with me for my salvation,
bore a single peach that year:

the hard, green bud of it. How
all the summer long I watched it grow.

There was something that I asked of you
in that worn-out orchard.
Although I don't remember what it was
I asked, I do know
I took the peach for answer.

* * *

What is "saved," or "redeemed," or "ransomed" in the act of writing? Mary Oliver suggests in her poem "The Journey,"[12] that the only life we can truly save is our own. That is what writing does for me. It saves my life. In writing, I literally save my own life. I "ransom" it, to use Dickinson's word, from silence. Something in me that was broken, cracked—becomes whole. The cracks, if I write them with utter honesty, are where "the light gets in." The present meets the past, and healing begins.

Often the things we fear to write turn out not to be monsters at all—in fact, we fear to expose them because we love them too much. To write them might mean losing them. Only it doesn't. We don't have to show the writing to anyone—we should not unless we are certain we will not be rejected, not be ridiculed or made to feel ashamed. As I said earlier, we must hold the most sacred writing in privacy, in silence, until time passes, and it becomes safe, psychologically, emotionally, to share it with others.

Some things we write may never be shared. For most of us there are things that cannot be published, not if we care about the safety and happiness of people whose secrets we hold. But we can write them. Writing takes it out of the inner place where it grows parasitic in the dark, brings it out to the page where my eyes can see its form, my ears hear its groans, my fingertips touch the words that tell it back to me. And then, because I choose to honor the privacy of another, I may burn the page or shred it—that act helping to purge my own tender heart of the temptation to take power from someone else's weakness or vulnerability.

To write like this—to write concretely what our inner eye sees, our inner ear hears—is to break silence. If we read it to others, or allow them to read, it fully breaks silence. If we write and never show it, even perhaps destroy the written words, we have nevertheless broken an inner silence, and in the very act of writing will have let some light in to the inner space that needed light. That act can be a kind of ransom—a kind of redemption. It allows me, the writer, to see more fully, more explicitly, and to name, perhaps even to bless, what before was hidden.

* * *

As writers, it is important to allow the material we are writing to find its own form. That statement by Ben Shahn, "Form is the shape of content,"[13] is a basic principle for us, both for the art of our writing and for the personal healing work that it often is. I am suspicious of a writing life that limits itself to one form. Work that is allowed to find its own form will allow us to grow, to experiment, to imagine. And it will allow the emotion underneath what we are writing to find its appropriate voice. For example, in the story above I instinctively moved from the "I" of first person narrative to "the child" of third person narrative when the story became too hot to handle emotionally. Writing "the child" helped me to step back, gain a bit of perspective on an intensely emotional experience. So does using metaphor as I did in the story about the sensitive plant.

The subconscious helps us, gives us the perfect form or metaphoric image for what our words are trying to express. It sometimes nudges us to change from third person to first person, which is always a move closer to the material. Later, when the first draft is done, we look at it, recognize the shift, and ask ourselves whether it should have been first person all along, or whether we need to honor the shift and tweak the writing to make the transition work. There are two kinds of "craft" at work here: the first kind is learning how to get out of the way and allow first-draft material to flow freely. The second is the learned craft of polishing a first draft without destroying our own inimitable voice, the good help we have received from our "dreaming place," the subconscious mind.

I have been asked by writers who are just beginning to work with autobiographical material, "Why does the same old story come up again and again?" "Does it ever stop? Will there always be more pain to dig up?"

Because I've worked with so many writers over thirty-two years of leading workshops, and because I've written so much out of my own childhood, I can say with certainty that yes, the same stories come again and again, and for most of us mortals, there is always more pain to discover. Strangely, though, as writers, that's one of the good things. Not only because we discover more deeply who we are and why we are who we are. Not even because discovering who we are helps us to change who we are into something better. There is another, more writerly, reason. Janet Burroway, author of the excellent textbook, *Writing Fiction*,[14] says, "Only trouble is interesting." At least in creating story, I think she's right.

The good news is, under pain, there is joy. Under grief there is love. Under betrayal there is the possibility of change, and/or of forgiving. A famous (perhaps apocryphal) story about Carl Jung says that a patient tells him, "Doctor, I dreamed that I was in a vat of boiling oil, and you were beside it, saying, 'Not out! Through!' "

Trouble that comes up again and again is not always the same. Some trouble, some pain, really does get healed as we write and re-write it. That healing is greatly facilitated if the writer is not putting rocks into her pocket and walking into the river, as Virginia Woolf did, or as the old stereotype of the writer goes, writing alone in a freezing garret while drinking himself to death. A bad workshop can kill you as a writer in short order, but a good workshop can help a lot.

Poet Louise Glück wrote in "The Wild Iris" that "whatever/ returns from oblivion returns/ to find a voice." I believe that with all my heart.

In my workshops I always write, or try to, in response to the writing prompts I have suggested, and I read aloud among others who choose to read what they have written. I am deeply committed to this practice as one way of decreasing a sense of hierarchy in our writing community; it means there is no one in the room who is not taking the same risk—of failure, of exposure, of a bad first draft—as everyone else. We are all in it together, a wonderful leveling practice.

But for the leader, this can be a challenge. For example, because I have taught writing for so long, there are central images that I use as "triggers" again and again in working with different groups of people. One of those is to suggest to writers that they imagine a doorway, or a breakfast table, or a hallway. Then I ask three simple questions to help them see more clearly what they have imagined: "What is the quality of light?" Poet and novelist Maureen Buchanan Jones has written, "This particular question is essential, I think, because it makes the listening writer feel the atmosphere he or she is remembering or imagining. We are animals, acutely aware of light whether we are conscious of it or not. As soon as the precise peculiarity of light becomes clear the writer knows exactly where she or he is." The second question is, "Where is the light coming from?" And after a beat of silence, "Is anyone near you, or are you alone?"

When they have had another brief pause, I ask them to begin to write down something that they "see" and then go anywhere they wish with their writing, departing from that image or staying with it.

Over the years, this prompt always took me back to the same scene—the terrible tenement in St. Louis where I lived for most of my adolescence: the same doorway, the same table, the same hallway. After a while it was very uncomfortable, difficult, if not impossible to find anything fresh and original about that apartment. One day I rebelled onto the page and wrote in twenty minutes the following poem, which was taken with uncharacteristic quickness by a literary journal, and has survived into my first "new and selected" volume, *Another River.*

IMAGINE A HALLWAY IN CHILDHOOD

It is always the same goddamned hallway,
the same smell of darkness
at the center of my mind.

I won't go back there this time.
Not again.

I will make myself a hallway. Let it be
light. Let there be sun
falling through a window and carpeting
a stair. Let there be space and a clock
ticking fifteen minutes before noon.
Let it be morning. Let it be June.

Let there be biscuits baking in the kitchen
and the smell of nutmeg rampant in the house.
Let there be some dust between the rungs
at the stairway edge,
but only half a week's worth. No more.
Let there be a baby's picture book
abandoned on a table in the downstairs hall
and a slight puddle standing
at the tip of an umbrella
in an old umbrella stand.

Let there be privacy possible here,
let there be no Mr. Costello smelling
of cheap wine, grouchy, waiting in line
outside the bathroom door with his urine
in a milk bottle in his hand;
let there be no stale smell of sauerkraut
from the room of the unhappy woman upstairs,
no screaming Nigger! Nigger!
coming up the furnace ducts
from the apartment below. Let there be
an absolute absence of cockroaches.
Let there be no fear of the police,
no chain lock on the door,
no grease across the windowpane.
Let there be no shame.

And it is so.

I have made a hallway for myself,
and I am walking down it.
I walk in sunlight and nutmeg. I walk
in the still magic of imagined space,
and almost at the end, on the left,
there is a door. It is standing open,
and I go in
and close the door behind me,

like this...

* * *

What I did not expect, and what surprised me greatly, is this: ever after writing this poem, I have not one, but *two memories* of that apartment; the fictional image is as real to me as the remembered image.

Furthermore, and even more startling, perhaps a year or more after writing it, I dreamed that the tenement building where I had lived was on fire. I stood and watched the huge, encompassing flames, and I knew that the fire was utterly cleansing the inside of that old, roach-infested, filthy brick building. There would be nothing left but the smell of ash and the shell of bricks. Then the dream shifted, and the building was still there. I walked up the scarred concrete steps and opened the door. Inside, the stairway was the same, but no longer sticky with dirt. The smell was no longer a sickening mixture of urine and roach poison. At the foot of the stairs, there was a small, glassed-in booth with a woman guard seated inside. The building was safe. It was clean, and I no longer lived there.

I came to that redemption through writing. Over, and over, and over again writing the images that had so wounded me as a young girl. And then finally writing a different, fictional version.

Sigmund Freud reputedly said that dreams are the royal road to the unconscious. Whether night-dreams or daydreams, whether writing or in some other art form, that redemptive work is begun in the unconscious, and with all my heart I can say that Emily Dickinson is right. *Silence is all we dread. There's Ransom in a Voice.*

INSTRUCTIONS FOR THE JOURNEY

The self you leave behind
is only a skin you have outgrown.
Don't grieve for it.
Look to the wet, raw, unfinished
self, the one you are becoming.
The world, too, sheds its skin:
politicians, cataclysms, ordinary days.
It's easy to lose this tenderly
unfolding moment. Look for it
as if it were the first green blade
after a long winter. Listen for it
as if it were the first clear tone
in a place where dawn is heralded by bells.

And if all that fails,
wash your own dishes.
Rinse them.
Stand in your kitchen at your sink.
Let cold water run between your fingers.
Feel it.

—P.S.

CHAPTER | **4**

Fear

Perhaps the world ends here.
—JOY HARJO

I HAVE BEEN GIVEN a book of poems. In fact, this week, three books of poems have arrived, all from people I care about. I ask for the gift of brand-new, unpublished words in every workshop or writing retreat I lead, and I confess I fall in love with almost every writer in almost every gathering where we do the audacious act of writing ourselves onto the blank page. Our imaginings. Our dreaming. Our memories. Ourselves. Then I go home, and soon I am in another circle of writers, falling in love all over again with new voices.

But at home, where I am supposed to do my own writing, I simply can't read all the words sent to me as gifts from writers I know. So, when I received the book of poems day before yesterday, a book by someone I have never met, sent by my friend, Sharon Groves, whose work I do know and love—I didn't expect to read more than a sample poem here and there.

Instead, I read every word of the book, from the title on the front cover through the blurbs on the back cover. And now I've lost it. I know it's somewhere in this book-cluttered house, because I'm recovering from a hip replacement, and I have not been out of this house. I've searched everywhere, three times, and it hasn't surfaced. I tried blaming my husband; he searched his basement office. It's not there. I wanted to quote from it to begin this chapter. I wanted to talk about it onto the page. I wanted to, and I will.

What does it mean, this kind of losing? A strange mix of wanting to know, and protecting something by not knowing. This book that I have lost, the name of which I can't remember, nor can I remember the name of the author or the design of the cover—all of which makes it harder for me to find where it is hidden—has touched on something that apparently a part of me doesn't want to deal with. At least not now.

But I am also really annoyed. I want that book. I want to write this page. I want to be brave and honest and...

Don't I?

Well, maybe not.

* * *

The book is by a woman. It is her first book as a woman. She has two books published and well received, written when she was a man. To read this book of poems is to take, vicariously, the incredible journey from one gender to another. It begins with the author as a man, and ends with the author as a woman. In the middle, between the two identities, is a section on the soul—where, and what is the soul, the poet asks, when the body is neither one identity nor the other? Brilliantly the poet wrestles, and the reader—this reader, at least—wrestles with him and her. What comes clear is this: The poet must die as the person he was, in order to begin to live as the person she will be. That dying, in order to be reborn, is nothing short of terrifying. Not the gender change—the abyss of feeling a lack of *soul*.

I have not been using the word "soul," but I have been writing about personal spiritual identity. I have said, "The end of the world is a private thing," and I have written about an experience that some call "being born again," although I was only five years old at the time. How do those ideas—my own, and Harjo's, and the writer of the lost book—relate to writing?

* * *

Last evening, my weekly women's workshop was led by poet Peggy Reber, who has participated in it so long she knows my routine better than I know it myself, and she has improved upon it with her own grace and ability. I attended half the meeting, my left leg propped up on a footstool. She settled us in to write and read aloud as a prompt a poem by Joy Harjo. The first line of the poem is, "The world begins at a kitchen table…" Peggy suggested we might want to write about a table, but we were free to write anything.

I have used that line as a prompt myself many times in leading workshops around the United States and in Europe. I remember well the poem's title: "Perhaps the World Ends Here." The image in my mind as Peggy finished her prompt was a table—the table in the tenement—the table that appears first in my brain when any kitchen or table is included in a prompt.

Each one of us has a personal mythology, central lived images that are the emotional, if not the literal, foundation of our stories, our poems, our artistic voices. They are our own hieroglyphs, carved in the bedrock of our emotional lives. A number of famous writers have said that they have spent their lives telling "the same story" over and over again, in different images, different plots, different tones. Responding to Peggy's prompt, I first saw the tenement table. But I had written about it, and I had dreamed it burning. I didn't want to—and didn't need to—write exactly those images again. At least not in the way I had done previously. But I didn't know where to go, or why the image came back after I thought I was "shut of it," as my Ozark grandma might have said.

In our writing practice, though, I teach my workshop members that the *open sesame* into writing is almost always a concrete image, almost never a general idea. And so there was nothing to do but begin with the table. Never mind that it was already familiar to the writers around me, from other times when we wrote together.

Jan Haag, a professor of journalism at Sacramento City College who uses my method in her classrooms and workshops, writes, "I've said to the workshop folks, the re-told story is the 'wind up' before you throw the ball… though you have little or no idea what you're throwing at, where it will go or land."

Here is what I wrote, taken from my journal:

There was a kitchen table in one of the two rented rooms we lived in all through my high school years. It was round, heavy, scarred from long use. It would have opened up into twice its size if it had not long ago lost all its leaves. The top was perpetually cluttered with dirty dishes, opened packages of unfinished food, scraps left on plates, crusted into the bottoms of pans. Through it all, roaches moved. I was newly home from the orphanage where everything had been clean. If I cleaned here, clutter bloomed immediately as my mother readied herself for her night-shift job, dropping things where she used them. She was exhausted. I was a kid. My younger brother was seldom home, most of the time in foster care.

When I was a student in the MFA program at U Mass, I tried to write about that table...

And there the story shifted into something I had *not* written before. That's how the *open sesame* works. The first image that comes in response to a prompt is a nudge. It is a tiny lightning bug in the mind. It's a trick the unconscious has for leading us as if we were children with Mason jars, chasing lightning bugs. When we sit down to write, we may run for a while from bug to bug before we catch the light that is our real writing material.

"When I was a student in the MFA program at U Mass," I wrote, and all at once I was into the story and forgot that I was writing. That's where we want to be when we are writing. That wonderful inner place where the world falls away, and we are living the story again as our pens move across the page. It doesn't matter whether the story is funny or sad, comic or tragic, memoir, fiction, or nonfiction. What matters is we are living it, or reliving it, and our unconscious minds have free range to use our natural, most experienced, most uniquely personal voices. What I wrote that night in workshop was a furious rant. I tell it here in a different tone, more appropriate, I think, for this book.

I came into the MFA program in my mid-forties as a published poet and playwright. I wanted the advanced degree in order to teach writing, and I felt my greatest weakness was in fiction, so I enrolled in the fiction track. My first attempt, in my first class, was a story about—guess what—the kitchen in the tenement.

What I described as happening to a young boy, I had done in actuality. First I described the kitchen, the stove with its dirty pan, maggots moving in the remaining peas. The sink was small, metal, with no dish-drain. It was not attached to the wall; old pipes rose visibly from the floor behind the sink to two separate old-fashioned faucets. I described, too, the broken grate on the floor—the furnace duct where rats came up at night into the two-room apartment, and the bare light bulb hanging from a cord in the ceiling in the middle of the kitchen. All literally true.

The boy sees a roach crawl from the top of the table down under it. He gets a can of roach poison, goes down on his knees and looks up at the bottom of the tabletop. There are hundreds of roaches there, more than he has ever seen in his life. He begins to spray, and roaches fall to the floor. Some scramble to get away. Some of the females drop half their bodies—their long, brown egg sacks—and struggle in their dying. The boy imagines himself to be Pharaoh. He is king of the Egyptians. He is as mighty as the Sphinx. He is killing the Hebrews who are trying to flee, trying to get back to the promised land.

It was memoir, of course, not fiction. It was what I had done, and what I imagined myself to be doing in order to bear the act of slaughter I was committing. My professor handed the paper back to me with only two comments written on it: *A bare light bulb is a cliché*, and *The poor don't talk about the Sphinx*.

Writing in workshop with Peggy, I ended the piece with this:

> *Well, yes, the hell they do, Mister Professor.* They talk about what their mother talks about, and this mother happened to love ancient Egypt. She took us to the St. Louis Art Museum to see the mummies. She talked about King Tut's tomb and the Pharaohs and the Sphinx. She had considerable portions of the Psalms memorized; she certainly did talk about the Sphinx. And as for a bare light bulb being a cliché—is a table lamp beside a leather couch a cliché?

*   *   *

In Florence, Italy, in order to see Michelangelo's statue of David face to face, you walk toward him down a long hall between massive blocks of marble with half-finished—or deliberately left imprisoned—angels. As glorious as the David is—as unforgettable—

the angels, whether one experiences them as emerging or as imprisoned, are equally, if not more than David, unforgettable.

Teachers of writing at all ages in public and private schools must deal with their institutions' criteria, with government regulations, with school committees, parents, and with students who don't want to be in their classrooms. Their task often is close to impossible. Elsewhere I have written about problems caused by the grading of imaginative work, and about an alternate methodology of assessing progress in students.[1] Teachers everywhere must work within the confines of grading systems, and most of them are heroic in their efforts to minimize damage done to the creative process by requirements to grade. Peter Elbow has done pioneering work in helping teachers who must grade writing, using terms such as "ranking," "grading," and "liking."[2]

I have had wonderful teachers. And I have had some who simply didn't recognize the "angel" in the unfinished work. What was not understood in our traditional ways of teaching writing, and still is not understood in many settings, is the function of the unconscious mind in creativity, its absolute centrality to creativity, and how it can be evoked, protected, and taught. Those are the primary issues, with techniques, practices, and prompts, that I wrote about in *Writing Alone and With Others*.

Strangely, a similar misunderstanding operates in most of the major religious traditions, in my opinion. In spirituality, as well as in the art of writing, we replace the natural voice of the creative unconscious with rules and boundaries. In writing, it takes forms like, "A light bulb hanging from a cord is a cliché." In spirituality, it takes forms like, "You're not a Christian unless you have been baptized." At bottom, the systems we have for controlling the unconscious have one thing in common: *If you don't do it like I do it, you are outside.*

And so we are afraid. Deeply afraid to be who we really are, to reveal who we really are. To trust once again that someone is not going to put a minus behind the grade at the top of our page of paper. Minus. *Not quite good.*

*   *   *

In spite of fear, if we are writers, we continue to want to write. Our art dwells in the unconscious, and when it is denied, it is under pressure. When we intend to write the truth of what we have experienced or imagined, and set our pen to paper, the unconscious spews out invitation. Images. Concrete details that are clues to something significant. So give me a table as a writing prompt and it will be the table at 4039 Olive Street, St. Louis, before they tore down the tenement and built neat little townhouses. Those central images in our personal myths are cracks through which light comes. But going there is always the hero's journey back toward the treasure. And the treasure is never unguarded. There will always be dragons, or the great dogs of Andersen's fairy tale.[3]

* * *

I opened this chapter with a lost book, a book that suggests that in order to be free to live a new identity, we may have to kill the old one. The book seems to me to be a profound spiritual exploration. A line from *Macbeth* comes to mind where a certain queen was "Oft'ner upon her knees than on her feet, / Died every day she lived." I had the sense that the poet was having that kind of experience, the changing of the self was so raw, so real. We do change all the time; we know that every cell in our body dies, and is reborn over and over again. Maybe in other senses, also, that process never ends. Maybe the dying, and the being born again, never ends. Maybe that's what spiritual life is all about. Maybe that's what writing, at its deepest, is all about.

I used Joy Harjo's line again as a prompt in a later workshop, in another place. I had been working on this book, knowing that my next chapter would require writing about being in the orphanage. It would demand looking closely at my complicated mother and reliving some experiences I had not yet ever written. This time, responding to Harjo's line, we had thirty minutes in which to write. Once in a while, writing seems to come from somewhere so deep, the music, the thought, flows almost effortlessly. Here is the poem I wrote in that workshop session, with no revision:

PERHAPS

Perhaps the world ends here.
—JOY HARJO

You have undone the weave of the garment
the old ghost habitually wore,
the ghost who forever meets you
inside the tenement door.
She is naked now, and so thin
you can't see her anymore.

But ghosts don't have to be visible
for you to know they are there.
She never stands at the table
or sits down in a chair.
She is naked, and cold as a shiver
under her long, grey hair.

In dreams you've unwoven her garments
and set fire to the tenement wall.
Nothing is left of the building –
a tumble of ashes is all.
You can't see her in that absence.
In the silence, you can't hear her call.

The world begins at a table,
says the poet. The world ends there, too.
And the ghost you try to dismantle
clothes herself in you.
Then her silence speaks only to silence,
and there's nothing more you can do.

You have railed at the fetters that bind you;
you have asked the inevitable "Why?"
You have stripped her of clothing and lodging—

what else can you possibly try?
If you kill the ghost of your childhood,
It is you who will certainly die.

* * *

There. That is the fear. How can we be reborn, unless the person we have been dies? The person we have been is the only person we know for sure, and that person is afraid to die.

I have read somewhere that we grow to love our own suffering. I'm not sure about that—it sounds like a guilt trip to me. Terry Jenoure, violinist, visual artist, and sometimes writer in my workshop, says that the phrase, *we grow to love our own suffering* does not suggest to her being satisfied or joyous or ecstatic. "It's that our suffering is the object/subject of our attention," she wrote to me, "in the way that you say that God's love is his attention. . . . Our suffering is our attention (over and over again) to the cruelty, the inhumanity."

Once I asked a therapist, "Why do I keep going back to that building?"

She answered, "Because you left something of yourself back there."

I find both Terry's and the therapist's comments helpful. Still, there is another chapter to write, and at least until it is written, I feel as if I am dragging something along with me like Linus dragging his blanket in Peanuts cartoons. If I lay it down, I won't be me, just as Linus wouldn't be Linus without his blanket. We do cling to our suffering, because it's what we know. It's familiar. It's the house the soul has inhabited, and if that house burns, if that habitation falls to ashes, the soul wanders, homeless, until it can take up residence in a new self that rises from the ashes, no longer defined by the old pain.[4]

* * *

My writing has taken various forms: first and always, poetry. Then plays, then fiction—twice a novel; once a memoir; three times books of nonfiction. To some degree all of them have required going back to the same old table, either to write about it, or to refuse to write about it. Two of my plays, *After the Applebox* and *Berries Red*, all of my other books, and many of my poems have dealt all or in part with poverty. As I have lived my life, though, more and more I am able to invite other tables into my work—the table here in our 140-year-old house; the altar rail "table" where I knelt as a teenager to receive little cubes of Wonder Bread and tiny glasses of Welch's grape juice; the table in the library where I sat across from the man I would marry, watching how light played along his sturdy farmer's fingers as he wrote a term paper; the table where I fed my children. Today it means sitting at this table in this house in Amherst, facing this computer.

I will never be finished. Maybe the poet whose book I lost is right. Her name is Joy Ladin.[5] I found it, finally, in a file labeled for a writing retreat that I hoped she would attend, and I read it through again. I was just as moved the second time, and I sent her this chapter. She has graciously given me permission to use it.

Maybe she is right. Maybe the old self has to die for the new self to be born. Or maybe, for me, the old self doesn't have to die. Maybe who I have been is not erasable on the tablet of who I am, or in the book of who I will become. Maybe writing, like painting, can be pentimento—one layer over another, the early layers now and then showing through.

For both the writer and the spiritual pilgrim, an "answer" is not always the greatest gift. Rather, coming to deeper and deeper understanding of the question itself can give us a place to stand in the presence of mystery, in the cloud of unknowing. Answers build walls that sometimes seem protective, but they may shut out the light.

Frances Balter's craft has been honed by several art forms. When she was young, she danced with Martha Graham; later, using the work of major artists and poets, she created in Philadelphia "Poetry on the Buses," used now in many cities around the world. And finally she has written poetry. In a slim volume titled *Zeal*[6] she includes these two:

NOT KNOWING

how God thinks *or how he creates*
an opaque cloud, random vine,
or screech of color,
I sit beside a stream
veiled in shadow,
until my anger lessens.
Yesterday,
He blinded my daughter.

I have not known suffering like that. Nor do I have an answer to *Why?* But the poem with which Frances ends her book gives me something that I value more.

PLEA

Like the Navaho who sings
With the first light rays
Encouraging the arc of day,

I long to speak of light
So flagrant with color that
Beyond my valley of silence

My voice might be heard.

Teach me.

. . .

"Teach me," I say now, into the mystery of all that I do not understand.

I thought, after the hallway poem and the dream of fire, that I was finished with Olive Street. I thought I would never go back there again. But there are questions under questions. There is another locked door, and it is very solid. At this moment, carved into the wood of it are the words: *Chapter Five.*

THIS IS A RIVER

This is a river underground,
row; row. A sideshow clown
stands immobile on the shore.
Row the riverboat. The door

opening to the vanished fair
must be up ahead somewhere.
Lighted faces behind glass
leer and disappear. We pass

an empty boat. An eye
is painted on the stern. I cry,
"Where did all the riders go?"
No one seems to want to know.

In the morning, was it fair?
Was a sign, a promise there?
Was there a doorway and a clown
or was there only going down?

Row the riverboat. The door
stands immobile on the shore.
Row; row. A sideshow clown.
This is a river underground.

—P.S.

CHAPTER | **5**

The Dark Night
of the Soul

Follow, poet, follow right
To the bottom of the night...
—W.H.AUDEN, "In Memory of W.B. Yeats"

...our lives, any life, is worthy of poetry.
The experience of any human being
is worthy of poetry.
—PHILIP LEVINE

WHILE WRITING, ESPECIALLY in the chapters on "Ransom" and on "Fear," there sounded in my mind again and again the title of a book by a medieval mystic, St. John of the Cross: *The Dark Night of the Soul*. What is "the dark night" that both Auden and St. John write about? Where is "the bottom of the night"? It became clear to me that if I am to understand writing as a spiritual practice, I need to understand that part of my own life.

In some texts the words "dark" and "light" have had negative/positive meanings—neither of these is my meaning. My use of "dark" and "dark night of the soul" include both suffering and secrets (what is not yet known or understood), but I hold suffering and secrets as sources of what may be our deepest and greatest potential, both as writers and as human beings just trying to make sense of our lives.

Follow, poet, follow right / To the bottom of the night…" I have often offered that quote from W. H. Auden as an encouragement (en-*courage*-ment) to writers in my workshops, because it has been permission and a guide for me. What is—or was—the "bottom of the night"? What if going in search of it, telling it, is itself a "dark night?" I am afraid of it.

And so I have procrastinated for several months by reading other writers. I researched Mother Teresa's now-famous forty-year interior darkness in which she could find no joy and no sense of the presence of God, yet all the while continued her work within her religious tradition, developing it from thirteen sisters in Calcutta in 1952 to more than 4,500 serving 517 missions in 133 countries worldwide.[1]

I bought texts, read and took notes, wrote short pieces like this one:

> This exploration is not a research project. Neither is it an existential search for meaning. It feels more than anything else like one of those pictures made for children where if you look closely enough there are pictures hidden within the picture—a hammer in the tree branches, a fish in the cloud, a kite in the spokes of a wheel. It feels like going in search of what is there, what I know is there, what I might find if I trace the outline of it.

And like this:

> Yesterday I saw something about the dark night of the soul—*felt* something, really, and let it slip through the fingers of my busyness. Several times I caught it again, as one does a fragment of a dream, and then it completely evaporated. All that is left is a foggy space where it for a short time stood clear, as a mountain will do on a misty day when the air is moving and clouds open and close in front of the shapes of a not-entirely familiar landscape.
>
> It had to do with the fact of "darkness" in us all, an integral part of human experience, expressed sometimes psychologically,

sometimes emotionally, sometimes spiritually. The deep dark in which we best see stars. The positive dark, the inviting dark. And the deep dark of war, oppression, slavery. The negative dark, the fearsome dark. The darkness of not seeing, of knowing how little we do see. At times in all our lives, darkness threatens to overwhelm us. Suicide. The violent kind and the quiet kind where we turn our faces to the wall, eat or drink ourselves to death, give up, let go, cave in.

Or memory. Or nightmare. How the terrible event happens again behind your closed eyes, or to your body, and if you could, you would never take another breath. You would go out like a single flame in a very large night. But your body itself breathes for you. Not because you will it, but because it insists on its own survival.

Trying to find my way into this writing, in the middle of very ordinary nights, I woke not from nightmares, but with strange dreams. In one dream, I had sores on the bottoms of my feet; I could not go forward. In another, beautiful, seductive grasses hid waves that became larger and larger until they washed over me, where I held on to wooden structures that did not feel very secure. Even as they threatened me, I felt awe at their ecstatic beauty, and at the beauty of the grasses that moved around me. In a third dream, the father I lost at age four appeared with his large, complicated family of men who drank, went to war, and died of alcoholism or violence. I was the outsider in that dream, the educated one, the one who did not belong among those rural Ozark folk. Some nights were dreamless, but I awoke anyway with Auden's command, "Follow right to the bottom of the night." Then my question, What does that mean?—and only tantalizing, buckshot pellets of answer-pieces.

Trying to write felt fragmented, too. My research seemed to be taking me further and further away from the center of what I needed to explore—so much so that I questioned whether I could, after all, write this book. Maybe I would have to be satisfied with an essay on writing and mystery. But my own disappointment kept me from giving up. It was August, time to lead my annual workshop at

Pacific School of Religion (PSR) in Berkeley. Surely, I thought, there in that center of theological schools I would be able to write about the dark night of the soul. But what came to me was exultation and awe. No dark night.

On the wall of the archeological museum at PSR where my workshop met, there was a gallery of photographs by Hilary Marckx, a theologian as well as a photographer. One of the black-and-white photographs showed a person's naked shoulders with the head thrown all the way back so the viewer sees only the shoulders and an almost geometric line of chin. I couldn't tell the model's gender or race. To me, it had the quality of Mapplethorpe's nudes, human bodies as beautiful as the marble sculptures of Michelangelo. Maybe in another place it would not have moved me into a gape-mouthed inner silence, but this museum used to be the library at PSR when Peter and I were students, and it was there, in that room, that I first knew I loved him.

As the two weeks of workshop progressed, more and more deeply the image affected me. At first, I experienced its meaning as exultation. Slowly, however, as I stood before it during workshop breaks, having just listened to written work that moved me both to laughter and to the shock of pain, it came to hold for me simply an image of extreme feeling—possibly joy, but also, perhaps, anguish. Light in the photograph falls on the neck and torso of the figure, while the face and the lower body are lost in shadow. As days passed, something came into focus that I already knew: Darkness and light are inextricably bound together.

Not long after that experience I led a workshop in Sacramento at the Sutter Medical Center. The participants were people with life-threatening illnesses, caretakers, and medical professionals writing together. Maybe writing there, I thought, I would be able to "follow...to the bottom of the night." I did think, now and then, of my own diagnosis of a slow-moving form of leukemia, but I didn't write about that much, just as others didn't write much about their illnesses or caretaking or medical practice. We wrote as writers in my workshops usually write—about anything we happened at the moment to imagine or remember. And even though I consciously wanted to explore the meaning of "the dark night," every attempt felt wooden and dishonest.

Among the workshop participants was a therapist to whom I felt drawn, Susan Flynn. I asked her for a private session, thinking maybe in conversation I could find access to something in myself that would connect to the feeling of "dark night."

I was tired. I was at the end of one week leading fourteen people and about to begin a second week with fourteen different people. I was stretched and vulnerable, as one often is in the midst of intense writing and teaching. Nevertheless, I told her that I was trying to write about the dark night of the soul, and described to her an image recurring in my mind: a little girl, in an office.

Susan asked gently, "What's under that?"

I heard the question, but reacted with an acute need to prepare for the coming week of workshop. I didn't even try to answer her question, but it lingered with me.

*   *   *

Back home, I asked myself, Is it possible to do what Auden asks? It was 2007—my country was torturing prisoners with dogs and waterboarding, and allowing the poor in New Orleans to perish while the whole world watched. In the face of global catastrophes, how could I justify writing to discover my own darkest night? But maybe awareness of the suffering in the world makes it even more crucial to attempt the "following" that Auden demands. He wrote his poem as Europe rushed to war, as Hitler was preparing to invade Poland. And the problem was not just Hitler—another line in his poem says, "All the dogs of Europe bark..."

Writing is often a struggle between the personal and the universal, and the way writers deal with that struggle varies. Poet John Ashbery was asked by the *New York Times* whether Americans are too enamored with their own life stories. He answered with a flat *Yes*, and said his own autobiography is uninteresting to him. In the same issue, Aleksandr Solzhenitsyn was quoted as citing an old Russian saying: "Dwell on the past, and you'll lose an eye. Forget the past, and you'll lose both eyes."[2]

I can't help it—I belong with Solzhenitzyn if he includes in "the past" his own past, and I believe he does. Delving into the past—personal or societal—may be painful, even dangerous, but if we forget the past, we become blind—or worse, we act out blindly. Ray Bradbury, master of imagination, said, "My field is myself, as it should be for any writer.... A writer must have the firm, hard ability to turn his eye inward upon himself...you're turned back on your hidden self, aren't you? That's all you'll ever have." The interviewer asks then, "Is that why you write? To understand yourself?" Bradbury answers, "I know this now. I didn't know then."[3]

The issue for me, both as a writer and as a spiritual seeker, is courage—the courage to be there myself, and the courage to allow the reader to be there—*to see, to touch, to taste, to smell, to hear.*[4] It is in the particular that we intuit the universal. The particular, concrete image is the lens through which we see the world. Not "torture," but the naked prisoner faced with a dog and a grinning woman soldier with a camera. Not imprisonment, but one prisoner forcibly fed through a soiled tube. How can I begin to understand the darkness that is in the world if I can't name the bottom of the night within myself? If I can't try to speak what has so far been to me unspeakable? I already have worked on this for so long, at least touching it in everything I've written—

> But you can't change your nature and mode of consciousness like changing your shoes. It is a gradual shedding. Years must go by, and centuries must elapse before you have finished. Like a son escaping from the domination of his parents. The escape is not just one rupture. It is a long and half-secret process.[5]
>
> —D. H. LAWRENCE

I pull up the image that I named to the therapist: a girl, eleven years old, in an office with three adult women. The girl's hand is on the shirt, on the shoulder, of her younger brother. This image is not the bottom of my night, but it is as close—right now —as I dare to go. I am not quite ready for that little girl.

*   *   *

Sy Safransky, editor of the literary magazine *The Sun,* writes in his essay "Bitter Medicine" that after many years, remembering the death of his infant son is "a thought with dark wings that drag the ground." He says, "I push it off the edge of my mind and it falls and falls, turning like the seasons, smashing against the rocks below."[6]

I have not lost a full-term child, but I have felt the brush of those dark wings. Once it came in the fourth year of our youngest child's life. It was summer, around the Fourth of July. I saw that occasionally one of her eyes did not seem to focus exactly with the other. We took her to our family doctor. He said, looking into her right eye, "This is strange—I can't find her retina." But it was a holiday weekend; specialists were on vacation. He told us to take her home and watch her carefully.

I looked up "retina" and found "Diseases of the Retina." The retina, I learned, is the back of the eye and functions as the front of the brain. It is there that often the first signs appear of acute diabetes, acute leukemia—I don't remember the rest of the horrifying list.

Bethany was sitting at the table, her lower lip held gently by her upper teeth in intense attention to her work with colored pencils, crayons and paper. I asked her to cover her left eye. Then I picked up a pencil and held it before her. "What do I have in my hand?" I asked. She couldn't tell me.

I called the doctor at his home. "Can you tell me that this is not a life-threatening situation?"

"No, I can't," he answered.

"Then I want a specialist to look at it right away."

"So do I," he said. "I'll call and make an appointment."

We saw a local specialist who immediately sent us to Boston, to the Massachusetts Eye and Ear Institute. There, in the very first examination, an old and wise doctor explained that a parasite, toxicara, had gone into Bethany's bloodstream and landed on the retina of her eye and fed there, leaving scar tissue that destroyed her sight. He said the damage was already done—there was nothing to be done about it. He asked permission to keep her in the hospital for a few days and to put her under sedation on one occasion so all the doctors and interns could see the scar pattern. He said most of the adult population have taxicara scars somewhere in their bodies, but it occurs on the retina only one time in a million, and it would help doctors to recognize it if they ever saw it again. We agreed to allow them to study her, and I sat beside Bethany's bed for those days and nights. She had lost the sight in one of her beautiful eyes.

In the other bed in that hospital room was a tiny two-year-old girl who was blind in both eyes. One eyeball had become enlarged; she was there to have it removed. Over and over, standing up, holding onto the sides of her crib, she asked me, "What Bethany do now? What Bethany do now?"

While Bethany slept, I struggled with grief for what Bethany had lost and my awareness of how much more the other child had lost. I could find no words with which to pray except words I had memorized as a young girl. They were written by an unknown, ancient Psalmist. Perhaps his name was David, but linguistic scholars cannot tell us for sure. Perhaps it was a woman who wrote the poem as she waited beside the bed of someone she loved:

> *Whither shall I go from thy Spirit?*
> *Or whither shall I flee from thy presence?*
> *If I ascend up into heaven, thou art there!*
> *If I make my bed in hell, behold, thou art there.*
> *If I take the wings of the morning,*
> *and dwell in the uttermost parts of the sea,*
> *even there shall thy hand lead me*
> *and thy right hand shall hold me.*
> *If I say, Surely the darkness shall cover me*
> *even the night shall be light about me.*
> *Yea, the darkness hideth not from thee;*
> *but the night shineth as the day:*
> *the darkness and the light are both alike to thee.*[7]

* * *

In those days and nights beside Bethany's bed in the hospital, I had time to think, and an earlier experience of mothering came back to me. Soon after our second child was born, my neighbor, an older woman, an artist who seemed to me to be successful and wise, offered to watch my children. We were gone for less than three hours, but when Peter and I returned home, our two-year-old was tied into her high-chair, screaming, and the baby had cried so much she was asleep but still sweaty from the battle. The woman scolded me, telling me that I was irresponsible not to more adequately control my children. "I kept my own boys in a play-pen until they were four years old," she said.

When Bethany lost the sight in her eye, I could not keep from thinking that perhaps I did something wrong. The doctors said that toxicara usually comes from the feces of a dog, and a child playing barefoot picks it up and somehow ingests it. In the night, alone by her bed, I felt I had failed to keep her safe: *If only I had more frequently cleaned out the plastic wading pool!* If only I had not let her play barefoot! But the story of the playpen was a merciful reprieve. Bethany was four years old. If I had kept her in a playpen, she might not have lost her vision, but neither would she have run free in the yard, felt rain on her face, squished mud between her toes, discovered what was in the lower kitchen cupboards and pulled it all out onto the floor, climbed the stairs before she could come down safely and learned from every dangerous thing inside and outside the house.

That experience first taught me that human suffering is the price we pay for freedom—our own, and the freedom of others. We are free to make mistakes, free to be cruel or kind, free to hurt or help one another. We are free in a dangerous world; Bethany was free in a dangerous world. My attentive hover did not keep her from blindness in her right eye. If the mystery that I cannot name, but experience as personal, does not keep me from suffering, I cannot translate that into absence or indifference or cruelty. In the heart of the earth, in the human heart, in the heart of the mystery, darkness and light are inextricably bound together. Who was he—or she—that ancient poet who wrote the words that comforted me so in the hospital in Boston?

. . . even the darkness is not dark to thee,
the night is bright as the day;
for darkness is as light to thee.

Writing about this feels like going down on my knees. Who am I, to think I can write about these things? Dare to approach mystery, face to face? Dare to write directly to mystery? Dare to approach an image of a little girl in a long-ago office? As I write those words, other images rise, almost like comforters, or supporters. I see in my mind's eye the faces of my closest friends, my husband, my children. I see the faces of writing workshop members past and present, and retreat companions. I see the faces of those close to me who have died: my mentor, Elizabeth, and my brother, Sam. I see the faces of those I most love and most trust, and through their eyes, beyond their eyes, in their eyes, holding me in love, I see mystery. And so I write to you, all of you, even those of you I do not know by name but who might have been my best beloved: Here is what I think about the dark night of the soul. Here is what I think *now,* somewhere past the middle of my journey on this river of my life.

Am I moving away from the child? Yes, I guess I am. No, I think I'm not. The image that comes now is a desert snake, sidewinding his way toward his destination. If he takes a straight line, he can't get there. I'm writing toward what I experience as mystery—into what I used to call "God." Writing *to mystery,* writing about mystery. Only there, only as a spiritual practice, might I be able to side-wind my way back to the child in the office.

These words are a garment I am trying on. This writing is patchwork, the art form of my grandmother Emma, my grandmother Elzina, my great-grandmother Susan and their mothers and grandmothers—the art form of our foremothers everywhere. The best parts of old garments, cut and saved and stitched together with scraps of leftover new fabric, to make something beautiful and useful. That kind of garment. Soul garment. Spirit garment.

Some of the primary scraps are from my own childhood, including those I've already named: gospel music sung in four-part harmony floating across the gravel road from a country tabernacle to the rented farmhouse where I ran barefoot in the front yard, catching lightning bugs in the twilight. The creek at the bottom of the hill, its fossils and crystals and crawdads.

It would be self-satisfying and romantic to claim that my experience of the natural world is rooted in the legacy of my Indian grandmother and great-grandfather and their ancestors—that their Cherokee or Creek reverence for the earth is somehow in my genes. Romantic, yes, and maybe not true. That grandmother was my father's mother, and she was denied access to me from age four by my mother. It was my mother, a child of English and Welsh immigrants, who stood beside me at a darkened window and taught me to love the lightning and thunder that terrified her. She hated and feared snakes, but she brought me garden snakes in her bare hands and told me to feel their skins—how clean, how beautiful they were. She taught me to value the fossils in the Ozark creek that ran at the foot of the hill where we lived, and to let the little box turtles go back to their homes when I brought them to her in the farmhouse kitchen.

And yet, this same mother later put me and my brother into an orphanage.

Years ago I wrote in a poem these words: "It is what we love the most / can make us most afraid / rocking in a dark boat on the water / taking the long way home." At the time, as is so often true of words that we write, I was only beginning to understand what I meant by that. E. M. Forster famously said, "How do I know what I think until I see what I say?" What we mean is usually a mix of memory, knowledge, and imagination. Myth is woven of those three. So is fiction. So is memoir. So is all of the writing that we do, even that which we consider most "objective," as is pointed out in postmodern thought. What I meant in that poem is rooted in my own childhood: I meant the mix of love and fear, light and dark.

Some writers compose their sentences in code to deliberately disguise autobiographical elements in their images. Some write purely autobiographical memoir. Most of us do both, often at the same time and in the same sentence. When I was a graduate student,

I had a private conference with a poet who was my professor. His own poems were collages of images with the whole so abstract I could never discern the story, if there was one, hidden within them. In our conference, he commented on the fact that I wrote openly about my own experience. "I can't do that," he said, and immediately, as if explaining, told me a story about a terrible moment in childhood with his mother. Later, thinking about what he said, it seemed to me that he meant he could not write the terrifying images of his own childhood. And yet his poems had frightening images—just not in a recognizable narrative form. From him and from some members of my workshops I have learned that writing in abstract or surreal images is one way to write autobiographically and still keep one's secrets inviolate, or protect others whose secrets we hold. I developed a writing exercise in which I read aloud abstract poems by Charles Simic and by James Tate, and led my workshop in thinking about abstract forms of visual art: *Are these poems more like surrealist or abstract art?*

Then I asked them to write for four minutes on some subject that was painful or unhappy or troubling. Then for four minutes on some subject that was comforting or joyful or happy. Then for four minutes on some images from the natural world. Finally I asked them to take fifteen minutes and try to write a poem that "makes no literal sense." They could use repetition, but they could not use any word that was not already in the material just written.

One writer in my Berkeley workshop told me that exercise was the most important thing that happened for her in the entire five days. "Now," she said, "I know how to write what I need to write without anyone else ever knowing what it is that I can't reveal."

Most writers mix fictional and remembered images. Eudora Welty was asked once in an television interview whether images in her writing were imagined or autobiographical. She answered with a statement that I cannot find in print, but I remember like this: *If I tell you it is imagined, you will feel cheated. If I tell you it is autobiography, you will be embarrassed. So I will tell you the truth. It's both.*

The writer who writes abstractly, like the novelist who uses personal memory in creating fiction, knows the lived experience that is expressed there, even if the reader does not. Perhaps my poetry professor allowed himself to see what he was concealing from his readers. I hope so, because I believe expressing what is within us helps to heal us, whether or not we share it with anyone else. In my experience, many men—more men than women—are hurt by their own silence. Pat Conroy observed:

> American men are allotted just as many tears as American women. But because we are forbidden to shed them, we die long before women do with our hearts exploding or our blood pressure rising or our lives eaten away by alcohol because that lake of grief inside us has no outlet. We, men, die because our faces were not watered enough.[8]

*   *   *

In Ashfield, a little town in the mountains of western Massachusetts, out on an unpaved country road, there is a quarry where Jerry and Johanna Pratt mine, carve, and sell stone, some of it schist, which is exquisite, with what they wryly call "crow's feet." When you look at it, you are almost convinced that you are looking at the tracks of a very energetic flock of crows on some prehistoric river bank. White lines form short, straight angles in the dark stone, and it is breathtakingly beautiful. They are not, however, the tracks of dancing crows. They are crystals, formed under intense pressure five or six million years ago, ten miles below the surface of the earth. They are the mountain itself, creating itself in beauty, in the solitude and privacy, in the *darkness,* of the inner life of the planet.

Darkness and light are inextricably bound together, *for darkness is as light to thee.* If I understand correctly, the ancient poet is claiming that human life has meaning, even in what we experience as tragedy.

*   *   *

The things we cannot talk about—or write about—are where the secrets lie that we keep from ourselves. Secrets, more than anything else, are the stones that make up writer's block. What we keep hidden grows in power, tempts us, teases us, "glows in the dark," and beckons; it causes every other subject to seem trivial and boring. Our own secrets are a Bluebeard's closet at the center of our creative life. Writing our secrets does not necessarily mean publishing them or ever showing them to any reader. But it does mean that we bring them to consciousness, name them—strangely, *honor* them by acknowledging their place in our inner life. Until we are able to unlock the doors of our inner closets, we are blocked in our writing. Many famous writers have said that we do not choose our subjects; our subjects choose us.

I first learned this lesson years ago. Poet Margaret Robison and I had just completed our MFA degrees in creative writing at the University of Massachusetts. Each married, with children, we saw no way to seek teaching positions away from our hometown, Amherst. We decided to co-lead a private workshop, and to advertise it we launched an interview series on WTTT, a small Amherst radio station. The first broadcast was a reading from our own writing that caused a crisis for me.

I had tried only once in the MFA program to write about my childhood in poverty, and the response I described earlier shut that topic down immediately. In my friendship with Margaret, however, I had become safe enough in my writing to venture into some of those images. One of those pieces, she said, was the strongest thing I had ever written, and she insisted that I read it on our program. I responded adamantly: *Absolutely not.*

Margaret didn't bend. She said, "Well, if you are satisfied with reading something less than your best..."

I accepted her challenge. She read beautiful poems about her middle-class childhood in Georgia, poems that had been published in a book, *The Naked Bear*.[9] Then I read my unpublished piece about a tenement pantry full of milk bottles. Probably one hundred unwashed milk bottles, many of them with dead roaches trapped in dried milk in the bottoms. After I read it, my teeth were chattering so loudly that Margaret and Bob Paquette, the program host, could hear them. After a moment in which I couldn't speak, Bob said kindly, "Pat, *everyone* has a pantry full of dirty milk bottles!"

As a writer, I am coming to believe that I have no recourse but trying to accept Auden's challenge: *Follow, poet, follow right to the bottom of the night.* I have no choice but to pursue the deepest truth my life has given me.

That doesn't mean my writing needs to be memoir. Fiction writer Deborah Gerlach Klaus told me her experience of writing her short story, "Sins of the Flesh,"[10] whose protagonist is a woman who years before gave up her baby for adoption. She is searching for her child. Deborah wrote the story in a workshop in which the professor kept pushing her to take the story further. Each time she brought him a draft, he sent her back with a challenge to be more brave, go deeper. (Wow, what might have happened for me, if the professor who heard my story about the roaches had been so wise?) Finally, Deborah broke through, surprising herself with her own discovery. The mother finds her adult child in a circus—to say more would spoil the story—but Deborah accomplished what all great stories must do. She went beyond what she knew to what she discovered and therefore, so does her reader. The result is unforgettable. I have no idea what in Deborah's life caused her to understand what she finally sees in that story—nor do I need to know. Perhaps Deborah herself doesn't know where it came from.

John McGahern, one of Ireland's most distinguished writers, says that every person has an inner life known to no one else, and his or her writing comes from that inner life. He also says writing itself is not alive until another person reads the words, takes them into the inner life of the reader. Reading, McGahern says, brings the words to life. He goes on to describe reading as a state from which the reader wakes, saying repeatedly, "When I awoke from reading…"[11]

Similarly, John Gardner writes in his classic book, *On Becoming a Novelist,* that both reading and writing are a form of dreaming; the reader dreams the writer's dream after the writer.[12] That is an artistic act, and it is a healing act. It is also an act of profound communion that can heal the heart of both the one who creates it out of the depth of the writer, and the one who receives it into the depth of the reader—but only when the writer has dared to go beneath the surface to that place where he or she is breaking through to discovery. In some of our material, then, if we can, we must *follow…to the bottom of the night.* That is a big "if," because it is possible to remain stuck somewhere this side of the bottom. Yes, I did open the door to the shameful pantry, and I did in my writing look straight at the dead and dying roaches trapped in the bottoms of the slick glass bottles. But as the therapist in Sacramento asked, *What's under that?*

*   *   *

Poverty is under that. For years I have written into poems the images of childhood poverty and shame. *And what's under that?*

The orphanage is under that.

In an earlier book I wrote one small chapter about my childhood experience of being placed in an orphanage.[13] It begins with the words, "The orphanage wasn't bad." That was the truth—all of the truth that I had access to at that writing. In one sense, it is still true. The orphanage wasn't bad because it was better than being at home. It was clean; there were no roaches, no chain lock on the door, no Mr. Costello holding his milk bottle full of urine in the line for the bathroom. There was, for me, shame in the orphanage, but it was different from the shame I felt in dirty tenement rooms.

There are many kinds of poverty, and the word "poverty" has been used to mean very different things, all the way from the dying homeless people on the streets of Calcutta to whom Mother Teresa ministered, to the educated and in many ways privileged "poverty" of those who choose to wear religious robes and carry begging bowls. Was my problem in adolescence "shame" more than it was "poverty"?

I have tried to look clearly at that possibility. Which is deeper, the poverty, or the shame? Images, words, angers, hurts, passionate feelings pour out onto my pages, a brew hot enough to burn me and deep enough to overwhelm this chapter. And so, for now, I put the lid on it. I will let it "steep" and come back to it later in this book.

* * *

Two images. A girl, eleven years old, stands in an office. Three women and the girl's younger brother are also there. The girl keeps her hand on her brother, on his shoulder. She straightens his collar. She intently watches him; she glances only now and then at the women.

In the second image, the girl stands with one of those women, the one who is her mother. They are at the bottom of a long hill of grass. At the top of the hill is the stone building that holds the office.

The girl, of course, is me. I see *out of her eyes.* In a kind of double-dream-vision, I see the office and the grassy hill, but never the girl's face. These two images have always been acutely clear to me, as sometimes upon awakening a dream is acutely clear. But they don't fade as a dream fades. They are as solid as the world around me now as I sit writing on this rainy day a thousand miles and sixty years away from the events that gave me the images.

And what's under that?

Here I stumble. Telling the story alters the story. If I weave a cloak of words around that eleven-year-old girl, will I lose her?

Perhaps. Is that why it is so difficult to write the specific details of one's own dark night?

Is it that we love our pain because it is so familiar, so long a part of who we are?

Or is it that we fear what opening those images might reveal to us?

Or is it that we are shamed by our own history—shamed for our own sakes, and for the sakes of others who may stand revealed by our writing?

Yes, Yes, and Oh, Yes.

But it is time to tell the story.

* * *

On the day her mother places her in an orphanage, a girl eleven years old keeps a hand on her brother. He is nine years old. He is the one she has protected from the mean kids in the new school-yards as her mother changes places of residence hoping for a better job, a better school, a better apartment, a better neighborhood. He is the one she comforted when her mother pounded his favorite toy with a hammer to punish him for wandering away to play with neighbors instead of staying in the yard as he'd been told. He is the one who threw his white baby shoe off a small bridge into fast-moving water. He was two in that memory, and she was four, but what she remembers is her mother's helplessness, and the shoe floating away, floating away. She remembers, too, the day her father sang as he repaired his old car in midsummer heat. How she sat in the car happy, hearing him sing. And then he, too, floated away, drove away, disappeared.

In the office, the girl touches her brother. She fixes his collar. She keeps a hand on his shoulder. Sixty years later, that little girl will have disappeared into an old woman, but the old woman will remember the feel of his cotton shirt, the three women, the office with the big desk and the big window.

After I published the book with its little chapter beginning, "The orphanage wasn't bad," someone sent a copy of the book to the director of Edgewood Children's Center in Webster Groves, Missouri. I had no idea that the institution still existed. The direc-tor read the book and wrote me a long letter of appreciation. She included my sixth grade report card. It took about a month for me to move from shock to a realization that if she had a report card, she had a file. I wanted a copy of that file.

Before I asked for the records I discussed it with Sam. He said, "Oh, Pat, that was so long ago. Why can't you just forget it?"

I replied that I didn't know why, but I couldn't just let it go. When I saw that he needed to let it go, I told him I would ask only for information that had to do with our family, not with him per-sonally. He told me it was all right—"If you want it, you can ask for all of it." But I needed to respect his privacy, even from me. So the lines in the reports about his being sent away are blacked out.

Then I wrote to the director of the orphanage and requested their records. When a large, manila envelope arrived, I put it away at the back of a file drawer without opening it. In that same file drawer there were the two small five-year diaries—one of them given to me by my mother on the day she put me in the orphanage— that I had not ever read.

For a person whose life is given to helping other people write, one would think I would know that diary was important, and I would be eager to read the contents of the envelope. But in my experience the writer's own story is often the one that is hardest to enter. After all, it is the cave holding the dragon that knows us by our original name. It is the closet in Bluebeard's castle. It is the treasure at the deepest level of the tunnel, guarded by the biggest dog, requiring the greatest courage and the most magic to enter.[14]

* * *

We were living, Mama, Samuel, and me, in one room in the base-ment of a house on Pine Street. It was a good neighborhood, but the room was small, dark, at the back of the house. The door to the rest of the basement, to the furnace and open coal bin, was loose on its hinges. One day the woman upstairs who owned the house came down raging with anger. She knocked loudly, came in and stood before the three of us. She told us to get out, we were dirty, we had brought roaches into her home. That is when Mama put us into the orphanage. She gave me two reasons. The first was "so you can learn good table manners." The second I think was too fright-ening for an eleven-year-old to hold. I repressed it until sometime in late middle age when I wrote my way into remembering it. She said she was afraid she might hurt herself *or us.*

* * *

It is months later. Sam is far away in a different orphanage. Beyond the window of the administration building, the director sits at a large, wooden desk. Her office is neat and spacious. A huge window at the side of her desk looks out on the long, sloping yard of the orphanage. In my memory, her face is both warm and intelligent.

Three adults—the housemother, a very young social worker, and the director—have taken the place of my mother. All three are kindly, and remote.

My remembrance of the housemother is as a hen with a brood of chickens—busily seeing that we were dressed, fed, in bed at the prescribed hour, neat, clean. That no one fought or got lost or too untidy. None of this felt negative to me. I came from chaos. I was there to learn order. Mama could not teach us to be clean, to be orderly, to be survivors. She was none of those herself. She was forever shipwrecked, storm-tossed, a tangle of passion, emotion, brilliant ideas and dreams, even laughter—but no harbor, no anchor, no lifeboat. Fear was the wind, and shame was the calm.

Mama was a haunter of second-hand stores. She loved stitchery— she sewed as an artist, not practical things like skirts and blouses, but decorative things, hobby things, satin pillows she made from old dance hall formals, crocheted doilies, things no one could really use, or even find a place for in a crowded, dirty, one-room base- ment apartment. She collected things—and among them was a box of beads and buttons that she gave me to take to the orphanage. I asked her why, and she said, "You just might like to have it there." I think at that moment I realized I was going away from her for more than just a few days.

She had taught me to make little dolls by stringing buttons and beads onto fine wire. Before the orphanage we lived in many places: I transferred from one school to another twelve times in my first eight grades. In one of those apartments I made several dolls, and Mama attached safety pins to the backs of them as brooches. She encouraged Sam and me to take them to the street corner and sell them from a little box lid. Her purpose was not to make money— the money would be mine. I think her intent was to be creative, to entertain us and teach us. She said, "People won't think it's strange— you're *children!*" Two people bought dolls at a nickel each. I was both pleased and sorry. I earned enough for two candy bars, but my best dolls were chosen.

* * *

Each morning and each afternoon I walked with exaggerated slowness past the orphanage administration building as I went to and from public school. I passed the director's window as slowly as I possibly could, because I hoped that she might see me.

I made a man doll with a hat that had a button for a brim. He was exceptional; he could stand alone; I liked him a lot. I attached a smaller one, a tiny doll, to the hand of the bigger one. Both of them stood, side by side. I was really proud of them, and I remembered a phrase I had heard somewhere, which I thought was clever and fitting for the dolls. I made a little card and printed on it, *Like Father—Like Son.*

I took it to the administration building, went into the director's office when she was not there, and stood the dolls on her desk. I put the card with them, and I place a note I had written to her next to them. I remember stepping back to look at them— how fine they all were on the clean, orderly desk—how fine a gift it was.

How much time passed I don't know, but I was called to the director's office. I went in; she closed the door. She asked me to sit down. Something was wrong about this. This was not what I was hoping for. Her voice was gentle. I think she might have started with, "Honey...Honey, did you make this because you are afraid your brother will turn out to be like your father?"

I feel again, writing these words, the vertigo, the loss of control, the swirl of chaos. *My brother? Samuel? My father? That shadowy, invisible, lost shape, that bad man Mama told me never never to have anything to do with?*

"No," I said.

And then everything was awkward and kind and polite and distant, and she said some words and everything was soggy and confused and disappointing, and only now do I clearly see that she missed the mark totally. *I had chosen her*—chosen her as the only possible friend—her face intelligent, her grace, her power, her control, her kindness. As I write these words, I think I hear her laughter—a musical, inviting laugh—*I chose her*—the dolls were not Sam and my father. The dolls were herself and me. There was no one else. She didn't get it. She either didn't get it, or she didn't want it.

* * *

I'm not a person who practices magical or even spiritual rituals, other than a moment of silence before meals, but finally, after months had passed with the orphanage records still untouched in an attic room file, it did come through to me that I needed help to open that envelope. A friend who was my former therapist, Joan Mallonee, offered to read them with me. She announced, in fact, that she was flying from Alabama to Massachusetts to do it, and asked if I wanted anyone else to join us. I tried to imagine opening them, tried to imagine how to make myself safe for that experience. A ritual seemed a good idea. And so I contacted my closest friends and asked each one to send me some token of her presence to place in a circle of candles and tokens around me for the reading. I borrowed another friend's cottage beside a small lake. There, Joan, Evelyn, my longest-time friend, and I prepared the space. Joan brought a bundle of sage; we lit it and waved gentle smoke around the room, inviting any spirits who might live there to depart for a while, and any spirits who could be helpful to me to enter for the time of our reading. Then I sat on the floor and placed the candles and the friendship tokens to make a circle around me that included Joan and Evelyn. I had never done any of these things before, but this situation seemed so unusual it called for unusual measures.

* * *

Joan had read the record the night before and reassured me before she began reading that it was going to be all right. The first page she read aloud was the note I had put on the director's desk with the bead dolls while I was living there. Joan held the page so I could see my childish handwriting as she read.

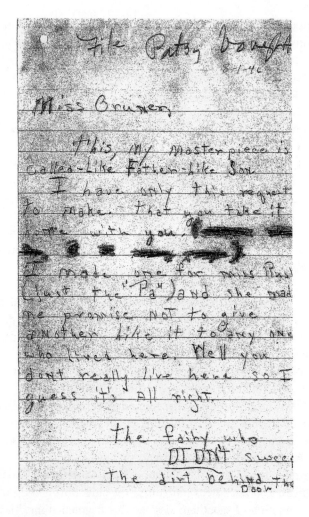

I have no idea what the "fairy" referred to. The records reveal me as a complicated child, confused about sex and afraid of it, resistant when social workers tried to prepare me for menstruation, capable of aches and pains that relieved me of duties I didn't want to perform, resistance to talk with social workers about what troubled me most deeply, and (most bothersome to the staff), fearfully and religiously troubled by the other girls' sexual experimentation, frequently alienating them by reporting their secret activities to the housemother or a social worker. I worked hard, did well in school, and they wondered in the records why I worked so hard, and why I was so sad.

There were a few surprises in the dozen or so additional pages. The first report was by a social worker. It detailed the "intake" of myself and Samuel, as he was called then, that day in the office. How I kept a hand on him. The memory of my hand on his collar is vivid, but the social worker's description of my behavior goes beyond a casual touch. The new information and the old memory are indistinguishable now. My adult perception complicates the child's experience. It was painful to hear the social worker's concern about what to her was my obsessive touching of my brother, my hand on his shoulder, straightening his collar. My attentive hover.

In my memory, they separated us immediately and totally. He lived in the boys' cottage and ate at the boys' end of the dining room. All of my memories of him there after that day are across a space too large for us to speak to one another.

As for the housemother, her reports match my memory. She smiled, but when the smile was turned toward me, it didn't seem real. She wore an apron over her roundness of bosom and belly and sat in an armchair most of the time in her room on the first floor across from where we little girls slept. She didn't much like me, both in my memory and in her reports.

Stories the older girls told about boys worried me. They sat together on the back steps sometimes, the older boys and the older girls. Sometimes I saw them kissing. That frightened me. The big girls took a little girl and a little boy into the bathroom and made the rest of us smaller girls stand where we could see. They told the boy to lie on top of the girl. In my eyes, the little boy was laughing, but the little girl was afraid. That, too, frightened me. The big girls giggled in the doorway to the bathroom. In my memory, I tried to talk to the housemother about it; she smiled at their pranks and told me my concern was out of place. She also let the older girls

know that I "told on them." In her reports she seems to take it more seriously, saying that it would not have happened if she had not been on a day off.

I was truly surprised to learn that after a time my mother wanted me to come back home, and that I didn't want to go. Someone intervened, supported me, and convinced my mother to let me stay. I have no memory of wanting to stay, but I also have absolutely no memory of wanting to go home. Home was a disaster area. As I listened to Joan read, I could understand the housemother's annoyance with me, and yet I felt proud of the child I had been, that even though I was not happy there, I understood that I needed to stay, and with someone's obvious help, was able to ask for it. The record also contained a dangerous possibility; they seriously considered sending me to live with a family that wanted an "older girl" to be companion and baby-sitter to their young children. The report says they finally figured out that the host family intended the "older child" to have full responsibility for two children under the age of three and decided I was too young at the very beginning of my twelfth year.

The last report in the envelope was from the housemother. The first words are, "Patsy has been upset lately." After several complaints about "my temperament," which she suggests could be because I am about to begin menstruating (something that did not happen for another year and a half), she says:

> She must have told her mother that I had her put some of her rocks in the attic, and her mother wants to get a little cabinet of some kind for her so that Patsy could have them at hand whenever she has the inclination! Really, all she did was clutter her chest of drawers and her locker with them and she rarely took them out. I suggested she put them all in a box and in the bottom of her locker; another time I suggested that she had so much extraneous matter which she was not using at all, wouldn't she like to put some in the attic so that her clothes would not always be in such a state. She did, and among other things, carted the rocks to the attic.

I can feel it even now, in my bones. The violation. I was not like the other girls. Those rocks were my safety. They were the ground I stood on, fossils I gathered in the creek at the bottom of the orphanage hill. I belonged to them. They were my ancestors. They endured. For millions of years they had endured.

That's the last report. There is no information about what happened then, and I have no memory about it. Except that I went home, and I took my rocks with me.

*   *   *

Home, when I got there, was no longer the basement room. Mama had moved us a few blocks away into a tenement on Olive Street between Sarah Street and Vandeventer. We had two rooms on the top (third) floor of a tenement that stood between an abandoned doughnut shop and the Congress Theatre, where on weekend afternoons a double feature (two movies) with a newsreel, a segment of a serial and a cartoon cost twelve cents. The neighborhood was small stores, a pawn shop, several taverns, and one or two other tenements. Two street-car lines ran in front of our building. The lock on the front door was broken; the stairs were filthy, smelling of urine and roach poison. Seven families used one bathroom, and nobody cleaned anything.

At night I sat in the window of the room that served as kitchen, on a cot that was my bed, or my brother's when he was home briefly between foster homes. In the other room, Grandma, who was in her eighties and had moved in while I was in the orphanage, shared a bed with Mama. All of her possessions were in one dresser drawer. There was no closet. Out the window, above the rooftops of stores, I could see in the distance the lighted dome of the St. Louis Cathedral. It shone golden in the darkness. Below me, streetcars rattled by, lighted inside and I could see women there. They appeared to be looking out the windows, but I had ridden streetcars at night many times. I knew they could only see their own reflections in the glass. They could not see me in a dark, upstairs window.

I thought they were women in fur coats, riding to the opera downtown, and I hated them with a pure hatred because they were blind—they could not see me, trapped in a tenement window. I wanted to go to the opera. I would look then at the golden dome of the cathedral and swear—*I will get out of here, and I will never forget!*

It would be many years, and it would be in the act of writing, that I would realize: Those were not women in fur coats, going to the opera. They were waitresses and maids, going to night shift jobs, and they were wearing fake fur. Women going to the opera didn't ride streetcars on Olive Street. They rode in big private cars over on Kingshighway and Lindell Boulevard.

* * *

In the first image, a child stood in an office. In the second image, the child is at the bottom of the hill, standing at the entrance to the orphanage. The hill seems huge—a long slope of grass with the buildings at the top. She stands with her mother. It is only five weeks after they stood together in the office. The mother speaks:

"They won't let Samuel stay."

"Why not?"

"I don't know. They say he did something sexual."

In the child's mind, the world stops turning. Her heart stops. There is a dreadful silence in the world, and nothing exists but that moment, that grass, those buildings, those words: They won't let Samuel stay.

"Did he?"

"I don't know."

* * *

He was all I had. We weren't allowed to sit at the same table in the dining hall. But I could see him across the big room, on the far side of the dining hall. I could see how light caught in the yellow of his hair. I could see him laugh with the other boys. Then, after only five weeks, he was gone.

* * *

Sam went from foster home to foster home. Not until we were both in our sixties did he tell me about bad things that were done to him there, things I promised never to tell. After I had read the record where all the words about him were blacked out, we were sitting one day at my kitchen table, eating brownies left over from my writing workshop, telling stories and laughing as we always did when he stopped in for a cup of coffee. He was a truck driver, a big bear of a man, and my best friend all the days of his life. Finally I cracked open the question. I told him what Mama had said at the entrance to the orphanage, and I asked, "You were only nine years old. What can a nine-year-old do that is bad enough to get him kicked out of an orphanage? Did you do something sexual?"

He gave me a long, straight look, and said quietly, "I didn't *do*, but I was *done to*."

* * *

"Follow, poet, follow right to the bottom of the night."

Mama was standing beside me, and Samuel was in the boys' cottage, but in that moment at the bottom of the hill I realized that I was completely alone. The word that I had never even thought, I have now written my way into. The word is: *abandoned*.

How can I say that moment was the deepest point of dark my life has given me? How can I, when I have felt the shadow of dark wings hover over the lives of two of my children? When I have lost into death some of the people I most loved? When I am not unaware of the trouble in the world?

I say it because it is true. Tomorrow, it may no longer be true—writing changes us. But in the moment of this writing, the darkness at the heart of who I am, who I became as an adult, the darkness that formed both my strengths and my weaknesses—was abandonment.

* * *

My mother said she put us into the orphanage "for your own good" and "to learn good table manners." When I thought about that in my young adult life, I was angry. Only later, did I realize that, in fact I did, "learn good table manners," and that what she meant was she wanted me to be able to change class. She wanted a different world for me—one where people sat together to eat at a table, and had good manners—different from the world I returned to when I came home from the orphanage.

In that world, which I have already described, one day when I was in high school I wore a Salvation Army formal dress to school rather than stay home. I did it because I couldn't bear to spend the day in the two rooms as Mama slept all day in order to work all night. There was no place to store clothing except in piles in the corners, everything rumpled, soiled, shameful.

I decided to pretend I was going somewhere after school. The formal was pretty, but it was satin, full, with straps over bare shoulders, and it was long. I didn't think saddle oxford shoes would look good, so I wore a pair of Mama's high-heeled shoes.

This would be funny if it wasn't so awful. How I thought I could pull it off is beyond me now. I walked a long block down Olive Street to Vandeventer and took the Vandeventer bus to high school. By the time I got to school, the shoes were so painful I could hardly walk. By that time I knew I looked utterly ridiculous, but I was desperate to be in school. I went to my locker and got my gym shoes. I gritted my teeth and walked the halls from class to class all day looking neither to the right nor to the left.

* * *

My world did change. Before the orphanage, the life we lived was the only life I knew. After the orphanage, it was impossible *not to see* the home I returned to. As a thirteen- fourteen- fifteen-sixteen-year-old, I swore I'd get out and never forget. And it came to be: I did get out. For now, writing as a spiritual practice is working on the "never forget" part.

At the beginning of this chapter I quoted D. H. Lawrence: "But you can't change your nature and mode of consciousness like changing your shoes. It is a gradual shedding. Years must go by and centuries must elapse before you have finished. It is a long and half-secret process." It has taken me many years of writing to find my way to the heart of my own darkness: to the origin of my fear of loss; to the origin of my desperate need for reassurance that those I loved would not go away; to the origin of my inability to walk away from relationships that a wiser person would have let go; even to the origin, perhaps, in the year before I began this book, of my desire to follow Sam when he died.

* * *

Abandonment. I say—no, I *write*—"abandonment," and when we talk about the chapter, my friend who is a therapist tells me that he has a question about my use of the word *abandonment.*

I think, Oh, what I experienced *wasn't* abandonment—the word so hard to write, so slow in coming: *a – ban – don*…No. Not that. Try again: *a – ban*…No. And finally, more than twenty pages later, the whole word—all the way through "ment"—what I meant, what I could not write, but meant, was *a – ban – don – ment.*

My friend said he had a question about my use of that word, and I thought, it's just as I feared—that's not the right word, after all. It was a while before he could ask his question, because he loves me, which he did not say, but I know because I love him and I can see it in his eyes, the love of a friend—a longtime friend for a longtime friend. And also he had difficulty asking his question because he is not my therapist, which he did say, and because writing that word had made me vulnerable, which he also said. He said these things several times, and all the while I was certain that his question was that I had used the wrong word. Finally he asked his question: *"Have you really gotten to the bottom of the abandonment—have you seen the whole of it?"*

I hung there on the cliff edge of that dark for long enough to let the question in. He wasn't saying the word was the wrong word. He was saying it was maybe more the *right word* than I had allowed onto my page. Was there more that I had not let into my conscious mind? Had I gone all the way into the meaning of that word in the life of the child that I was on the day when I first knew myself to be alone?

Immediately after writing the word "abandonment," I had written, "Not that my mother abandoned me, but that I experienced abandonment." He quoted that line to me, and asked, "Are you stepping back? The father left. The mother left. The brother left. That child was *abandoned*. Are you letting your mother off the hook?"

Soon after, writing about it, I stumbled into these questions: If I am letting my mother off the hook, is that letting myself off the hook? Is letting myself off the hook also letting the reader off the hook? After all, the reader "dreams" the writer's dream after the writer. In my heart I know that what my friend said is true. But I also know something of my mother's history, her character, her limited education, her own entrapment in poverty, her desire to have her children escape it. I know the good gifts she gave me— poetry, a desire for an education, a love of writing, laughter. The dark and the light, mixed together.

But in this chapter I am attempting to obey Auden's command to follow right to the bottom of the night. I thought the word "abandonment" was for me, in fact, reaching the bottom. But what if Auden's command (or invitation) is like Jesus's command (or invitation) to give up everything and follow him? What are the specifics of those imperatives—Jesus's and Auden's? Is Jesus saying sell your house, go homeless, give your last penny to the poor and become the poor yourself? Where in that is the care of the self? And where is the limit to Auden's imperative? If we go all the way to the bottom of the night, do we become the darkness?

Listening to me reflect on these questions, Peter reminded me of the biblical statement, "If then the light in you is darkness, how great is the darkness!"[15] But thinking about that now I hear an echo reminding me of words I quoted earlier. I can't separate light and dark. "The darkness and the light are both alike to thee."

* * *

The friend who questioned my word, "abandonment"—or rather, my compromising it—may be right. Maybe I was more totally abandoned than I admit in my story. Maybe I was, in fact, eleven years old in this world with nobody at all able or willing to love me. Maybe what I have called "love" was not love at all, but other people's need.

Maybe the dark abyss below/in front of me can swallow me, can overcome my light. Maybe the bottom of my own night is a darkness I cannot descend into without "the light that is within me" becoming dark. "How great is that darkness!"

I step back. I say to my friend, You may be right, and I am deeply grateful for your honesty and love in asking your question: *Have you really gotten to the bottom of your abandonment?*

I say to myself, perhaps my mother did *not* love me, was not able to love me. But believing that she loved me—that she did the best she could, that she *wanted* to love me wisely (is that not love?), *believing* kept the light that was within me from being overcome by dark.

Lane Goddard, a wise friend and marvelous writer in North Carolina, asked me, "If I receive the love another is able to give, even if it is not the love I want, am I not loved?"

I say to Lane, "Thank you."

I say to Auden, I have followed this far today. But for now, I step back. I remember the dream at the beginning of this chapter. My soles (soul) are covered with sores. I cannot walk farther in this direction at this time. I know now that the bottom of my own night was abandonment. But for now, I keep the belief. I say, *she loved me.* I choose that much light.

* * *

Writing as a spiritual practice is one of the ways we can trace the outline of the mystery. Writing allows the darkness—the *tehom*—to take form, and strangely, the end of darkness is a breaking into light. Dante wrote about this in *Inferno:*[16] at the very bottom of hell the pilgrim breaks through to Purgatory, which is the way to Paradise, giving Dante glimpses of "store upon store of delight." Auden himself goes on to say:

Follow, poet, follow right
To the bottom of the night,
With your unconstraining voice
Still persuade us to rejoice;

With the farming of a verse
Make a vineyard of the curse,
Sing of human unsuccess
In a rapture of distress;

In the deserts of the heart
Let the healing fountain start,
In the prison of his days
Teach the free man how to praise.[17]

It may feel as if *centuries must elapse* before we write our way
home. But for writers, those inner earth-shifting events make up
the texts of our personal mythologies. No matter what our personal story, it is the dark and the light out of which we come. None
of us grows to adulthood without experiencing darkness as well as
light, and that darkness, whatever it is, is one of the lenses through
which we see the world.

Each of us has a private inner life, and in that life there are
secrets that drive us to be who we are. Writing is not the only way
for a pilgrim to identify, name, and find his or her way through the
dark night of the soul. But writing, I suggest, is where we humans
most make our own minds visible to ourselves and to others. There,
on the faint lines of our pages, we can take down our masks. Ironi-
cally, even when we think we are building masks, creating entirely
fictional characters, our very mask-making reveals us. In writing,
we see, sometimes with fear and trembling, who we have been,
who we really are, and we glimpse now and then who we might
become.

WELCOMING ANGELS

Between the last war
and the next one,
waiting for the northbound train
that travels by the river,
I sit alone in the middle of the night
and welcome angels.
Welcome back old hymns, old songs,
all the music, the rhyme and rhythm,
welcome angels, archangels,
welcome early guesses
at the names of things,
welcome wings.

I have grown tired of disbelief.
What once was brave is boring.
Welcome back to my embrace stranger,
visitor beside the Jabbok.
Welcome wrestling until dawn,
until it is my hip thrown out of joint,
my pillow stone, my ladder
of antique assumptions.
Welcome what is not my own:
glory on the top rung, coming down.[1]

—P.S.

CHAPTER 6

Tradition: Religion

*There are hundreds of ways to kneel and kiss
the ground.*
—R U M I , Sufi poet, 13th century c.e. tr. Fatemeh
Keshavarz

*The great way has no gate. A thousand paths
lead to it.*
—L A O   T Z U , Chinese Taoist philosopher (B.C.E. 600)

SOMETIMES TRADITION HOLDS US when we cannot hold
ourselves.

Once when I was tangled in problems and desperately unhappy, a good friend listened to me describe my dreams. There had
been a sequence of three. In each dream I was standing alone on a
stretch of beach. In the first dream, a bomb was about to go off
close enough to me to make me afraid. The next night it was an
atomic bomb, and I knew it would kill me. The third night it was a
nuclear holocaust, and the whole world was going to blow up.

My friend said, "I want you to let me hold those bombs for you
for a while. I'll hold them, and you tell your mind that you have
received the message. You understand, and you don't need any
more bombs."

It was brilliant. She took the bombs, and I could breathe.
I didn't dream even one more bomb. Slowly, I worked my way out
of what had seemed an impossible situation.

In the orphanage, there were two things that held me—my
rocks, as I have described earlier, and one hymn. Each Sunday,
someone from a suburban Methodist church picked me up and

returned me to the girls' cottage. Each Sunday I sat in approximately the same pew, and the first thing I did was look at the wooden board on the wall to the right of the pulpit where the numbers of the hymns we would sing were posted. I knew the number of my favorite. It was seldom there, but I found it in the hymnal and read the words until I memorized them. I didn't at all understand why they were important to me until one day many years later as I was writing about the orphanage. I was briefly again that eleven-year-old girl. I sat again in the pew, saw the deep rose and blue stained-glass window above me to my left, felt the heavy hymnal in my hands, and in my mind, I began to sing the antique words, "O Love that wilt not let me go…" —and inside, I laughed. How could I have missed their significance?

> O Love that wilt not let me go,
> I rest my weary soul in Thee,
> And give Thee back the life I owe,
> That in Thine ocean depths its flow
> May richer, fuller be.
>
> O joy that seekest me through pain
> I dare not try to fly from thee,
> I trace the rainbow through the rain
> And know the promise is not vain
> That morn shall tearless be.

The church itself, the people in it dressed in their Sunday best, the different faces on those who picked me up and returned me to the orphanage, the minister who admitted my age group, perhaps six or seven boys and girls, into membership and had us turn around to face the congregation and then talked about me being from Edgewood Children's home, as if that was a special privilege, as if it wouldn't make me embarrassed and ashamed—the church itself was nice, but it didn't give me any significant shelter. It was the hymn itself, the words that connected me to the moment in the orchard at Mount Zion that I have described earlier—it was the *Love that wilt not let me go* that sheltered me.

Karl Marx called religion "the opiate of the masses." I don't agree. It is not the opiate. It is not escape or "feel good." It is a life-preserver in a stormy sea. It is the tree branch in the flood. It is the hand of a stranger when you are drowning. Religious tradition is not Presence. Religious tradition is not holy. But it is sometimes survival when everything else fails.

As I write these words, the news reports are telling the world that as many as 150,000 people may have perished in an earthquake in Haiti. This morning's paper has a section of poems and prose pieces by Haitian writers. Some of them describe Vodou experiences.[2]

Religious traditions, all the way from Vodou to the most formal orthodoxies in Jewish, Muslim, Buddhist, Hindu, and Christian practices, can become a community of the living and in some cases, even of the dead, who may hold what we cannot hold— "hold the dreams" for us when we cannot bear the bombs. In some Native American traditions, those who hold our dreams are called "the Keepers."

Nevertheless, many of us have to walk away from our own deepest traditions.

* * *

I am leading a five-day intensive writing workshop in Sacramento. We are meeting in a Quaker meeting house. On the first day, four-teen women and men sat with me in a circle in this quiet, unadorned room. In the center I spread on the floor a beige cloth and on it I placed about seventy objects: a battered baseball; a stained and used wooden spoon; an old Jack Daniel whiskey bottle; a long, heavy, nun's rosary; a set of jacks and its ball; a battered pack of Camel cigarettes; a small blue Buddha; a horseshoe; a bright red bra; a yarmulke; a bit of crochet; a metal replica of an ancient goddess; two pipes, one for marijuana, one for tobacco; a comic book…and on, and on.

I picked up an object, held it in my hands, and began the piece below, which I continued on the second day while others worked in response to new prompts. The poem that is included here was only mentioned in the first draft writing in the meeting house.

I have in my hand a small replica of a prehistoric goddess. She has a name, but at the moment of this writing my 75-year-old brain will not give it to me, and for some reason I'm glad that it won't. I can't remember where she came from, either. Her hair looks maybe African. She is naked, and every important exterior part of her anatomy is there except a face. Even the part my mother called "down there." What name does it have, anyway? I am stunned that I can't be sure of the name of my own body part, even now, 75 years after my "down there" emerged from my mother's "down there."

I have not ever been drawn to goddesses. Early in my life, influenced by church doctrine ("the only begotten son of God" doctrine), and by superstition ("Catholics worship idols and they worship a woman!"), I was insulated against goddesses. Later, along with many other women of my generation, I became uncomfortable with "Father God," and with singing, "Rise up, oh men of God" and "God our father, Christ our brother..." In short, when I realized that my personal "down there" caused me to be pretty much absent from the language of liturgy, I was not drawn to substitute a holy "her" for a holy "him."

So this morning I sit here with a small, metal reproduction of an ancient goddess between my thumb and my index finger, and wonder why all at once I am at least drawn to her enough to pick her up and hold her in my left hand as I write.

It occurs to me that it might be because I lost my cat, Nellie, ten days ago. I held her head in my two hands, put my face close to her face on the vet's table, and whispered to her as the vet gave her the shot. I didn't cry—not right then. But the vet cried.

When Sam and I were kids in the two-room tenement apartment in St. Louis, we frequently took the bikes that the "Red

Feather" people gave to us, and headed for Forest Park. His bike worked fine. Mine had all the threads worn off the axel of the front wheel, so every time we crossed a street I would have to lift the wheel and hold it up against the bike frame as we crossed to the sidewalk on the other side. There were streetcars in the streets; kids rode bikes on the sidewalks in those days. Sam would stop and wait for me. I was thirteen, he was eleven; I was home from the orphanage, he was visiting from his foster home. Those days in the park were wonderful. He liked the mummies, but his attention didn't last long beyond the mummy room. He would play around the statues in front of the museum while I lingered to see my favorite statue. It was a cat. An Egyptian cat. What I loved about it was the curve of its back. That line. It seemed to me to be serene. Each time we were in the museum, I stood and gazed at the line of the cat's back, memorizing it, taking into myself the serenity, the curve, the safety. It was a fortification, a bulwark against the chaos at home.

Forty years later, I wrote to the St. Louis art museum and asked if they had a picture of the cat that was in their collection in the late 1940's. They sent a beautiful photograph—the cat is Bastet, *goddess of women and of joy*.

Maybe that is why I picked up the little goddess. After I went home from the vet's, and after Peter took my cat's body, wrapped in a shroud (an old, crocheted, linen dish towel) and buried her, I went to my computer and wrote a little poem to the vet who cried as she put my furry companion to sleep:

TO MY FAVORITE VETERINARIAN
ON AN UNHAPPY MORNING

for Deborah Lichtenberg

How can it be that we yoke ourselves,
make ourselves beasts of burden,
utterly servant to animal sweetness?
And how can you, high priestess

of animal sacrifice,
how can you bear to carry our sorrow
when we must lay our burden down?

That's why I picked up the goddess, I think. So. Goddess. My own body. "Down there." This goddess' body is so bold! Her arms lie across her huge breasts. Her "down there" – (is the word "pubis"?) – why is there no serious word in my vocabulary that isn't "cunt" or "pussy?" No easy, dignified word like "penis"?

There is a goddess named Kali. I think she's Indian. I think she is cruel. I know there's more to her than that, but I can't remember more. I think of my mother. Her brilliance, her frustration, her rage, her mental illness. How she held a match before my five-year-old eyes after she told me that my father had written me a letter. He had sent me a picture of himself. She showed me the picture. "He doesn't love you any more. He has another little girl now. You want to burn this up, don't you?" I looked at the picture—Did I say *Yes?* Did I nod *Yes?* Daddy's face. Kali. Fire on the face of my father.

* * *

My own tradition went off base a long time ago. I mean, a *long* time ago—a thousand years before Jesus, when King David began the business of turning a desert people's experience of mystery into a kingdom, an army, and a religion. The great prophets, more than five hundred years before Jesus, rose up from the ruins of Israel and the captivity in Babylon and issued their reaction to the idea of kingship and nationhood. They cried out for justice and righteousness. ("Righteousness," by the way, meant *right relationship* with God and neighbor. It did not mean cultic or cultural mores or dogmatic practices and beliefs.)

Jesus emerged from the rural north of Israel, steeped in the teachings of the prophets, and confronted a wild world of Greek, Roman, and Gnostic religious, political, social, and artistic beliefs and practices—a boiling pot of explosive ideas. He was a revolutionary who saw clearly that his resistance to all of these conflicting cultural religions would end in his violent death. Matthew, Mark, Luke, and John, the four books that chronicle his life, were written between A.D. 40 and 65.[3] Everyone except those who believe in the inerrant inspiration by God of all words in the Bible agree that the documents about Jesus are complex and sometimes contradictory, and that most of the sayings that the New Testament claims as his are not his literal words. We have only fragments, glimpses of who he was, small portions of sayings that language analysis allows us fairly certainly to attribute to him.

This is not only true of Jesus. The complicated scriptures and traditions, dogmas and practices of all religions ultimately throw us back, I believe, on our own individual, lonely, heroic journey to discover who we are, where we are, and what our relationship is to this body, this life, and this mystery in which we find ourselves. It is up to us, guided by mystery, to discern what in our tradition is truly holy, what is simply wrong, and what is terribly dangerous.

* * *

And so, what in the world can we do with the torn and tattered remnants, the potsherds, the very *fossils* of tradition that we carry around? It is the second day of workshop; I have offered another writing prompt in response to which we are all writing. When we have finished, Joy Policar reads a story about a woman *not* being Jewish. The woman's husband is Jewish, and she has worked faithfully to take their son to synagogue, to Hebrew school. Now the husband and the son remind her that she herself is *not* Jewish. She goes to Buddhist meditation and feels "weird." She has no religious tradition. It feels, Joy's narrator says, "like a hole in my soul."

Joy's narrator, who has no tradition, wants one. I, who have one, push it around like a beggar's shopping cart full of plastic bags. Years ago, soon after leaving the church, I wrote a poem trying to make sense of leaving, and of where I found myself outside the congregation. I had been a child caught in grinding poverty, rescued from it by scholarships from a local church. I had been a minister's wife for twenty-five years. I had sat in pews, in the meetings of the administrative board, in the pot-luck suppers, in the Sunday school rooms. I had lived in the parsonages.

Writing the poem, I sprawled on the floor of the parsonage living room that we would soon leave, piling up drafts of a poem that I wrote in rhymed and metered form. I needed the form to try to contain all that was boiling around in me. We were leaving the organized church. We were leaving the only life I had ever known except life in poverty.

There is tradition in writing as well as in religion, and I will say more about that in the next chapter. For a writer who is also a spiritual pilgrim, the traditions often overlap.

When I was a young poet in college, rhyme was out of fashion. That was hard on me, because I grew up with rhyme almost as a second language: nursery rhymes, country-western music, hymns. It was still out of style in 1980 when I was writing for the first time about leaving the church, but something told me instinctively that *I needed the structure of form to hold the chaos of my experience.*

When I finally got the poem into quatrains with lines ending in rhymes in an a/b/a/b pattern (sun, rags, one, bags), I still wasn't satisfied. It wasn't enough. It wasn't firm enough, contained enough. I needed it to be like the line on the back of the cat—so exact, so pure, it could hold what I was feeling. I decided to try to rhyme the left-hand side of the poem, as well as the right-hand side, although I had never read a poem that did that. I worked through thirty-seven complete drafts. I couldn't get it to rhyme on the left in the first syllables, as I had on the right, but I captured the rhyme in the second or third syllable on the left (As a, Peels, Astonished, Reveals). I couldn't get it all the way to a/b/a/b, but I got it to a/b/c/b ("astonished" doesn't rhyme with anything, although in a different poem I might have worked playfully with the "ished" part.) Finally it was enough. I had said what I needed to say.

LETTING GO

As a beggar, resting in the sun,
Peels off layers of her outer rags,
Astonished to discover that each one
Reveals another under it, her paper bags

Filling with the garments she had worn
When everything was harder, darker, colder;
As she feels the chill of being born
Again, wiser now, and older,

So I. Having shed the church in the belief
That one particular chill of letting go
Might be a kind of ultimate relief,
(A flat sun of contradiction, saying "No"

To winter, to the ice around the heart),
Under vestments I am finding near the skin
Ragged garments where all distinctions start.
I blunder toward the person I had been

Before costuming for the beggar's part
And trying out in someone else's show.
Living now is nakedness of heart;
Dying—just another letting go.

*   *   *

It was the church—a dwindling, pathetic little Methodist congregation in a grand old lady of a stone building on Grandell Square in St. Louis—that saved me from poverty, sent me to college, and paid for my every need while I was there. After college, I went immediately to San Francisco where my brother was in prison and my mother was living out of suitcases in a tiny apartment. In less than two months, what seemed like the end of the known world to me suddenly changed. Although I had not applied for it, I was offered a full scholarship to Pacific School of Religion in Berkeley and began graduate school. There I met my husband. For twenty-five years we served Methodist churches in New England while living in parsonages and raising our family. We loved our people and felt loved by them. In hindsight, I understand that we were exhausted, in need of a sabbatical, and happened to be working under a bishop who was distant from us and a district superintendent who was a better businessman than pastor. The Vietnam War divided congregations like ours, and our emphasis on poverty and outreach rather than increasing members and budgets got us into trouble with the hierarchy. It was no longer a place where we fit. Leaving the church in my forties was for me a huge divorce. In childhood, Father God and Mother Church had taken the place of the father who left me and the mother who could not take care of me. Máire O'Donohoe, the nun who invited me to Ireland soon after I left the church, caught me in mid-flight and saved my heart from utterly breaking. Catholicism was not an option for me, which she understood, but after I led a five-day workshop in Sligo one summer, she took me to Knock, where pilgrims gather to reverence a long-ago appearance of the Virgin Mary. This is a phenomenon unlike anything a Protestant girl from Missouri like myself would ever have experienced.

Along a side wall in the very large courtyard of the church was a row of water spigots. These were not fancy spigots at all. In fact, they were exactly the same as the old spigots in the tenement of my childhood. You turned a knob on the top and water came out of a spout. At Knock, people were lined up, filling little plastic bottles with water from the spigots. The bottles were from a store across the street, and they were shaped like a statue of the Virgin Mary. Bottles in all sizes, but in only one shape. I asked Máire, "What are they doing?"

She answered reverently, "They are filling their bottles with holy water."

We walked around for a while, looking at the Stations of the Cross and at the statues that were behind glass, replicating the experience of those who saw the Virgin. Máire gently told me about the stations, but I could not stop thinking about the holy water.

Finally I had to ask. "Máire, what makes the water coming out of those taps holy?"

"Well," she said, in a tone more question than statement, "a priest has blessed the water."

"All of that water, from all of those taps? All at once?"

She turned and looked me in the eye. We knew each other well by that time, and Máire is a very clear-eyed country woman from Donegal. She is nobody's fool; she knew exactly what I was thinking.

"Pat," she said. "*All* water is holy."

Oh. I was beginning to get it—*there are a hundred ways to kneel and kiss the ground.*

* * *

Outside this Quaker meeting house a dog barks. California sun heats this semi-desert soil, pulls a blanket of heat up to the chin of the day. Yesterday it was over 100 degrees here. Peter told me this morning at 5:30 West Coast time, 8:30 in Amherst, that fog is heavy in the Connecticut valley—that he remembered to water my new hydrangea last night, but forgot to turn the hose off until this morning. He said the hydrangea is very happy. Maybe it is. Or maybe it is drowning.

I want to write about tradition, but even the thought of it makes me tired. *I believe in God the Father Almighty, maker of heaven and earth, and in Jesus Christ His only begotten son, who was born of the virgin, Mary...*

Is that the tradition I am talking about?

If tradition were a garment, it would be a heavy, velvet cloak. The Catholics have that right. But you can't move freely in a Pope's outfit.

If tradition were a dinner, it would be a feast. It would be a table laden with dishes of food, the recipes passed down through generations. Methodist women's groups have that right. But you can't move very freely after eating one of those pot-luck dinners, either.

If tradition were a Quaker meeting house, it would have no sign nor symbol on the walls of its meeting room. It would be plain, unadorned. I thought, when I left the Methodist church, that the Quakers had that right, and I joined a Quaker meeting. But I soon learned that tradition is as alive and well among the Quakers as it is among the Methodists or the Catholics. When the time came to speak, at the end of the silent meeting, an older man almost always stood up and droned, *We as Quakers believe...*

Tradition.

It is easy to point out what is wrong-headed, what is boring, what is downright silly, what is dangerous in any religious tradition. It is not so easy to become free of the tradition you yourself have taken in with your mother's milk. And every human alive has taken in tradition that way, whether our reaction is conformity, non-conformity, overt rebellion, or perhaps suppressing or forgetting the fact that we were ever influenced at all. I suspect there are saints in all of the traditions, and they are the ones who remain, who stick it out through error and boredom, wrong-headedness, foolishness, and/or cruelty, trying to make it better. Trying to make it true.

I am not a saint.

*   *   *

There is an old story in which a child wants her mother to stay with her at night. "I'm afraid of the dark!" the child cries.

The mother says, "You shouldn't be afraid of the dark. God is here."

The child asks her mother what God looks like, and the mother explains that God is spirit. The child listens, and finally protests, "But Mommy, tonight I need someone with skin on!"

When I was a child, I was introduced to a God "with skin on." That attentive Presence had a face, the face I had been given by my mother, my race, my culture, my class, and my own place in history. The tradition I was born into. The face was a bearded white man with blond hair and a long, flowing robe. On my knees I prayed to the God I imagined from my mother's hymns and stories. In a long life I have come to understand that the God I imagined as a child was a mask for mystery, but something was wrong with the mask. The historical Jesus was a Semite, a dark-skinned, dark-haired man. The white-faced mask was created by a society (my own) that institutionalized oppression of people with dark faces.

Not all are seriously flawed, but even the best masks in religion hide a mystery that is more wonderful than any mask. We are created in the image of the creator. That means to me that our own creations—children, poetry, fiction, art, dance, theater, music—can be the "faces" of mystery. The natural world, its creatures, its rocks, its waters can, and often do take us into spiritual experience.

But the fundamentalism I was born into held that only scripture was the pure Word of God, and it revealed a God who impregnated a virgin and sent his only son to death on a cross. I became increasingly confused as I began to doubt that Jesus was born of a virgin, and that a God who loves, as Jesus taught, could send his children to hell. I became so disturbed, I wanted to leave college. What mattered most to me was crumbling.

Fundamentalism in all religions teaches that faith requires unquestioning acceptance of its doctrines and its social, moral, economic, political, dogmas—closed and locked systems of belief that are held to be the only access to God.

Perhaps a comical poem written in the middle of the nineteenth century by Oliver Wendell Holmes describes the fundamentalist problem best. "The Deacon's Masterpiece or the Wonderful One-Hoss-Shay: A Logical Story" describes a small, horse-drawn buggy, or "shay." The shay is built to last forever: It is magnificent, perfect. But on the day that the shay is one hundred years old there is an earthquake, and the shay shivers. Then, the poet says

> *You see, of course, if you're not a dunce,*
> *How it went to pieces all at once,—*
> *All at once, and nothing first,—*
> *Just as bubbles do when they burst.*[4]

It is not accidental that the builder of the shay is a parson. Holmes could not better have described the tight dogmatic structure of fundamentalism or how, when one bit shivers in the mind of a believer, the whole shay can shatter. In my case, it shattered.

The earthquake in my fundamentalist faith happened during my first two years in college when a professor argued convincingly that many of the stories in the Bible were oral tradition written down hundreds of years after the historical events occurred. Language analysis, historical records, common sense—none of that I could deny. The crisis became personal when I myself began to question the truth of the virgin birth of Jesus. That threw me into such a panic I convinced the local church paying my full scholarship to allow me to change schools.

Questioning a single verse in the Bible was not to me the crumbling of a romantically sweet vision of hay and manger and angels singing on high. It was not at all a personal fear of going to hell—I had *experienced* God as loving, and so I did a good job of ignoring hell. This crisis was worse than any of that. My very here-and-now self was in jeopardy. I was in agony, terrified that if I could not believe that Jesus was born of a virgin, if one word in the Bible was less than true, then none of it was true. It was all a lie, and if it was a lie, so was my own *experience* a lie. That loss is the central fear of the fundamentalist. A friend who had a similar origin in fundamentalism calls her break with it "a personality meltdown." Meltdown. Breakdown. That is how it felt. It took many years to fully understand that what broke for me was not my *experience* of encounter with the holy, but *the locked box* of doctrine that tried to contain it.

The scholarship committee of my church allowed me to transfer from Central College (now Central Methodist University) to the more religiously oriented Methodist school, "Scarritt College for Christian Workers" in Nashville, Tennessee. I expected there to have my old beliefs in the literal inspiration of scripture (every word is the "inerrant Word of God") restored and under-girded. Instead, my new professor, Lindsey Pherigo, gently and slowly helped me to understand that the ancient stories in the Bible are deeper, more complex, and therefore much greater than the tight fundamentalist doctrine in which I had bound myself. "God is greater than any text, greater than any doctrine," he said.

I could almost feel some tight iron bands loosening around my heart. Maybe I could *think,* maybe I could *change my thinking* and not lose the experience at the heart of my own spiritual life.

* * *

It is the third day of the Sacramento workshop; I talk about differ-ent forms in poetry, and lead a playful section on trying to write a sonnet. Several read what they have written; we laugh and clap. Before I read, a man in the workshop circle tells us that the word I was looking for the day before, the word for my mother's "down there" is *pudendum.* Then a woman says the goddess' name is Venus of Willendorf, and the word for the *female* "down there" is *pudenda*, not "pudendum."

We write again. I write:

Workshop—Third day. Sacramento. April, 2009:

> I still need to write about tradition. Lines by Edwin Markham
> that I learned by heart years ago rise in my mind: "Now is the
> holy not afar/ In temples lighted by a star/ But where the loves
> and labors are." I love those lines, but I can't go all the way with
> Markham: "Now that the King has gone our way,/ Great are the
> things of everyday." I don't want a king, any more than I want an
> old white man with a long white beard pointing down the ceil-
> ing of the Sistine Chapel. But I do want "the holy not afar." I do
> want the holy "where the loves and labors are."
>
> I don't have adequate language for my own most private body
> parts. *Pudendum? Pudenda?* I wasn't the only woman in this
> meeting room yesterday who was surprised by that name. I
> wasn't the only woman who had no comfortable name for a part
> of her own body.
>
> I don't have a comfortable name, either, for the mystery that is
> beyond all language, beyond all tradition. But oh! I do love the
> mystery! I do love the brush of the hem of its garment. And I
> have come at last to understand—to at least *begin* to under-
> stand—that sometimes the garment is in fact heavy velvet.
> Sometimes it is an orange robe. Sometimes it is macaroni and
> cheese casserole at a pot-luck dinner in a church basement.
>
> Sometimes it is a plain round room in a meeting house with
> no symbols, no ornaments, just a humorous little 3x5 card on
> the casement of the door to the meeting room that says in old

English script: 𝕻𝖑𝖊𝖆𝖘𝖊 𝖘𝖍𝖚𝖙 𝖔𝖋𝖋 𝕿𝖍𝖞 𝖈𝖊𝖑𝖑 𝖕𝖍𝖔𝖓𝖊. Sometimes it is rocks, thrown into a river on a high holy day. Sometimes it is meditation in a room with a golden statue of a smiling, fat man. Sometimes the brush of the garment of the mystery is the expression in the eyes of a long-loved animal. Often it is the face of someone I love, or have loved and think I have lost, but there, in my mind, she is. Or he is. And in that face is the face of the mystery.

I have become free. There is nothing now between me and the mystery. I behold, and I am beheld. I hold, and I am held. The mystery moves, changes, becomes, comes, and comes, and comes. But the mystery never goes. I can sing the old songs, even the ones with the antique and for me impossible theology, and tears can run down my cheeks—delicious tears of love and remembrance and recognition.

But tradition is not where the holy dwells. Tradition is just a garment that the holy now and then puts on. *Now is the holy not afar,/ In temples lighted by a star,/ But where the loves and labors are."* The holy is where I am. Wherever I am. Wherever any of us are. The holy is not myself, but I am held within the mystery, and the mystery knows me every moment. The mystery loves me, and calls me by my name.

* * *

My friend Al Miller writes brilliant and heart-breaking poems about the Vietnam War. Last night here in my Amherst workshop, he wrote and read aloud an amazing prose piece about having to end the life of a young ewe on his farm—the loveliest and best ewe of the year's flock, he and his wife Suzanne agreed. The ewe had been battered by a ram; forced up against a fence and left to die. And she did die, after four days of heroic attempts in the house to medicate, hand feed, and save her, but for mercy her death was brought to her through the barrel of a borrowed gun, in the hands of Al, who had written so many images of guns in the jungles of Vietnam.

In the piece, Al mentioned a goddess with many hands, and on each hand an eye. The hands, he wrote, were for action. The eyes were for understanding. At least that's what I thought he read. This morning I called and asked him about that goddess, and he directed me to an essay by Thich Nhat Hanh, a Zen Buddhist monk, peace activist, scholar, and poet who was nominated by Martin Luther King for the Nobel Peace Prize in 1967. The goddess is Avalokitesvara. In Buddhist iconography she has one thousand hands, each in a different position, and an eye in each hand. "When you have an eye in your hand," Thich Nhat Hanh says in his *Commentaries on the Five Wonderful Precepts*, "you will know how to practice true nonviolence."

> In Buddhist iconography, there is a bodhisattva named Avalokitesvara who has one thousand arms and one thousand hands, and has an eye in the palm of each hand. One thousand hands represent action, and the eye in each hand represents understanding. When you understand a situation or a person, any action you do will help and will not cause more suffering. When you have an eye in your hand, you will know how to practice true nonviolence.[5]

I still don't know very much about goddesses, Diamond Sutras, and holy water. I suspect I have to do more work about tradition. Al reminds me gently that tradition is only a recipe. "You don't have to follow it," he says.

I think I need the grace of more compassion toward bishops, district superintendents, backward collars and orange robes. But I do know now that there are a hundred—no, *countless* ways to kneel and kiss the ground. And I wouldn't be surprised at all if my lost little four-legged Nellie knew how to kneel and kiss the ground. She kept me company on my bed all day and all night through all of the weeks I lay recuperating from falling on the ice and breaking my hip two years ago. Or maybe she is part of the ground that I need to kneel and kiss. In the spring, when the snow is all gone, forget-me-nots will bloom over her grave.

YOUR BOAT, YOUR WORDS

Your boat, they will tell you,
cannot leave the harbor
without discipline.

But they will neglect to mention
that discipline has a vanishing point,
an invisible horizon where belief takes over.

They will not whisper to you the secret
that they themselves have not fully understood: that
belief is the only wind with breath enough

to take you past the deadly calms, the stopped motion
toward that place you have imagined,
the existence of which you cannot prove

except by going there.

—P.S.

CHAPTER **7**

Tradition: Writing

What I want to say is this:
I liked those little balls
on my mud pies.
—PAT SCHNEIDER

TRADITIONS IN WRITING, LIKE TRADITIONS in spirituality, are both bane and blessing.

Peter Elbow has written that many of the problems people have in writing "come from its permanence and cultural weight." We write, in part, because reading has mattered to us. The writing of others has mattered to us. But that very importance can be a weight we carry as we put our own pens to paper: the importance and weight of tradition.

Tradition is a house that we live in, but we keep adding rooms, stairways, even elevators that take us to parts of the house we may not have even imagined were there. The house itself is a living thing. It is made of bricks and glass; morning light comes in, and the glass thinks, *I am the best part of this structure.* But the bricks say, *Oh yeah? Where would you be, if we didn't hold you upright?*

Thinking about tradition in writing, I see the bricks as writers and literary critics who have gone before us, and the glass as the work of the newest, bravest, most innovative writers and literary critics working now as this day begins dawning and I sit writing. It is 5:45 in the morning in Amherst, and the sun has not yet risen. Another writer in California just emailed me, and it is 2:45 A.M. there! We are writing to each other, and we are talking about our writing—being "literary critics" for one another. Writers and literary critics need one another, just as those who are on spiritual journeys need theologians, and theologians need those who care about spiritual search. Critics and theologians—those who *think about* writing and religion—help us understand where we came from, how we got here, and make it possible for us to move, change, innovate, and grow. But there are traditions in which the unwary, the uninformed, can be seriously knocked off course.

I had published a good number of poems in literary journals and magazines when another writer's particular literary tradition ran head-on into me, and, like some of the writers in my workshops who have been stopped in their writing by certain critical responses to their work, I had no idea what had hit me. A friend in a neighboring town asked me to trade some poems in manuscript; each of us would critique the other's work. I had not published a book of poems at that point; she had two books published, and I was impressed. I gave her several free verse poems and a couple of formal poems. When we gave back each other's work with our comments, I was stunned. She had filled my pages with suggestions for changes that seemed to me to destroy the poems. For a number of days I went around thinking I must be a terrible poet. Surely she knew best; after all, she had two books published.

Again and again I looked at her comments, and I could not do what she suggested. Finally one of her comments was the key to a huge lesson for me. I will come back to that.

* * *

Most people for the first time studying creative writing in classes or in my own workshops assume that the teacher or workshop leader must "know best." Similarly, many writers who are just beginning to offer their work for publication have no idea of the deep currents of tradition that lie hidden under the surface of all forms of published writing, and so beginning with their first rejection slip, their reaction is, "I must not be a good writer." They don't know where their internal critics are coming from, nor where those who judge their work are coming from, or for that matter, what history influences their own work.

Older writers frequently say to me, "If a poem doesn't rhyme, I don't like it." Writers in their thirties and forties write free verse and look dismayed or completely befuddled if I suggest they write a villanelle or a sonnet. Some young graduate students in MFA programs are now calling themselves the "New Formalists." They listened to rap and rhymed up a storm creating it in middle school and junior high. Now it is not unusual for them to bring me a ballad or sonnet or even a villanelle without any prompt from me. Most beginning writers in all of these groups have no idea that the teacher or friend who is responding to their work may very well come with traditions peculiar to his or her own age, traditions that come straight out of the history of literary criticism. Neither do they understand that their own words on paper are influenced by personal traditions and their generation's literary preferences and prejudices.

Styles in writing fall in and out of fashion: By the 1950s, rhyme and meter were mostly out, and "free verse" was in. Early twentieth-century writers and teachers had reacted against the Romantics of an earlier generation. T. S. Eliot led the charge, shooting down Tennyson and making a doctrine of the "impersonality of poetry."[1] Today rhyme and meter are back in style.

The New Formalists are weary with the predominance of free verse in the work of their predecessors. There are trends in writing just as in clothing design, furniture design, music, and all the other art forms. Like teenagers, every generation of writers will question, if not reject, the teaching that went before. The very strength of one generation of writers is fodder for revolution by the next.

In the 1950s my college English professors were still teaching the poetry of the Romantics, those old masters of feeling like Alfred, Lord Tennyson and William Wordsworth, who said, "Poetry is the spontaneous overflow of powerful feelings: It takes its origin from emotion recollected in tranquility."[2] But the same professors, teaching us to write, distrusted personal feelings. "Subjectivity" was bad. Feelings—especially *personal* feelings—were "self-indulgent." Poetry should be "impersonal." The Romantics

used rhyme, yes, but we should not. It was old-fashioned, senti-
mental, *verboten!* They wrote about love and nature; those were
"sappy." I was taught that "modern" writers not only *could be* but
must be what was called "objective."[3]

* * *

In the 1970s, when my three older children were in elementary
school and I pursued my MFA in creative writing, the battle was no
longer subjectivity versus objectivity, or romanticism versus mod-
ernism. (William Safire once quipped, "all the 'is'ms' are was'ms.")
In the world of writers and writing, the prejudice against personal
feeling continued, but there was a new word for it. What was bad
was *confessional.*

"Confessional" writing has its origin in the monasteries and
convents of Europe, as monks and nuns wrote about spiritual pil-
grimage. Augustine, sixteen centuries ago, wrote his masterpiece,
later named *The Confessions of St. Augustine.* It is a monologue addressed to God. The reader travels with Augustine as he does battle
with himself, with ideas that come to him from his time and place
in history, and with God. In Augustine's text and in much of traditional devotional literature, the distinction between "writing" and
"spiritual practice" disappears. They are one and the same. The
poetry of Gerard Manley Hopkins; the journals of John Woolman,
John Wesley, Thomas Merton, the commentaries of Hildegard of
Bingen on her illuminations, and the confessions of John of the
Cross, as well as Augustine are a few of the classic examples.

The term "confessional" as a negative came to power in literary
circles out of this legacy, but also partially as a defensive response
to the emergence of writing by people who were still mostly outside the mid-twentieth-century literary establishment: women,
people of color, gay writers. It questions the *content* of writing,
under the ruse of questioning style, craft, and skill. The female director of a major MFA creative writing program (who shall remain
nameless) in a major American university was overheard by one of
my workshop participants to say, "If I ever hear another poem
about an unhappy childhood, I'm going to puke." Note the word

about. What was being faulted was not craft, style, or skill, but what the poem was about. In other words, its *content.*

I find in my workshops at the start of the twenty-first century a lingering distrust of writing personal subject matter—I feel this distrust in myself. Writers tell me apologetically, "This is self-indulgent," or "This is too personal," or "I know this is too much about me." They seldom use the word "confessional," and most have no idea that the prejudice they are voicing has a lineage, all the way back to the 1950s.

Yet confessional writing has always been with us, in poetry, journals, memoir, and veiled, in fiction, songwriting, and drama. What else was Arthur Miller doing, if not "confessing" the anguish of an entire nation, in *All My Sons*? In that play, a father has compromised the safety of soldiers by using inferior materials in the construction of airplanes. Only when his own son goes down in one of those planes does the father understand what he has done. The line, *They are all my sons!* is a lens through which a warring nation might see itself and be healed.

Jack Kerouac, in his 1951 novel, *Visions of Cody,* writes this:

> I'm writing this book because we're all going to die—in the loneliness of my life, my father dead, my brother dead, my mother far away, my sister and my wife far away, nothing here but my own tragic hands...that are now left to guide and disappear their own way into the common dark of all our death, sleeping in me raw bed, alone and stupid: with just this one pride and consolation: my heart broke in the general despair and opened up inwards to the Lord, I made a supplication in this dream.[4]

Allen Ginsberg, in "Meditation and Poetics," quotes that passage and then comments, "As a motive for writing a giant novel, this passage...is a terrific stroke of awareness and *bodhisattva* heart, or outgoingness of heart." Kerouac not only "confesses" that his motive for writing fiction came from his own lived experience; he also "confesses" a religious experience.

It does not matter *why* the writer writes—to confess, to heal, to publish, to talk to him- or herself, to record family stories for descendants. None of those reasons for putting words on paper prevent those words from *also being art*. The writer pulls content (images, actions) "from the dark"—out of the interior of his/her private life. What is left for us but some form of *confession?* Even when we write imagined images and story, are we not confessing what we have imagined? When we write the results of our research, are we not *confessing* our own discernment?

* * *

Having said all of this, and knowing that I am going out on a limb of some of my own prejudices and preferences, I spoke with someone who knows this history better than I. She told me that I could quote her, but not name her, reminding me that it has been said, *amateurs borrow, professionals steal.*[5]

> I don't think this train of thinking ["confession" as a negative] would necessarily be against memoir per se—or memoir that pushes for facts and real stories. And so I feel that you actually have a debt to this movement: that is, you are the beneficiary of this tradition when over and over you say that it's the concrete detail that communicates the idea or the general feeling. This is a good insight, and you benefit. But you also insist on telling how you feel—even how you feel as you are writing about how you feel. That's what got forbidden.

Tradition is with us, whether we like it or not, whether we accept it or rebel against it, and as we mature as writers, it is helpful to us to be aware of the tradition from which we come.[6] When someone talks to us about narrative form—the form, for example, of "the short story"—it helps us to know that some Native American story forms are cyclical, very different in their form from the sacrality of beginning, middle, denouement, and end that I experienced in college and grew up assuming was proper narrative form.

Finally, whether we know a lot, a little, or nothing at all about the literary tradition that underlies our own voices, it is our own voices we must protect and trust. They are full of nuance, full of unconscious craft, full of character, because they are full of the voices we heard around the kitchen table—the voices that Paule Marshall called "the poets in the kitchen," and John Edgar Wideman called "the language of home."

In my own original voice lies the foundation, the authority, the orientation, the perspective I need in order to use other voices. I find it nothing short of a tragedy that so many teachers of writing have not understood the primal need for young writers to use first—and be affirmed emphatically for—the power of their own voices of home. Almost all of the primary problems of beginning writers are rooted in their effort to *sound like someone else.* That first voice, the voice of home, is the one the writer must protect from the contempt or disdain or disregard of any critic, no matter how famous or capable that critic may be. It is not all that a mature writer needs; surely every writer needs the tools of literary criticism and as much knowledge of various traditions as possible— but a profound acceptance of and trust in one's own voice is the first and most important thing the writer needs.

*   *   *

And that brings me back to the story of the friend who offered me the gift of her critical response to my poems. After some days of seriously doubting my own ability to know what a good poem is, let alone to write one, a particular comment that she wrote in the margin set off a comic-book lightbulb over my head.

The poem was titled "Mama." Her comment on my page was this: "'Mama is a childish name for 'mother.' Change to 'Mother'?"

But where I came from, "mothers" were "mama," "stones" were "rocks" and "fireflies" were "lightning bugs." My friend was cleaning southern Missouri out of my speech. Through that lens I looked at all of her comments, and most of them simply did not fit with her imagery or her usage, perfect though that was for her poems reflecting her origin in New York City.

I felt a kind of shock of recognition then, wondering how many notes I had put on manuscript margins that betrayed my own preferences and regional speech. We are all, to a greater or lesser degree, provincial. We are all capable of ignorance across lines of dialect, locale, race, gender—all of our marvelous differences. I began to laugh, because I could see how strange the language must have been to her. Not only the word "mama" but the syntax, the rhythm—in other words, the entire *voice*—must have been almost a foreign language to her. "Mama" was published soon after I recovered from her critique and offered it to the literary journal, *Excursis,* and it was included later in my book, *Olive Street Transfer,* and then in the "new and selected" poem book, *Another River.* I would never have had the courage to do that if I had not discovered that it was my *voice*—the unique Ozark twang, the flavor, the very originality of my voice—that she was rejecting. Here are the first few lines:

MAMA

Kerosene, gasoline, Maybelline, Vaseline—
Mama said she knew a family in the Ozark mountains
named their baby Vaseline Malaria
because the words were pretty.
Mama's dead now seven years, and I don't visit
the shallow grave where she wanted her ashes buried.
The one time I did walk there alone,
a big, black dog stood guard,
his legs braced far apart, fur
on his neck rising.

Mama was powerful. . . .

Partially in reaction to that critique, and to disappointments that were more bitter in my writing life, I wrote the following poem as a kind of personal manifesto, in the voice of an Ozark kid. It's fun to read at public readings.

WHAT I WANT TO SAY

Well, I was playing, see,
in the shadow of the tabernacle.
I was decorating mud pies
with little brown balls
I found scattered on the ground
like nuts, or berries.
Until some big boy came walking by
and laughed. "Hey,
don't you know you're puttin' goat doo
on your mud pies? I bet
you're gonna eat 'em, too!"

That day I made a major error
in my creative life.

What I want to say is this:
I liked those little balls
on my mud pies. I was a sculptor,
an artist, an architect. I was
making pure design in space and time.
But I quit
because a critic came along
and called it shit.

BRAIDED RUG

The rug is braided and the braid
is the hair of a woman and the air
is full of birds that are not singing
and I am very tired. What am I
going to do if this is not the clue
to something   and here it is
almost October and no crocuses
are planted on the lawn and here
         it is
     halfway through my life
         and
the rug is braided and the braid
is a path and the crimson
is the blood of a boy
dying by himself in a swamp
in a war that he does not believe in,
does not understand, and the blue
is his father's eyes trying to believe,
trying to understand, and the white
is the blank evidence of blue
and crimson   The stitches
that hold the braid coming around this time
to the braid that came around last time,
         the stitches
     are the mother. She holds
         it all together.
But maybe if she didn't, maybe
the crimson would flow off to a flower
in the corner of a pasture under gooseberry
bushes and blue
would maybe go back into sky and white
would not be absence any more
but presence
of snow cut to puzzle pieces by stalks
of wild iris
in the center of the circle
where the first braid turns back on itself,
like an iris in the eye of God.
                              —P.S.

CHAPTER 8

Forgiving

What did I know, what did I know
Of love's austere and lonely offices?
—ROBERT HAYDEN

THREE MONTHS AGO, when I finished the chapter on the dark night of the soul, I thought I was finished with darkness, and I expected light. In fact, I expected *ecstasy*. My next chapter was going to be called "Writing and Ecstasy." That seems silly now, because I know that my own process of writing is more like going through a dense jungle with a machete than it is a walk down a well-marked trail or a lighted street. I can turn around and see where I've been, but I can't see where I'm going until I get there. *Not seeing* is necessary to my own excitement with writing. Writing is an act of discovery, not an act of repetition.

As I wrote about darkness, it seemed that the old cliché, after all, must be true. Isn't it always darkest just before the dawn? The embarrassing truth is, I was so wrung out by the journey I was taking into darkness, I actually, secretly, thought that after I finished, I would *deserve* some ecstasy. So I took notes on my computer under the heading "ecstasy": quotes by Carl Sagan and Emily Dickinson; Gordon Bok's song, "The World Is Always Turning Toward the Morning"; a couple of poems of celebration and praise by Mary Oliver; the title of a C. S. Lewis book, *Surprised by Joy*.

But ecstasy did not follow. Rather, as I drew near the end of the chapter on darkness, the word "forgive" kept coming into my mind between darkness and light. Not as a command, not as, "*You must forgive!*" Rather, just a disembodied word, first in one form and then in another: *forgiveness; forgiving; forgive.* And the words *forgotten, forget, forgot.* And finally, *let go.*

I did battle with it. What does it mean to "forgive," anyway? Does it mean, "Don't think about that?" Does it mean, "push that down inside somewhere and forget about it?" Where and when does "forgive" go awry and become "repress"? How can I forgive, if I don't even know what it is that I am forgiving? How can I forgive what I don't fully understand? What if the people whose actions hurt me were "doing the best they could?" Forgiving was not a word I wanted to think about or knew how to think about. Whatever it meant, I didn't know how to get there.

But each time the word "forgive" or "forget" came up, I noticed it, acknowledged it, sometimes wrote a note about it. It seemed to be a kind of unexpected break in the jungle foliage, a glimpse of mountain or water up ahead—something to go toward, something to watch for, but not to act upon immediately. Like Scarlett O'Hara, I met it with, *I'll think about that tomorrow.*

Now, tomorrow has come, as tomorrows will. Winter snow has given way in my New England town to the steady rain of April. I sit in my little attic writing room and watch icy bits of rainwater collect into patterns on my skylight windows. Two months have passed, in which a journey back to Missouri has occurred—a journey that is so deeply related to the writing I was doing in the chapter on the dark night of the soul, it seems to me to be one of those amazing movements of "mystery." At least for now.

* * *

A few days after I completed the first draft of "The Dark Night of the Soul," and while I was still reeling from where that chapter took me emotionally, my son, Paul, called. He was going to take an exploratory trip to Arkansas to research a possible new book subject, and do a travel piece for the *New York Times.* He invited me to go with him; we could spend a couple of extra days in southern Missouri—the part of the Ozarks where I was born.

"We'll go anywhere you want to go, Mom," he said.

To say that his invitation was a coincidence is impossible for me. I had just waded through internal Ozark images up to my nose holes, even thought I might be "shut of it," as they say in those hills. But here I was, about to go to the very scenes I had just described.

I am home now from that journey. I've written close to eighty pages of journal about the experience—but totally blocked in trying to begin this chapter. "Writer's block" is a common experience. It almost always is rooted in emotions—most often, fear. I've written extensively about fear and its causes and its effect on the writer in *Writing Alone and with Others* as well as in earlier chapters here.

Looking back at the two months when I tried again and again to begin this chapter, it seems to me that my problem this time wasn't fear. I experienced two other kinds of writer's block. First, the experience *was still happening*. Wordsworth's somewhat antique saying, quoted above, says it best: "Poetry is… emotion recollected in tranquility." A writer needs the perspective of "recollection." I have said that when I write, I "explore." That's true, but writing that is creative is *re-creative* as well as explorative. It is the past and the present woven together. Even when the work is fully fiction, it is made up of countless fragments, mosaic tiles of memory, rearranged and enlivened by a new energy, a new alignment. Words themselves are remembered from our first learning and our practicing of them. I tell my writers who are going to travel or attend a significant family event to take notes rather than try for finished work. Rather, try to gather details, images—mulch for the writing they will do later, when the experience has had time to settle into remembered images.

Second, I was blocking myself by trying to write a *chapter*, rather than simply writing what I needed to say. "Form is the shape of content," and yet, full of the content of my journey, I was putting "form" first, trying to make my experience fit a preconceived shape. Not "what happened" but "make a chapter." It was too soon to make the content into a chapter. After I came home from the Ozarks, the experience was still happening in my first processing of it. It was not true that I couldn't write—I just couldn't write what I *wanted* to write—a chapter in a new book. My own habit is, *if all else fails, write a journal entry.* This time, that is exactly what I needed to do—eighty pages of journal. Because I couldn't do anything else, and because it was appropriate to catch an experience—the details of that experience—for possible use later.

Since this book is about writing, how it can work to take us to deeper understanding of our own spiritual journey, finally I understood that this chapter needed to include that process—some of the journal entries themselves. Some letters to Sharon. Some repetitions in letters and journal entries written in my workshops or alone in my attic room. Maybe I will leave the repetitions, because telling stories over and over is one way to find the sort of holographic meanings of our memories.

* * *

Shortly before the trip with Paul, I handed out as a writing prompt in my two weekly workshops a couple of lines from a poem by Robert Hayden: *What did I know, what did I know / of love's austere and lonely offices?*

This is what I wrote in response to those lines:

My father left when I was four years old. The next year Mama received a picture of him in the mail. She brought it to me where I sat playing on the front porch. She said, "Your daddy doesn't love you any more. He never loved you. He has another little girl now. You want me to burn up his picture, don't you?"

I watched the match come toward my daddy's face. Saw my father's face on fire. Saw it fall to ashes. Gone.

When I was thirteen, newly home from the orphanage, my mother's mother was dying. We went to help care for her at my aunt's and uncle's place—they lived in rooms behind their filling station on Route 66 near Fort Leonard Wood. Mama called me to her one day and said, "Your daddy is in the filling station. You can see him if you want to. Just bend down and look through the keyhole. She cautioned me not to go out there, and reminded me again that he had "another little girl now."

He was facing me, far away at the other end of the filling station. He had yellow, curly hair. He was laughing, leaning against the ice chest, drinking a Royal Crown cola.

I had started menstruating that week. As I looked at him I wondered, do other daddies know when their little girls start their periods? *What did I know, what did I know / Of love's austere and lonely offices?*

When I was fourteen, after Grandma died, I was living in two rooms in the tenement in St. Louis with my mother, and now and then with my younger brother who was mostly in foster care. The telephone rang. My mother was at work at her all-night job as a practical nurse.

A man's voice. "Patsy, this is your daddy." The voice a hot bolt of blue lightning somewhere in my body.

In shock, all images disappear. There is a brief, blank, open space in which all your animal senses are alive, and nothing exists except shock.

When the voice on the telephone said, "This is your daddy," it was the voice of an enemy. I was alone. It was night. I was afraid. I answered, "The only Father I have is in heaven," and hung up on him.

The next morning when my mother came home from work, I told her what had happened. "You did the right thing," she said. "He called me, too. He was drunk. He just wanted money."

*   *   *

When Paul invited me in February of 2007, we planned first that he would do his research in Arkansas. He was preparing to write his book *Bonnie and Clyde: The Lives Behind the Legend,* and since he would be in Arkansas researching them, he also accepted an assignment from the *New York Times* to write a story for their travel section on the Whitewater area since Hillary Clinton was a candidate for president of the United States, and interest in her was high.

When he finished his work, we would travel north to see the little settlement called Mount Zion in Douglas County, Missouri, where I was born, and to find Brown's Cave, a huge cavern that had figured in my family's history. Only at the very end of our planning did it occur to me that I was ready to meet one of my father's other children.

Six years earlier I had gone to Missouri to find his sister, Leona, and her daughter, Bernice. At that time I told them I had no desire to meet my father's second family. Now I had to call Bernice (Leona had died) and ask for information about my three half-siblings.

"Which one of them should I meet?" I asked.

She answered emphatically and immediately, "Sharon!"

"Will you go with me?

She hesitated, and then said, "Sure."

Later I learned that Sharon first refused, then agreed to meet me only if Bernice would go, too.

Old scars and traumas being what they are, this meeting felt dangerous and I at last felt brave. But not too brave. I allotted only an hour and a half for the meeting. Paul and I would have to leave to catch a plane back home to Massachusetts. If meeting Sharon turned out to be a disaster, at least it wouldn't last too long.

* * *

When Paul finished his work in Arkansas, we drove north to Missouri, visited Mount Zion, five miles from Ava, and followed two local spelunkers into Brown's Cave on land owned now by a Trappist monastery. Then we drove farther north to Waynesville where my father's people lived and met Bernice and her husband, Aaron. They took us to three cemeteries where we found my father's grave and the handmade concrete tombstones of his parents and siblings, decorated with bits of broken glass. We found the graves of Indian, German, and English ancestors, with probable Welsh and possible Dutch mixed in. My children were forged in an American melting-pot.

Finally it was time to meet Sharon. We would have only a quick lunch with her before we had to leave for St. Louis and the flight home.

As Bernice and Aaron drove us to the restaurant, we all fell silent. I felt as if every cell of my body was on full alert. My expectation, after all, was more than half a century old. It was an old sack somewhere inside that held hurt and anger, betrayal and forsaking, confusion and fear. Once Sam went to see our father. He brought me school pictures of the three other children—Sharon's appeared to be a high school picture. Sam said, "You look so much alike it's scary." I didn't want the picture, but I never could throw it away.

When we arrived at the restaurant, Bernice, Aaron, and Paul stepped back from the door, and I stepped through. In front of me, seated on a bench, was a woman who looked as frightened as I felt. When she saw us, she started to rise. I glanced at her, then glanced away, and as she stood, I realized—*that's Sharon.*

I said, "Sharon?"

Her first words were, "You have the Vogt nose!" She turned quickly to greet Bernice.

Simultaneously I turned toward Paul and said, "Her eyes are just like Laurel's!" It is clear to me now that we each turned for safety to our "seconds" in the ring. We all laughed nervously, and moved to a round table with corner seats. I asked Sharon to sit next to me—we scooted in to the center, Paul, Bernice, and Aaron on the sides.

When we were settled and had ordered sandwiches, Sharon said, "We're all proud of you because you write books."

Bernice said, "How many books have you written, anyway?"

I mumbled something several digits lower than the truth, and then Sharon began, and Bernice joined in, a nervous and rapid-fire discussion of "We don't speak right.... We talk hillbilly..." This was one thing I had feared—my writing as a barrier to our meeting. I had told Bernice and her mother on my earlier trip that I'm a writer, but they hadn't seen any of my books.

After a bit I said slowly and seriously, "I love the way you speak. You use the language as I first learned it, and it is beautiful, and I love it." They stopped that line of talk then and didn't come back to it again.

Sharon Senovich is shorter than I, more petite, prettier—an expressive face, intensely blue eyes. It is said that more than 90 percent of what we ever know about another person, we know in the first four minutes.[1] Our animal selves, we are told, know instantly far more than we will ever learn later. My first five seconds with Sharon confused me greatly: I liked her. We could be sisters—I could see it. We look enough alike. There was a stunning strangeness, as if seeing myself unexpectedly in a mirror—for a moment both unfamiliar and familiar.

We talked nervously at first, then more easily, about our grandparents, Harv and Elzina—how they lived on a farm in a religious commune where the preacher claimed to be Jesus Christ for a while when they were young—probably not as converts. Harv was a farm laborer, doing jobs from farm to farm as a young man. Elzina, pregnant, insisted on leaving the commune, but the preacher refused to loan Harv a horse and buggy to take her to her parents. So one dark night Harv "borrowed" the horse and buggy, was reported by "Jesus Christ," caught mid-trip and put in jail, accused by the preacher of stealing his horse. Horse thieves were hung in that county at that time, so Harv dug his way out of jail and hid in a cave "for a long time" while Elzina's mother brought him things to eat. There was good laughter in the telling of the story; we all relaxed over plates of good southern food. Paul told them about our finding Brown's Cave, where Harv most likely hid; how a local spelunker led us inside as far as we could go without wading in water to our knees, how it seems a perfect place to deter lawmen.

Clearly their image of me had been of a privileged city girl. I told them that we were very poor, described briefly the tenement where we lived in St. Louis, and said that we were in an orphanage for a while, and Sam was in foster homes for most of his childhood. Both Bernice and Sharon were clearly and completely surprised.

I told them that I know now that my mother was mentally ill, but that the trouble wasn't all her fault. Our father drank and went to prostitutes, and when I told his sister, Leona, she replied with a little chuckle, "That sounds 'bout like Cleve, all right."

And then the surprise came. Sharon said, "Dad tried a lot of times to see you kids. One time he got all dressed up—had on a white shirt and everything; he looked real nice. He went up to St. Louis to see you. Your mother wouldn't let him see you, and so..." She paused and said, "I always think of it as *and so*—he got drunk." We were all silent for a moment, then she asked, "He drank before they got divorced?"

I nodded.

"I always thought he started drinking when I was born," she said. "I always thought it was my fault."

I was struck by her candor, the quiet dignity and strength of her responses. When Bernice said our father's death was caused by ulcers, Sharon replied, "Really? I always thought it was sclerosis of the liver." She was direct without being confrontational, honest, and even in her nervousness, warmly genuine.

"And so," she said again, "he got drunk. And while he was drunk someone stole his wallet." As we talked, the strong image that I had was of him, without wallet and without shoes. In my memory, Sharon said "shoes" but later, she told me she didn't know about the shoes. Perhaps I made that up—yet I felt I knew. He was drunk, and it was night, and someone stole his wallet and his shoes.

Slowly what she was saying superimposed itself on top of my own story: My father in St. Louis, his words, *Patsy, this is your daddy.* Mama said he asked for money.

Did he want to see me? Or did he "just want money"?

Someone stole his shoes. I'm certain now that Mama told me that, and that it was most likely true. She was not a liar. She loved a good story, and she would have liked the way those details belittled him. She must have given him money to go home on—she would not have wanted him in St. Louis.

My father got dressed up and rode a bus three hours to St. Louis to try to see me—he asked my mother for money to return home; barefoot or in his stocking feet he rode for three hours back to Waynesville on a Greyhound bus…

He rode away without shoes, not only rejected by my mother, but also personally and bitterly rejected by me.

*   *   *

May 10, 2007

Dear Sharon,

Let me begin with rain. Today it was announced before it arrived—thunder and lightning—they are rare in New England compared to Missouri. At some point in my childhood I imagined that thunder was God's belly growling, and I was in God's belly. It wasn't a scary idea—it was rather friendly, actually, because at that time I liked thunder and I liked God.

Today I knelt all morning in grass still damp from yesterday's rain, and made a bed for annuals. I planted cosmos, zinnias and marigolds, and in one sunny corner of the yard I planted hollyhocks, remembering that you told me our grandmother loved hollyhocks—*lots of colors,* you said. I talked to her as I put each seed into a little groove and covered it with a quarter inch of soil and patted it down. And then the rain came again, and all afternoon the seeds were watered.

You know I am writing a book, Sharon. For some time, even before my trip to Missouri in February, and my meeting with you, I've been trying to write about forgiving. Before going back to the Ozarks, this writing had nothing to do with you. In fact, I had no intention of meeting you. But after Paul invited me to go with him on his assignment for the *New York Times*, sometime in the planning process it occurred to me that I did want to meet one of the children of my father's second marriage, if any of the three of them would meet me. That idea surprised me almost as much as the shock of realizing I was going to go back at all.

The word "forgiving" (not "forgive" or "forgiven" or "forgiveness") came up as I finished a chapter about being in the orphanage. Not a command. More like an invitation, or a question.

Gradually, after the trip, I became aware that the word had taken root in my meeting with you, but every time I've tried to write, the overwhelming complexity of going back to Missouri, meeting you, hearing new information about the father I thought I had—I don't know what—just given up on, I guess. All of that complexity of feelings, memories, new information, made it impossible to write.

So today, after being on my knees in the yard, with my hands in rich, dark soil, and after talking to our grandmother—yours and mine—about hollyhocks, it occurred to me that maybe I could write this chapter—or parts of it—to you. This chapter in this book I'm trying to write. This chapter on forgiving. Maybe I will never use it. Maybe you will never read it. But maybe it will help me write it.

When I started talking to our grandmother, I called her "Elzina" and then I heard myself do that, and remembered how Bernice corrected me when I first met her. Every time I said "Elzina," Bernice would say "Grandma!" So this time again I said *Elzina* in my mind, and then—I guess to her—I said, *I'd better stop that. I'd better call you Grandmother.*

I think, Sharon, that my writing about forgiving is related to you. At first when I realized that, I sort of assumed I needed to forgive you for being born—for taking my place in my father's heart: *He has another little girl now; he doesn't love you any more.* You, Sharon, were that "other little girl."

But as time has passed, as we met and spoke face-to-face in Waynesville just for one hour and a half, and as we have exchanged our first few letters, I have stumbled each time I have tried to write. The first awareness of what might be wrong came as I realized I couldn't write about forgiving someone else unless I could write about my own need to be forgiven. But what of all my failures should I write about in order to seek forgiving or report on forgiving that had already been given to me? It all felt terribly convoluted, complicated, and just not right.

I came in from planting my seeds all muddy and sweaty, but a sweetness lingered in my mind from the act of planting hollyhocks as rain clouds gathered, and talking to our grandmother, telling her that I have learned from you that she loved hollyhocks, that she always had a lot of hollyhocks in her yard.

Before I was four years old, a woman bent above me and told me how she played as a child. She turned a hollyhock blossom upside down and said it was a beautiful lady in a brilliantly colored gown. I have always thought that woman was my mother. But I don't remember Mama ever having hollyhocks. She had petunias, nasturtiums, sweet peas—but not hollyhocks.

So now I think it was our grandmother teaching me, telling me what she pretended when she was a child. If so, that is my only memory of my grandmother. And so I claim it. I declare it. I make it so. *I claim her. She is mine, and I am hers, through this act of writing.*

Rain has poured down, now, and for the first time this spring it is warm enough to have the back door open and pantry window open, so the sound of rain and the smell of earth moves through the house. All at once I understand, Sharon, that what has been drawing me to the idea of forgiving is the welcome with which you have received me, the welcome you have continued to extend to me in your letters. The unmistakable blessing with which you reached across the chasm of my separation from my father and his family—how quietly, but unmistakably, you reached out, touched me, and took me in.

Love,

Pat

*   *   *

May 19, 2007

Dear Sharon,

I have written the stories about my father before, but never with the thought that you would read it. Now I feel the danger.

Always before, when I wrote about him as that young man I knew only for the first four years of my life, there was no one I could hurt. Sam didn't want to talk about him. He was only two when Daddy left, and he told me he wished I'd just forget. But I couldn't forget. Hurt hangs on, and you can't pry its fingers loose. However that freedom, that forgiving, happens, it's not by forcing hurt down out of sight.

But now, if I write about him, I'm not just writing about my daddy. I'm writing about your daddy, too. So maybe I'll never send this to you. Except yes, if I ever want to publish this book, I will, because I have promised you, in my first letter to you, that I will never publish anything about you without you seeing it first, and receiving your OK.

And I want you to understand the experiences that formed me, so I can give you the gift of knowing how great your gift is to me. In the summer when I saw my father through a keyhole in the filling station door, I took a Greyhound Bus alone from Waynesville to St. Louis. I was thirteen, old enough to stay to help Aunt Nellie with my dying grandma when Mama had to go back to St. Louis to work. Uncle Elmer took me to the bus, put me on, and went back to his car. I was in a seat near the back of the bus. A man got on the bus and something happened in my body—a kind of freeze, as if I were a wild animal cornered, suddenly in total danger, and nowhere to take flight. The man was Daddy. He had curly hair, he had a grin for everyone on the bus, he called several people by name. When he got on the bus, it was almost a party, and he was the source of the good time. *Was it my daddy?* Was I wrong? I had seen him only once since he left us, and that was through a keyhole. His face in the picture that Mama burned was burned onto my mind. But maybe this wasn't my daddy.

Perhaps an hour into the trip, he moved to talk to another man who sat in a seat behind him, closer to me at the back. He was turned around toward me, leaning out into the aisle, laughing with the other man. He supported himself with one hand on the seat back. One finger was cut off at the middle knuckle.

Time stopped. The world stopped. The Greyhound bus was forever. Mama had told me that he shot his own finger off to try to impress a nurse he wanted. She told it with disgust, with that "*See, haven't I told you he is a bad man?*" tone of voice.

No question. He was my father. He didn't recognize me. I wanted desperately to tell him who I was, but I was awkward, I was thirteen, there were pimples on my face. I was ugly. He would be ashamed of me.

Love,
Pat

*　*　*

May 28, 2007

Dear Sharon,

I stand forgiven and forgiving in the heavy internal rain of emotion that spills out over my eyelids and onto my cheeks. I hope you don't mind my writing this to you; I hope you will be comfortable allowing me to offer it out into the world. But if you don't, it is no less healing to me to write it. And this is not the first time I have written my soul out in letters. When I wrote *Wake Up Laughing,* I found my way through the tangle of leaving the church and beginning a search for my father's people by writing a fifty-five page letter to a nun in Ireland who hardly knew me. It was because she hardly knew me that writing my story to her was so helpful. A famous writer, John McPhee, once said that every book he wrote began, "Dear Mother…" Writing *to someone*—even if they never read it—is a tremendously helpful thing for a writer to do, because it focuses the story down to its origins, back to when women sat at a quilt frame or men sat at a checker board—back even to the prehistoric cave when we humans knelt around the campfire and told our stories: one teller, one listener who does not know the story.

At this point, I want to say *Dear Sister.* How strange. All through my childhood, when I thought myself to be alone against the chaos of home and the dangerous world, there was a grandmother who loved me and a little sister whom I would have loved, if I could have known her. In only three more days I will have a birthday. This afternoon I am going to a toy store to buy the best stuffed animal I can find. I'm going to send it to my little sister.

> with love,
> Pat

*   *   *

In the night last night I woke with the strangeness of knowing that my father tried to see me, the image of him on the bus going home with no money. With no shoes.

After a walk on the bike-path in early morning cool, I came to my writing room. My granddaughter's young cat, visiting with me while Sarah studies Spanish in Guatemala for a few months, is spread out near me, on top of my antique Singer sewing machine. Outside this little walk-in attic room with its steeply angled roof, a starling is moving back and forth feeding a single large chick in a birdhouse under the eaves.

All I know is the truth of Hayden's lines: *What did I know, what did I know / Of love's austere and lonely offices?* What did I know of the suffering that lay under my father's or my brother's alcoholism? Under my mother's divorce and mental illness? Under Sharon's personal tragedies and her lifetime caretaking of her family of origin?

I am bent double with grief and with gladness that my writing has brought me to this place, to learn before I die that my grandmother Elzina—who never learned to read and write, whose father was an Indian, probably Creek—who planted and loved hollyhocks and taught me to love them too, loved me. And that the father I lost at age four tried to see me.

Sharon shared with me pictures of our father. She let me make copies for myself and my children. One picture, she said, was for me to keep. It is very small; it fits in the palm of my hand. It is wrinkled, crackled, but the image is plain: a little girl about three years old holds a doll in one hand and has her other hand on her brother. He is about two years old. On the back of the photograph there are words written in pencil: a phone number and a man's name. The children are Samuel and me. Sharon said she thinks our father carried it in his wallet, and at one time had nothing else to write a phone number on. "I'm pretty sure," she said. "He carried it in his wallet."

With all his failings, which he surely did have, it must be that my father loved me, too.

Forgiving cannot be the silent shoving of things under the rugs of our hearts. Forgiving doesn't mean forgetting. Ancient Hebrew scripture says, *He remembereth our sin no more*. Pretty amazing. But *we* are human, and we have to remember, or we will forget the lessons that experience teaches us. If my young friend who is an addict forgets the danger of the dealer who supplies her, how is she to avoid heroin, that saber-toothed tiger in the jungle of the housing project where she lives? How can another friend forget, whose thirty-five-year marriage abruptly ended so her husband can have "one last, great love before he dies"? How can my neighbor across the street forget the eighteen members of his family who were killed by the Nazis?

If we can't forget, how can we forgive? I believe that forgiving can't be done by willpower alone. I can will myself to write out my own memories and feelings. I can will myself to imagine onto the page how someone else may have felt. I can will myself to research someone else's life in order to better understand what happened. But I don't think I can forgive by simply *willing* to forgive. Forgiving *happens to us* when our hearts are ready. Sometimes it takes the form of working on our own story until quietly, often surprisingly, we simply let go of hurt. Sometimes forgiving makes it possible to pick up the pieces of a broken relationship and begin again. Sometimes it means letting a relationship go. We can't forgive through willpower. What we can do is work toward readiness of heart. Writing as a spiritual practice can be that kind of work.

When our heart is ready, we often don't even know it until forgiveness happens within us. It is a gift.

THIS LETTER

If I thought I could write myself
out of this letter
that someone apparently wrote
one night on the arc of the sky
and sent like a streak of meteor light
here

I would not do it.

Never mind that this place
is full of grammatical errors,
p-e-a-c-e misspelled as w-a-r
and subjects subjected to verbs
one does not want
to imagine—

I would not do it.

I would stay here, editing,
if given the gracious "stet"
of yet another chance
to work the melodrama
of my worst mistakes
into understatement

I would

revise again and again this life
that is my manuscript
until in the end it might become
a letter worthy to have written
across my envelope of skin:
"Return to Sender."

—P.S.

CHAPTER 9

Receiving Forgiveness

... sweet honey from my old failures.
—ANTONIO MACHADO, tr. Robert Bly

THERE IS ANOTHER ASPECT TO forgiving—in addition to forgiving others, we need to be able to receive forgiveness, even from ourselves. Receiving forgiveness is as complicated as forgiving, whether our doing of harm is utterly personal, or is an act or failure to act within the darker sides of our corporate lives. I want to say something about both.

When we have caused hurt that is personal, we may not ever know whether we have been forgiven by the one we have injured. Forgiving is most deeply an inner, private act. Perhaps in time, here or hereafter, we are forgiven in the heart of the one we have wounded, and may never know it. Or perhaps the one we have hurt cannot or will not ever forgive. We may ask for forgiveness, even beg for it, and receive no response that offers relief or consolation. Dorothy Parker's quatrain is brilliant: "Sticks and stones are hard on bones / Aimed with angry art,/ Words can sting like anything/ But silence breaks the heart."

Refusal to forgive is often followed by silence. How do we go on? If we stand unforgiven, how do we forgive ourselves? How do I heal my own internal wounds, self-inflicted by my misguided, unwise, or deliberately cruel act or failure to act? Certain churches have long offered the possibility of confession to a priest who offers forgiveness. Some of us find that a good friend, a pastor, or a therapist can hear our confession, our contrition, and offer forgiveness, consolation, and healing love. Even with that assistance, though, we have our own work to do. There is shame, acknowledgment of what we have done, grief, and sorrow. Finally if we are to be whole again, we must crawl up out of the pit. We must find a place to stand, and begin again. Writing as a spiritual practice is a place where in total privacy we can hear our own confession and ease the wounds that we have caused in our own hearts.

Once, having hurt someone, I struggled for days before I went to my journal and wrote very slowly, each word seeming like a step—my first steps of turning from the absolute agony of knowing that I had injured someone I loved, someone who would not, or could not, forgive me.

The words came as a poem. My hurtful act occurred on a day when I had already been brought low by a visit to my doctor who for one hour made it clear to me that at an advanced age I had suddenly become a late-onset-type-one diabetic and would have to count carbohydrates for every bite I ate for the rest of my life. I hate numbers. I failed fourth-grade math and my mathematical abilities have gone downhill from there. The idea of my life depending upon arithmetic was for me a disaster. Only in writing the poem did I see how things were intertwined, and begin to understand how I could have so badly tripped. The "math" was metaphor for my other kind of error:

AfterMath

i am all right
all night
and all day
all the way
even though i might
not like myself
i am all right
all day

and all night
although my errors
multiply and divide
and i cannot subtract them
even though they may
cause long division
i will learn to dance
on the graves of my mistakes
whatever it takes
all my effort
all my trying
all my might
i will be all right

As the words lay slowly down on my page, I was able slowly to stand up. After admitting to myself and to the one I had hurt, what I had done, after asking for forgiveness, after receiving no word of it in return, after days of punishing myself, I began to write—for the first time ever, using the lower-case "i" for self reference: i . . . am all right. There was, of course, more grief work to do. But I was standing. Writing as a spiritual practice had made that possible.

* * *

My generation of white Americans was afflicted with a terrible innocence. Children burned in the ovens of Auschwitz when I was a child, but I did not smell the ashes that circled the globe. Americans went to war once again believing as they had in my mother's generation that they could wage a war to end all wars, but war was far away on an invisible shore named "Normandy," and I was safe in the heartland, a thousand miles from our own nearest shore. And race—race was on every face in America, but different colors went to different schools, and we who were white had not yet heard of anyone of color who had refused to give up a seat on a bus. No white person had yet ridden a freedom bus south; no black inner city had yet caught on fire. In St. Louis, I felt superior because we did not have separate seating on the streetcars and buses. I thought that meant we weren't racist in our city. But I did not question the fact that there was no black child in my school or in my Sunday school, no black child in the orphanage.

I was in my third year of college when a friend whom I deeply loved, Charlotte, said to me late one night in a dorm room, as I sat on her floor and she lay on her bed, on her side, propped up on her elbow and looking me in the eye, "Pat, I do believe you could be dragged through the deepest level of hell, and you would come back up without a bit of it sticking to you."

I had no idea of what Charlotte was talking about. At the time I thought she was giving me a compliment, although I didn't know for what. Now, fifty-seven years later, I believe she was talking about a terrible innocence.

I was white. Charlotte was black.

*   *   *

What do we look for when we write as a spiritual practice? When I started work on this book, I knew only that I wanted my writing to be *the thing itself.* I didn't want to write what I already know, like a teacher or a priest reciting facts already known or opinions already resolved, offered for someone else's edification. I didn't want to edify. I wanted to explore. When I finished writing the previous chapter on "Forgiving," I quickly realized that I had entered only the outer chamber of that subject—the easier part to explore. I left out my own need for forgiveness.

Writing as a spiritual practice sometimes necessitates going where the door is locked and the key has been misplaced. A lot of things may need to be turned over, looked under, opened up, to find the key that will open the door. It is clear to me that I can't write about forgiving only from the perspective of the one who needs to forgive.

But if I was going to write about my own need to be forgiven, what failure would I choose to explore? It was pretty funny, actually: I sat at my computer and began a list of possibilities: *No, not that—that would hurt _____. No, not that either—I worked that out in therapy. No, not that—never mind why—I'm just not ready.*

A long time ago I learned that generalities aren't worth much in writing. Pious statements, confessional narratives, if they are written in the safety of generality, are doomed to cliché. "I did a bad thing" doesn't move anyone to shock or awe. However, write, "I was a woman guard in Auschwitz," and you immediately have the reader's attention. So when I realized that I needed to explore receiving forgiveness, I looked around for a story. This past year I have lived through a hip fracture and an imperfect repair followed by an imperfect healing. It was a stupid thing I did, to walk uptown just before a predicted heavy snowfall—to lie to myself that I would be safe, I would have time to go and return safely before snow covered icy spots on the sidewalk. With a fractured hip, I've had a lot of time this year to think about my stupidities and my failures, and to work on trying to forgive myself.

But that story doesn't feel like a locked and protected secret. I'm ready for a cave with a dragon in the heart of it—a dragon that is a part of myself, wounded, not yet healed. A cave and a dragon that requires the sword and armor of spiritual practice.

Charlotte. There are feelings hidden in that story that are still unresolved in my heart. When I think of her, I am proud. And I am ashamed. There are threads in that story tied to many other parts of my life. Complications. Trouble.

And so, in spirit, I will wade down into the cave, into the mud and deep waters of this story. I will ask of it what meaning it has in my life. I will relive it by writing it, but with fifty-seven more years of life experience as lens for understanding. I will write as a spiritual practice.

*   *   *

I never forgot Charlotte, but I buried my remembering. She came slowly back into my consciousness when Kate Hymes and I began work on an anthology of the writings of women old enough to remember the Montgomery Bus Boycott. Kate grew up in New Orleans, I grew up in St. Louis—both cities racially divided, Kate and I on opposite sides of the division. There was also a difference in our class. Kate had both a mother and a father; they lived in a home that they owned. Her mother bought Kate's clothes in the department stores in downtown New Orleans. My mother was a single parent in a one-room basement apartment and then in a two-room tenement; she bought my clothes in the Salvation Army store.

Kate and I put out a call for manuscripts and received more than 300 from women fifty-five years of age or older, telling their stories of race as it was lived before the boycott. Kate came to Amherst, and we catalogued all of the manuscripts into the computer without reading any of them. Just before she returned to her home in New Paltz, we had the happy idea of opening one envelope and reading the story—as a kind of ritual beginning of our work on the anthology. We agreed that if the writer was black, Kate would read it aloud; if white, I would read it aloud.

The writer was white. In the stillness of my study, then, I sat facing a black woman as I read aloud the words of a white woman telling her story of race as she had lived it. It was a poem about a black woman ironing while a little boy who was described as blond and innocent and wide-eyed, looks up over the ironing board and asks, "Why are you so dark?" The black woman responds, "Because I drink too much coffee." The poem went on to say how much the family always loved that maid, and how good of her it was to protect the child's innocence.

When we finished reading, Kate and I sat in silence for a minute—one of the longest minutes of my life, because all at once the task we had undertaken felt truly dangerous to me. The poem was earnest and sincere. And in my mind, a terrible innocence was described in the poem, and was equally operating in the writer. What did my own whiteness hold that I only dimly understood? My own childhood rolled before my eyes—an old, black woman on the Sarah Street bus; a black child sitting next to me in a room with child-sized chairs; and Charlotte. A rag-pile of stories, each one marked with some kind of trouble. What had I gotten myself into?

Kate is good at silence. Finally I choked out a few words. "I would really like to know the tone of voice that woman used when she said she drank too much coffee."

Kate said, "Exactly."

Black writers described harm done, insults endured, hopes, and even lives destroyed by racism in schools, in homes, in places of employment. In manuscript after manuscript, my white sisters wrote about black domestic workers in their homes whom they had loved and lost. And time after time, Kate asked me, "If they loved their maid so much, how come they didn't ever get in touch with her after they grew up?" There were a few exceptions, but in most of the manuscripts there appeared to be a total break in the relationship when the domestic worker no longer was employed by the family.

After a while I began to steel myself against Kate's question, preferring to hear in the white women's narratives a loss of the person who had bathed them, sung to them, kissed their skinned knees, fed them their food—in short, mothered them. Wasn't that loss real? Although I didn't say so to Kate, I began to resent the judgment I felt in her repeated question.

In one sense, I felt safe—after all, my mother was too poor to have a "domestic worker." In fact, she *was* one. Although, as a private duty "practical nurse" (which at that time required no training) she was invited after a night of sitting beside a sick man's bed to have coffee at the dining table with the woman of the house, while the black maid was required to have her coffee alone in the kitchen. And it was true that my mother bought my clothes in second-hand clothing stores, but if she had been able to buy them in the downtown stores, I could have tried them on there. Kate's mother had to take a bus across town to the stores, buy clothes, take them home for her daughters to try on, and return the ones they didn't want by taking the bus again across town.

Why didn't the white women who grieved the loss of the black woman whom they loved ever contact them as an adult? I had no answer.

And then, one day, as Kate pondered her familiar question, Charlotte came into focus in my memory. How much I had loved her. How I had once—but only once—tried to make contact with her. Why did I wait so long? Why did I never try again?

* * *

We were students together. Charlotte Alston was a couple of years older than I, a stunning pianist and composer who had been chosen by Norman Cousins in New York City to be his protégé—he gave her a personal scholarship to study and supported her as an artist. I, too, was on a scholarship, given by my local church. Neither of us, Charlotte because she was black, I because I was poor, could have been in college without that aid.

I had never in my life had a friend of color. The Methodist school, Scarritt College in Nashville, Tennessee, had never had a black student before that year. It was a magical experience to be friends with Charlotte, not only because I loved her passion and her breathtaking musical gifts, but because friendship was slightly dangerous, forbidden, and exciting. I believe that was as true for her as it was for me.

We spent afternoons together as she practiced on the organ in the school chapel, and I sat doing homework in a choir pew near her. We spent late nights talking for hours and hours in her single room. My white roommate was incredulous that I should have such a friendship. I told Charlotte about my life—I no longer remember what I told her. She told me how when she was a young girl, her black piano teacher said that Charlotte was now a better pianist than the teacher; there was nothing more the teacher could teach her. How Charlotte went to the school of music in Greensboro and they turned her away because she was black. How she went back again and again, day after day, and sat quietly in their waiting room until finally they could stand it no longer and allowed her to have lessons.

The crisis in our friendship came when there was a spring break at the college and Charlotte invited me to go home with her to Greensboro. I wanted very much to go, but it was 1953, and I thought I needed to ask the dean for permission. Did I want to ask permission because I was afraid of the anger of the school, afraid I might displease, or worse, lose my scholarship? Or because I was afraid of Charlotte, afraid of her world? I don't know. Charlotte was reluctant to have me talk with the dean, but I insisted. The dean told us that we would not be allowed to ride in the same car of the train—she didn't think it was a wise idea for me to go. However, she said I could use her telephone to call my mother, and if my mother gave permission, the dean would not refuse. She asked Charlotte to step out into the hall and wait.

Now, so many years later, I understand that my mother was mentally ill. The problem is, when you are young and your mother is your only parent and is mentally ill, mental illness is your "normal." I had no idea that she wasn't well. I had been trained to be obedient, and I was obedient. I told her that I wanted to go to Charlotte's home for spring break. I had written to her that I loved Charlotte, that I was so happy to have this friendship. I thought my mother would be pleased. She had taught me that "Negroes" were my equal, that racism was bad.

But she exploded. She screamed at me over the phone that my relationship with Charlotte was sick—that I was a lesbian, that I was in love with Charlotte.

I had never in my life heard the word "lesbian." I didn't know such a thing was possible. I didn't know that women could fall in love with women. Which is not to say my mother was wrong in her analysis of the situation—I suspect, in fact, that she was right. But I was in a state of shock—dumbly, I handed the phone with my screaming mother to the dean. And the dean listened, spoke some comforting words to my mother, hung up the phone and told me that I could not go with Charlotte to North Carolina.

I obeyed.

*   *   *

Charlotte said—and I don't remember whether it was before or after that day in the dean's office—that she believed I could be dragged to the depths of hell and come up with nothing of it clinging to me. She was wrong. It does cling. Racism is one of the deepest rungs of hell, and it clings. It is a poison that my generation ingested with our mother's milk—if it was not hatred of persons of color it was hatred of that hatred, and a consequent self-consciousness, longing, and—yes, *need for forgiveness*—that clung to us and made it impossible for us to relate human person to human person without the scrim of race between our white faces and any face of color.

I did try once before I met Kate to contact Charlotte. I saw in the local paper that a choir from Greensboro College with Dr. Charlotte Alston as director was coming to Northampton. I went to the concert, found Charlotte, and invited her to come to my home. She came and we visited for an hour, but it was formal and strained between us. I wonder now if I ever told her what really happened in that telephone call. I doubt it—I know that I was afraid of my mother's wrath; I had never disobeyed her. And I know that I came away from the experience in the dean's office ashamed. How could I adequately tell Charlotte? I hardly understood it myself. I was ashamed of the dysfunction in my family, ashamed that the dean heard my mother's rage, ashamed that maybe my relationship with Charlotte was perverted, ashamed of my own cowardice in refusing to go with her, and grieving—yes, grieving, that's a big part of it—for not being able to go, and for the invisible wall that came down between the beautiful, gifted, friend whom I loved passionately, and my own miserable, white self.

Recently Kate and I co-led a workshop for black and white women writing together about race. I wrote about my friendship with Charlotte. I named the fact that I, too, as a white woman, had failed to follow through with someone that I loved who was black—failed precisely because I was white.

Then I tried to call Charlotte. She had died the previous year.

* * *

There are two rooms in the house called "forgiving." One room is where we work to forgive others who have hurt us, until finally forgiving happens in us. Like ice melts. Like wind blows. It happens. The second room is where we work to allow ourselves to receive forgiving from others and from ourselves. The second room often is the hardest to inhabit.

But there is in each room a way, and it is writing as a spiritual practice. Writing to understand takes us back into the story. Not necessarily into the factual events, but into the *story* that we have made of the events. We live into the story again, and the story changes. As I have written about Charlotte, I have in some deep sense confessed to Charlotte how I wish I had taken that train ride to her home in North Carolina. How I wish I had sat at her table and had received food from her mother's hand. How much more blessed that would have been than any kneeling and taking of communion from a white pastor at the altar of a church among a white congregation where no black person was welcome. Never mind that we could not have ridden in the same train car. I would have been changed by the ugliness of that separation. I would have been braver, wiser, and more powerful.

And yet, I am also proud of the young woman that I was. I am proud that I was a girl whom Charlotte loved and who knew that she was loved by me. I am proud that I wanted to go to North Carolina. I am proud that I went as far toward that possibility as my life at that time allowed me to go. I am proud that I survived, that I have lived long enough to come to this day when I could write my way back into that old story, and find myself. I sing to myself this beautiful poem by Antonio Machado, translated by Robert Bly:

> *Last night, as I was sleeping*
> *I dreamt—marvelous error!—*
> *that I had a beehive*
> *here inside my heart.*
> *And the golden bees*
> *were making white combs*
> *and sweet honey*
> *from my old failures.*[1]

I would like to believe that somewhere, somehow, Charlotte knows I have written these words. I can't quite believe it, but I can offer it outward from myself toward the mystery, and I can say, *Why not? Maybe it is possible.* After all, it was possible that a certain black girl in 1953 came to an all-white college (*miracle!*) and met a certain white girl with no money for college who was also there (*miracle!*) and for a short while, in a country where two girls of different color could not ride on a train together, they were friends. Deep, real, beautiful friends. And so, *here inside my heart…the golden bees [are] making…sweet honey from my old failures.*

THE UNDERTAKING

An excerpt from Scene One

NOTE: *From a one-act play in which two gravediggers have been given the task of burying a body. The body has turned out to be alive: a living prophet. They have spent the whole of the first scene procrastinating. This ends Scene One.*

FRANK: —Now! I shall go away and find some solitude and prepare.

BARRY: *(to himself)*
I feel sick.
—really sick.
Like something's rattling around in my emptiness.
Perhaps it's another attack of semantics...
    (remembers—half singsong, half serious)
"He who has clean hands and a pure heart,
who does not lift up his soul to what is false..."
    (Leans over, looks at prophet, spits into pit.)
Prophet, prophet in the pit,
what have I to do with it?
What have I to do with it?
Upside down, down under mud,
neither the mind nor the heart is good...
—stars go out, or spin like things—
—silly balloons, with miles for strings,
And here am I,
under the stars and above the mud,
after creation and the flood,
before the sickle and the fire,
...a blood clot in the world's bad eye—
here am I.
Prophet, prophet in the pit,
I can hit you when I spit.
Tell me, mudman, while you sit
—what have I to do with it?
What have I to do with it!
    (Lights dim out.)

—P.S.

CHAPTER 10

Doing Good

Your work is to discover your work
and then with all your heart to give yourself to it.
—HINDU PRINCE GAUTAMA
SIDDHARTHA, founder of Buddhism, 563–483 B.C.E.

The moment one definitely commits oneself,
then Providence moves, too.
—JOHANN WOLFGANG VON GOETHE

MY GRANDDAUGHTER, SARAH, only three years out of college, is excellently employed as a teacher in a private academy where students are encouraged to bring their own horses with them to school.

This week she left a message on my telephone answering machine: "Grandma, I love you. I have a good job, but I want to do good in my life." The message clicked off. I heard sadness and confusion in her voice.

Sarah is keenly aware of the world beyond the private school where she teaches. She has just spent six months in Latin America, learning Spanish and living in the homes of people whose daily sustenance depends upon serving Americans their meals and providing them with a place to stay while they study the language. A family member was ill; there was no money even for aspirin.

I thought for a long time about how to answer her. The fact is she *does* do good in the world, just by being here. She is a person who gives of herself with great generosity. Her question was a gift to me—how does one do good in the world? I began to think about all the mistakes I have made, trying to "do good," and wrote to her the pages below.

* * *

So much has been said, written, painted, danced, dreamed about how to "do good" in the world. I, too, want to do good, only my way of saying it has been slightly different: I have said, *I want to make a difference.*

Because someone made a difference in my life.

I sit here tonight in a nice house on a tree-shaded street in a college town, because two times someone walked up a flight of dirty stairs in a tenement, stood face to face with a younger me and spoke words that changed my world. The first was my seventh grade teacher, Dorothy Dunn. I will tell that story later. The second was Gerald Harris.

Reverend Harris was the pastor of a dwindling Methodist congregation, about to sell its historic Civil War period building at the edge of the slums where I lived, and move out to the suburbs of St. Louis, where there would be a new building among people who could afford to support a building campaign.

I had been going to church in the old building each Sunday. I was in high school, and teaching in their Sunday school. Reverend Harris knew what I did not know: It cost money to go to college. I thought people could go to college just like they went to high school. I didn't know you had to apply. I thought it was free.

Another thing he knew that I didn't know was that I was perilously close to disaster. The only thing ahead of me was a minimum wage job, although I dressed so strangely I doubt that I would have been hired as a waitress or a store clerk. My English teacher had taken me aside and asked, "Honey, don't you have anything better to wear?" That was after the day, described earlier, when I wore a satin formal and my mother's high-heeled shoes to school because no, I *didn't* have anything better to wear.

It was utterly embarrassing to have Reverend Harris come to our door. Mama was home; she let him in. I cleared off the clutter on the couch so he could sit down. A rich man had given Mama the couch to thank her for her nursing care. One night, as she sat beside his sickbed in his mansion on Kingshighway, she told him that she wanted to send her daughter to college. He responded, *Why do you want her to get an education? Who will run the laundries?* Reverend Harris stood watching me clear a place. Then he sat and said, "We want to send you to college."

I think I said, "Thank you." I don't remember anything more except the shock of realizing that it cost money to go to college. But I didn't say that. I just wanted him to go. I was ashamed.

*   *   *

Years later I made my first botched attempts to reach back across class and make a difference for someone else caught in poverty. I was a young mother living with Peter and our three children in a huge old parsonage in Gleasondale, a mill town in rural Massachusetts. Peter was a student of theology at Boston University, and was assigned by the Methodist Church to serve the Gleasondale congregation. The town was only "a wide place in the road," a stretch of Highway 63 where there was a bend in the highway, an old millstream, and a row of decrepit mill housing that had become apartments for families on welfare. There was a small country store that doubled as post office. At one end of the village stood the church and parsonage, at the other end, the fading, but still grand Victorian home of the Gleason family, who had built the church. In between, families at the bottom of the social ladder lived in substandard housing.

On the day we moved into the parsonage, a battered station wagon pulled into the driveway. The man who got out was wearing a work shirt and jeans, his belly hanging over his belt buckle. He told us quietly that there was an undesirable family living next door to the parsonage: a woman and seven kids. He said, with a roll of his eyes. "We'll build you a fence between the two houses, if you want us to."

I said that wouldn't be necessary.

So far, so good. That woman became a lifelong friend, and in fact she is the person who recently quoted to me the verse from Leonard Cohen that gave me the title and epigraph for this book.

We had been in Gleasondale for around a year when one day I walked alone to the small village store/post office. The postmis-tress/storekeeper knew everything about all of us in the village—

she told me once that she read all the postcards. "The people who write them don't care," she explained. "After all, they put it right out there for all the world to see."

Across the highway from the store there was a junkyard. The man who owned it roared the engine of his panel truck up and down the highway past our house every day, all the windows but the front ones blacked out. Sometimes his young son sat on the seat beside him. The postmistress volunteered to me the information that there was a shack at the back of the junkyard, and a woman lived there with the junkman and the boy. The postmistress thought the woman was ill; nobody ever saw her.

I felt I could not bear to live in a big house so close to a shack where a woman was ill and a boy was…I couldn't even imagine. I don't know what in the world I thought I could do about it, but on an impulse that day I turned in on the path that led into the junkyard. It was the scariest place I had ever been, and I had known firsthand some scary places in my life. It felt like another universe from my everyday world. Abandoned appliances, car parts, machinery, all manner of junk was not just piled—it was stacked into what seemed like solid walls on both sides of a hard-packed dirt path. There was no exit to either side, just a winding path forward, or back the way I came. No one knew where I was; all that I knew was that I had to go to that house and knock on that door. I had no idea what I would say if it opened. It was the woman I was after, not the child. I wanted to know if she was there, and if she was all right.

I knocked. Once. Twice. No one answered. Then I turn and fled back down the path to the highway.

How do I do good in my life?

* * *

Some time after that day, our car began to smell strongly of urine. At first I thought it was because we had babies in diapers, but there was no evidence of stains in the car, and the odor was strong in the mornings, when the car door was first opened, but dissipated during the day. Finally I guessed that someone was sleeping in our car, and I watched in the early morning through a window. Sure enough, the car door opened, and a boy perhaps twelve or thirteen years old got out of the car and walked to the school bus stop.

We knew who he was—the boy who lived in the junkyard. After a few more days of urine smell in the car, I came up with a plan, told Peter, and he agreed. I put a cot in the basement with a pillow and some blankets, and left a note on the back seat of the car. It said, *There is a cot with some blankets in the basement. The door is never locked. You can sleep there if you want to.*

The urine smell moved into the basement. After about a week of that, I left a note on the cot. It said, *If you are going to sleep in the basement, you might as well have something to eat—you are welcome to come upstairs.*

The boy ate with us, then. But the first time he had Sunday dinner with us, there was a crisis, and the crisis was mine. In those days I was living a fairy tale. The parsonage was a Victorian house with a curving staircase in the entry hall and huge built-in fireplace mantels, taller than I, ornately carved. Never mind that the rooms were so drafty our baby had pneumonia three times that rainy August; the house was an old dowager, proud, but somewhat down-at-the-heels. The church was next door. It was even more run-down than the parsonage, but originally just as grand. We had cleaned and painted and repaired the church, and found books and bits of silverware marked with its original name: RBC, for "Rock Bottom Church." I kid you not. That was the original name of the village, "Rock Bottom," because, we were told, it was built on a glacial drumlin. I saw no sign of a hill, let alone a drumlin.

Every Sunday I enacted the fairy tale: After church I served a Sunday dinner like I had read about in books when I was a child. *Dick runs, Jane runs, Father comes home with a newspaper under his arm, and Mother is in the doorway with an apron on, and a plate of warm cookies in her hand.* Not in the home I grew up in. But that was the storybook life I tried to create for my children. We had chicken and mashed potatoes, usually, and homemade bread and a pie for dessert. And I set the table with a tablecloth, cloth napkins, my silverplate that was a wedding gift, and candles lighted in the center of the table.

The boy ate with us for the first time on a Sunday. He was quiet, but halfway through the meal he looked carefully at his fork, and then at the candles, and said in an awed voice, "You must be *very* rich!"

After the meal was over, after the boy had left, I took all the silverware—not only the pieces that were on the table, but those that were in the silverware chest, too, out on the high back porch and threw them all, a handful at a time, as far as I could throw them, into the weeds at the edges of our yard. I was sobbing. He was right. I was very, very rich.

Peter, gentle person that he is, said only, "Oh, for goodness sakes, Pat!" and went out and gathered up the silverware. I don't know if he got it all; I never went looking for any of it. Soon the old truck with the blacked-out windows roared up to our front door. The father stomped up the front steps and told Peter that if we ever messed with his boy again, he'd send the sheriff after us. The boy never returned.

How do you do good in your life?

* * *

It would be a huge understatement to say that I didn't understand why I threw all that silverware into the weeds. But I understand it now—I was back on Olive Street in St. Louis. Back home from the orphanage. I was twelve or thirteen, just the age of the boy at my table. The orphanage had been clean. Too clean. So clean, the house-mother wouldn't let me keep my rocks on top of my dresser. I was home from a clean place, and I could see who we were, and how we lived. I could see the milk bottles with their crusts of soured milk, the roaches, the rats, the clutter everywhere in the two rooms where four people lived with no closet, and no one able to keep order.

The woman who threw the silverware was not just me, the young minister's wife, the young mother of three pre-school children, the young woman who wanted to make a difference in the life of that boy. That silverware was thrown by a twelve- or thirteen-year-old girl, trapped in a St. Louis tenement with no way to escape. She was desperate, and anyone with silverware on the table, with candlelight on the table, with good food on the table, was *enemy. Enemy.* She threw the silverware, and she *hated me.*

How do I do good in my life?

*   *   *

Those weren't my only aborted attempts to "do good." I have always regretted that I was not among the people who marched into Selma. I was at home with our babies. Nor could I go when Peter and our good African American friend Sam Turner took a group of high school kids from our church on a workcamp in an impoverished community in Appalachian Kentucky. In the middle of the civil rights movement, a busload of white kids with a black teacher raised the suspicions of the Kentucky police. Their bus was stopped, Sam and Peter were questioned, and allowed to go on. Sam was refused food in a roadside restaurant. The kids all walked out of the restaurant; the bus drove off, and then returned. They had left one kid in the restroom. Sam's wife, Flo, and I stayed at home changing diapers.

It wasn't until the buildup to the Gulf War that I had my chance to try civil disobedience. I had prepared by taking a course with the Quakers. We were trained to be nonviolent; we role-played how we would respond to insults, to violence, to arrest. Then I went to an air force base near where I live and stood with others blocking the entryway. I was earnest and committed. I believed that my country was wrong in the war we were waging.

I was arrested, taken in a bus to a police station, fingerprinted, given a court date, and released. Not for a single moment was I afraid. The police were polite; the people I was with were quiet and orderly.

Weeks later I was due to appear in court. I wore a skirt and a business jacket, and I took some work in my briefcase because I expected to wait before my case came before the judge. When I arrived at the courthouse, the hallway was crowded. I sat on a bench surrounded by mothers and children, teenagers, men, and women. Immediately, I became anxious. I knew those people. They were from the housing projects in that river city, almost all of them. Not one carried a briefcase. Not one wore nylon stockings. Not one wore a business suit. They were there because their lives were on the line, or they were there to support someone who was in serious trouble. Drinking while driving—a man who lost his driver's license would also lose his job. Dealing. Prostitution. Breaking and entering. Mothers desperate for their teenaged sons. Young women pregnant by guys who didn't give a damn. Guys who couldn't remember what happened at the bar that Saturday night. A weary judge. Bored public defenders. Accused people who didn't show up. A lawyer who didn't show up.

Who was I in that vortex of human distress? An overdressed, middle-class married and working woman, playing a game with the law. I was an imposter.

My brother was there, in someone else's skin. I saw his yellow hair in the visiting room at the army prison. I heard his words, "Pat, I wish you hadn't come. I didn't want you to see me here." My mother was there, helpless to save him as he was made scapegoat for another soldier's crime. I was in that courtroom in my mask of privilege, and I was in no danger at all. When I got my fine, I paid it, but I walked away feeling very confused, and certain that I would never again protest war by being arrested.

* * *

The mistake I made in going to the junkyard shack was trying to do something I was too young and too inexperienced to do—especially all by myself. Much, much later, I was able to go into a housing project—first supported by an agency and then for many years by myself, and to do consistent, long-term work there. But I can still feel the threat of that man, and so on that day, if there had been an answer to my knock, I might have caused harm to myself, to the boy, or to the woman in the shack. To act was right, but I was not yet wise enough to know how to act.

The mistake I made in protesting the war was different. It wasn't that I was inexperienced; it was that I had a load of experience I myself had not worked through. I had stood in line outside a maximum-security prison, waiting to see my brother. I wanted to be like Grace Paley, out there on the front lines, climbing fences, sitting, or lying in the street. But at that time I could not. Now that I have written about Sam in prison, now that I have read to him what I wrote, now that he gave me his permission to publish it and stood on the platform with me and read a portion of the book himself when it was released, now that I have written and made enough mistakes to learn a thing or two, I can do it now—I can protest. I can be arrested. Or I can write what it feels like to be the sister of a boy caught in an unjust prison system. That, too, is a way of being there.

* * *

"You have a foot in both classes," one person said to me. "But I don't. I wouldn't be able to work across class."

I want to say to him, "Yes, you can! Anyone can!" But that isn't true. It is true, however, that it doesn't take having "a foot in both classes." In the trainings I led for many years, trainings that now other, younger trainers lead for professional persons who want to use writing to empower those who have been silenced by poverty, illness, abuse, or other traumatic experiences, we have proven that it does not require "a foot in both classes."

Writing and teaching writing are amazing ways to work across class. When I began my first workshop for women in a housing project, I had a lot to learn. We all did, and we learned it together, writing together. I learned how to lead; they learned how to teach me how to lead them. Writing together with honesty and courage, the leader writing and reading aloud first-draft work along with the participants, requires a mutual honesty and vulnerability that simply crumbles the walls of difference.[1]

The most important lessons I learned were from the writers themselves. When I told one woman she could not bring her three children to workshop because I was not being paid and could not afford to provide child care, she brought them anyway, walking them for many blocks because there was no bus service anywhere near that housing project. She came every week, and every week the children were there. We learned to cope. I learned how much the workshop meant to that woman.

Some of the lessons I learned were from older, more experienced professional people working across difference. On one occasion, I was to give a major speech to three hundred people at Smith College School for Social Work as we premiered the film about the original Chicopee workshop, *Tell Me Something I Can't Forget.*[2] An administrator and good friend at Smith asked me ahead of time to tell her what I was going to say. I told her the stories I planned to tell, one of them ending with my buying a used washing machine and dryer for a woman threatened by a social service agency that her children might be taken from her. The school her children attended was complaining because they smelled of urine—but she had no car, no washing machine, and there was no Laundromat within walking distance. My point in the speech was trying to illustrate how difficult it is for single mothers where there are no public services available. How high the stakes are if your child wets the bed every night, and you have only a sink in which to wash sheets, and no place to hang them out in freezing New England weather. The administrator told me, "Don't tell that story. It goes too far against traditional social work practices. You can't tell it." So I didn't. And she was right. My audience would not have seen the woman and her dilemma—they would have seen a nonprofessional do-gooder failing to keep proper boundaries. I wouldn't have agreed with them, but we have to learn to choose our battles.

As tiresome as "inner child" references have become in some quarters, it simply is true that what happened to us in childhood continues to happen over and over again in our inner lives until we find a way to open the closed places inside us and heal the wounds that hide there. There is nothing wrong, I think, in the fact that the roots of my own passion for social justice lie in the part of me that sat in a tenement window hating "rich folks." The child part of me hated the "rich woman" that I had become in her eyes, hated me for living in a big (never mind drafty and rather ugly) Victorian parsonage with candles and silverware.

My work directly with low-income women and the writing I have done with both women and men in workshops has healed the rage that crippled me when I tried to make a difference as a young woman. In the process of working to heal others, those I worked to heal healed me. Through it all, the vow I made at twelve, *I will never*

DOING GOOD | **169**

forget, fueled my intention. Going into the places where other people were caught in poverty as I had been caught in poverty, even when I did it unwisely, helped me to grow in understanding, and to heal. And writing helped. Lots and lots of writing.

Here is the good that I want to do. I want never to disappear completely into the woman with education, with tree-lined streets, silverware, and candles. I want, with my pen and ink, with my fingers on the computer keys, to make visible the face of one child behind a tenement window. She was back there three-quarters of a century ago, but I want her to stand for the faces of children who are caught today without means of escape. The disproportionate number of young black men and women behind the bars of our private prisons, the teenaged white and brown mothers in low-income housing, the young absent fathers unemployed and on street corners, the children in war-torn countries who spend their entire childhoods in refugee camps or urban slums. I want all of us who are privileged *to see* those who are not. Most people care; most are kind. When we truly see and understand the world of the child with the empty rice bowl, the one with the bruises hidden under the shirt, the one kept by the john on the street, we want to change those worlds. I want to do battle with the *not seeing.*

But Sarah—I write this to my granddaughter—this is *my* place, *my* battle, *my* way to try to do good with my life. And it took me a long time to claim it. Maybe I fully claim it only here, now, writing these words to you and for my book on this November day in the year 2007. Looking back, I see the things I have written—books of poems, plays, lyrics for songs and three oratorios, an autobiography, two novels, a section in my book on writing—all of them dealing, some more and some less, with difference, especially with poverty. But here and now I am writing as a spiritual practice in order to make visible to myself what my own spiritual practice has become. It seems to have tended always toward this—putting words on paper, and with at least some of those words hoping that I might help to make visible the faces of those caught in poverty.

There are as many ways of doing good as there are people who want to do good. Finding your own way takes time.

TWO THOUSAND DEATHS

We will not rest or tire
  Until the war… is won.

—G.W. BUSH, October 26, 2005

Rain pounds New England,
lashes trees. The news.
The children of the poor. The wind
that brings the rain, tail end
of hurricane. The news. Two thousand.
My basement is flooded. Rivers
run to the sea.

A crow commands in early light.
This earth is angry. Hurricane.
The slain are from the poorest states.
A cardinal chirps a clear and delicate word.
Indian reservations. The deep south.
Vermont.

The rich man asked my mother,
Why do you want her to get an education?
Who will run the laundries?

Rain pounds the great spruce tree
beside my window.
The president's mother offered consolation:
The people of New Orleans, *she said,*
were so poor, they are better off as refugees.
Besides, without them, who will fight our wars?
It is the children of the poor we send
to kill the children of the poor.

Still the mountains. Still the rivers.
An iron moving on freshly washed cotton
smells sweet.

Changing the World

Be the change you want to see in the world.
—MAHATMA GANDHI

...they won't say: the times were dark
Rather: why were their poets silent?
—BERTOLT BRECHT

Yes, the work must be political...
—ALICE WALKER

"TAKE WHATEVER COMES," I tell my writing workshop participants. "Whatever image, whatever words. When you begin to write, take what first flashes into your mind, because it is a gift from your unconscious."

So here goes. Straight to the concrete foundation, the steel girder, the brick wall. I write my name on the wall.

I am in an airport, waiting for a flight. Across from me in the waiting area is a woman who smiles at me. She is attractive, younger than I am. She speaks, and I answer. We fall easily into conversation, and she tells me about her children. She has four. She tells me about each of her four, describes each one's marriage, and how many children each has, and ends each narrative with a detailed description of how that son or daughter is "doing the Lord's work."

And then it is my turn. I tell her that I, too, have four children. I, too, am very proud of them.[1] We smile at each other, acknowledging each of us how special a thing it is to be proud of your children. I tell her that all four of my children are writers, my three daughters are professors, and my granddaughter is in graduate school. I don't use the word "lesbian," but I use female pronouns to tell her that one's partner is a professor and another's is a community organizer. I tell her my son is a writer, his wife is a photographer and tennis teacher, their son is fifteen, in school.

She is pale, silent. Then she says in a shocked voice, "You have *two* of them."

I wish I had said, "No. I have *four* of them," as if she meant "children," not "sinners." But the bluntness of her statement, her dismissal of their lives, their professions, their identities, probably left me, too, pale. It certainly left me shocked.

I knew exactly what I was doing when I told her about my children. I anticipated what she would think in light of her children "doing the Lord's work." I knew the judgment she would level against my daughters and their partners. I knew the judgment she would level against me, if I told her the secrets of my own life's struggles. Even so, *"You have two of them!"* stopped me, left me breathless. We went on talking until our plane arrived. She quoted scripture to me that says homosexual sex is "an abomination." I quoted scripture back to her that says King David's love for Jonathan "surpassed the love of women."[2] She turned as we rose to board the plane and said, "Even though your daughters are sinners, a mother has to love them."

For almost an hour in flight I continued to tremble.

I want to change the world.

*   *   *

Everyone wants a better world. If I am educated, it is painful to know that the world has an enormous number of people who have limited or no formal education. If I am fed, it hurts to know there are those who are hungry. If some are denied justice by unjust laws or common societal practices, it hurts to see broken bodies and tormented minds on the evening news. But other than writing a check as a donation to some invisible charity, most of us don't know how to make the world better.

T. S. Eliot wrote, "Between the idea/ And the reality/ Between the motion/ And the act/ Falls the shadow."[3] We *intend* to do good, and we make mistakes. Jane Kenyon wrote about the *desire* to make the world better. For her, the "act" was writing: "the desire to really make art and to embody the truth, to make something beautiful.... That desire never goes."

The shadow that falls between our intention and our act frequently takes the form of an overwhelm of inadequacy so great we stop trying. That is what happened to me when I stood before the judge, described earlier. The world of poverty around me in that inner-city courtroom overwhelmed my safe, small act of civil disobedience, at least in my mind, on that day, in that place.

We watch on television as a single student stands in front of a line of tanks in Tiananmen Square, and we wonder at the courage of that young man. We read or watch our heroes: Sojourner Truth speaking to a hostile crowd, *Ain't I a woman?* Martin Luther King before the multitude in front of the Lincoln monument; Dietrich Bonhoeffer, the German Christian pastor resisting the Holocaust, refusing to stay safely in the United States, dying at the hands of the Nazis. We watch Rachel Corrie, the young woman in Palestine dying under an Israeli tank as she tries the stop the bulldozing of a house. We hear them, we watch them, and in light of their courage, our own attempts seem small, seem maybe of no effect.

When I was a child, my mother taught my brother and me a string game. A circle of string with a button in the middle was held between my two hands; moving my hands apart and back toward each other caused the button to spin. Sometimes I feel like that button when I think of changing the world. I spin between two perceptions: How small, how insignificant the intentions or the acts of one individual person seem—and how huge, how global, the acts of one individual person can be.

We are not often given the gift of knowing the effect of our acts. Young students grow up year by year, leave the classroom of gifted teachers behind, and live their lives out in the world. The teachers usually don't know whether what they did made any lasting difference or not.

But changing one person changes the world, and I am myself living proof that a single person, acting just once and never knowing the result, can change the world. Proof that sometimes the shadow *does not* fall between the intention to change the world and the act that actually does change it. As I said before, there were two people whose intervention dramatically changed my life for the better: my seventh grade teacher and my pastor. Both *intended,* and both went out of their way to *act.* I said earlier that I would tell the story of the teacher. Here it is, as I wrote it in *Wake Up Laughing.*

When I was thirteen years old, a knock came on my door. My door would open, if I opened it, onto a dark hallway in a tenement in St. Louis. Behind me would be two small rooms. The year was 1947. I had been told never, never to open the door when Mama was not at home. But the voice calling to me outside the door was familiar. The second time she called my name, I recognized the voice: my seventh-grade teacher, Miss Dunn, whom I adored.

It was unthinkable that a teacher would visit one of her students. It was unbearable that Miss Dunn had come up the dirty stairs, climbed three flights, smelled the heavy roach poison. Impossible that she see the clutter, the dirt, the shame in the rooms behind me.

The school year was over. It was summer, hot and sticky in that Mississippi river-bottom air. I opened the door just the tiniest crack, with the chain lock still in place. Yes. It was true. Miss Dunn stood in the dim light of the hallway, and she was smiling at me.

I unlocked the chain, opened the door a fraction more, tried to hide the room behind me with my body. She held out a book. Gray, with blue letters.

"Here," she said. "This is my book. I want you to have it."

I took the book, but couldn't speak. Her book. *She was giving me her book.* Once, when she gave me back a school paper, she said, "You can be a writer."

I held the door with my foot to keep her from seeing inside as I read the words on the cover: *Dark Was the Wilderness. Dorothy Dunn.*

When I didn't speak, she said, "I know what will happen to you when you grow up."

"What?" It was my first word, and my last.

"I won't tell you now, but come and find me when you are grown, and I will tell you if I was right."

And she turned, and went back down the stairs.

When I was in my thirties, and had a libretto performed by Phyllis Byrn Julson, Robert Shaw and the Atlanta Symphony Orchestra in Carnegie Hall, I wrote to the St. Louis Board of Education and asked for the address of Dorothy Dunn. They said she died within five years of the day she had knocked on my apartment door.

Both Dorothy Dunn and Gerald Harris, the pastor who convinced his inner-city church to send me to college, died before I graduated. Neither of them ever knew that what they did for one kid in a tenement set in motion a writing workshop almost fifty years later in a housing project in Chicopee, Massachusetts, a workshop that began a ripple effect into a network of workshops for writers and also for under-served populations that has become global in scope.

The mission of Amherst Writers & Artists[4] has been to keep in balance our passion for excellence in writing as an art form and our passion for using writing as a methodology to further social justice. From a single small workshop of twelve women meeting together in an office, then in a housing project, then in a library basement, and finally in a house owned by the town of Chicopee, Massachusetts, has grown a phenomenon of workshops in prisons, shelters, care centers, schools, hospitals, and many other venues across America, Ireland, Canada, Malawi, India, and other countries. The purpose of these workshops is on the one hand to affirm that art belongs to all people, and all people are capable of creating art with words, and on the other hand to affirm writing as a powerful methodology for healing and empowerment.

Muriel Rukeyser famously wrote, "What would happen if one woman told the truth about her life? The world would split open."[5] One woman, willing to let her bruises be seen; one young man, standing before advancing tanks in Tiananmen Square; one teenager hanging himself because of bullying. One.

Daring to be seen, daring to let the truth of the human condition be made visible by our telling, whether that telling be in words or in some other form of witness, splits open the world. Cracks it. And that's how the light gets in.

To tell the truth about our lives is a political act. In the housing project beside the Connecticut River where I led my workshop for women in public housing in my part of Massachusetts, there is no longer a grocery store or a Laundromat within walking distance, and there is no bus service. A woman with three daughters, one of whom wets the bed every night, and smells of urine in the schoolroom, is threatened by the school with having social services called, and fears she will lose her children. How is she to wash bedding every day in a cold winter climate with no washing machine, no dryer, no Laundromat, no bus service, no car, no other adult to help her? Her life is invisible to the well-meaning people who live on the other side of the river in my town, Amherst. She believes herself to be a failure, doesn't know that her story is important, or that her own words could be adequate to tell it—even to write it, with help. Unless someone "crosses the tracks" for her, as someone did for me, she will not escape, and her children, who live in the shadow of her fear, will have little chance of escape.

Whether as a private act or a public act, by writing we can howl, sing, or plainly and humbly tell what is true. When it becomes public, our howl of outrage can waken the world to injustice. Our singing writing can waken the world to beauty and to joy. When we plainly and humbly tell what is true, that telling can waken the world to itself. One moment at a time. One person at a time.

As Philip Levine writes in his poem "The Simple Truth":

Some things
you know all your life. They are so simple and true
they must be said without elegance, meter and rhyme,
they must be laid on the table beside the salt shaker,
the glass of water, the absence of light gathering
in the shadows of picture frames, they must be
naked and alone, they must stand for themselves.[6]

The power of writing to heal is being widely studied and affirmed. What those of us who have written at our kitchen tables and in our shops and offices have always known by heart is now being acknowledged by study and evidence in centers of science and medicine.[7]

Writing has the potential to heal culture, as well as to heal individual lives. Peter Elbow says,

Writing can help cultures resist change. So too, it can help individuals resist culture. Of course, insofar as the culture has infiltrated our minds, private writing has no leverage for resistance. But the infiltration of a culture over an individual is never complete. Individual experiences almost always present some potential dissonance to cultural assumptions.[8]

*   *   *

Writing as a spiritual practice, it seems to me, while it fully includes and involves the self of the writer must also include the other. The tradition of spiritual practice out of which I came, all the way back to the great prophets of Israel, stressed justice and righteousness ("righteousness" meaning, as I said earlier, not a code of behavior but *right relationship* with others as well as with God). Those who turn toward spirit, I believe, *must* consciously, actively, work to turn the world toward justice.

That doesn't mean that we write for the purpose of preaching and teaching. But it does mean some awareness that writing—unless no one ever reads it but the one who writes it—is a public act. To write and allow it to be read is to have a voice, and to have a voice is to be political. Physicist Fred Alan Wolf, in his intensely interesting book, *The Dreaming Universe,*[9] reminds us that we all dream, and he suggests that all of our dreaming makes up the dream of the dreaming universe. The dreams that we dream, in his vision, not only change the world, but change the very universe itself. It may be so. A friend told me that the Maya calendar predicted the end of the world on the winter solstice, December 21, 2012. He says the prediction meant not an apocalypse, a fiery Armageddon, but unimaginable changes that technology creates. The world as we know it is ending, he says. Things are deeply connected that until now have been separate. He sees this as a wonderful new world coming into being, and the change, he says, is happening. I am told that the Maya people talk about this as "rebalancing." Perhaps he—and they—are right.

For now, though, the great majority of the world's people live below the poverty line. So many in our world are voiceless unless someone gives them voice. Amherst Writers & Artists workshops have given voice not only to ordinary people in ordinary workplaces, graduates of MFA and PhD programs in writing, but also to extraordinary people who are in jails and early release programs in Ireland, Canada, and the United States, to teachers who were themselves refugees teaching in a refugee camp on the border of Kenya and Somalia, in villages in Malawi, as well as in shelters, nursing homes, schoolrooms, housing projects, among the homeless and many other under-served populations in the United States. If we cannot empower their own voices, then let us use ours, for them. Writing the truth is a political act. The form doesn't matter. Only the voice matters, and the truth of the content. Gandhi said, "Whatever you do may seem insignificant to you, but it is most important that you do it."[10] If you write the truth, you will change the world. If you write privately, you change your own inner world, and that changes the outer world. If you write publicly, you give voice to what is, and that assists what is becoming. If you help someone else to write the truth, you may not live long enough to know it, but you will have changed the world.

THIS FLIGHT

for Sarah

This flight, then, before the last.
Distance won,
centering in.

There were wild birds,
were there not? Feeding
from my fingers?

Or were they children?

This feathering is not down
bedding of ducks
wintering
on the pond, wings folded,
feeding from the fingers
of my children,
their bright faces bending
toward reflection.

This feathering is for flight.
I might think this
to be that other time,
mistake the wild bird for its image,
but for pinions.

I am still a long way from home
but turning now,
banking on air,
coming in.

                                          —P.S.

CHAPTER 12

The Body

And the body. What about the body?
—JANE KENYON

The body knows things a long time before the
mind catches up to them. I was wondering what
my body knew that I didn't.
—SUE MONK KIDD

IT IS TIME to write about the body.

Body my house
my horse my hound
what will I do
when you are fallen

May Swenson wrote those words a long time ago. Now her
body has fallen, and she has not come back to tell us the answer.

There is the body of one's writing, and there is one's physical
body. And there is (really, there is!) something to us, or in us, or of
us, that is not the body. It might be called "spirit." But spirit, at least
here and now, seems to be housed in body. Body, my house. House
of my spirit. House of my mind. Body. Figuring it out, for me, is
one function of writing. Often, that function is private writing—
much of it that I truly do not write to an external audience, not
even a small workshop audience.[1]

At the moment of beginning to write this chapter, about all I
am sure of in relation to my own body is that it is my house. It may

also be my horse. I'll have to think about that one later. And if not my hound (I don't know much about hounds) perhaps my house-cat? My crawdad? My inchworm? I don't know.

For now, it is my house.

A few days before Christmas last year, my body fell. And some time later, somewhere inside my body, I fell.

*   *   *

It is amazing how the body continues to teach us. I stand, wobbly, hands on my walker, taking baby steps, humbled before the patient servitude of the body. Here's the full May Swenson poem:

QUESTION

Body my house
my horse my hound
what will I do
when you are fallen

Where will I sleep
How will I ride
What will I hunt

Where can I go
without my mount
all eager and quick
How will I know
in thicket ahead
is danger or treasure
when Body my good
bright dog is dead

How will it be
to lie in the sky
without roof or door
and wind for an eye

With cloud for shift
how will I hide?[2]

When my body falls, Swenson suggests, I am utterly exposed. Exposed to myself, actually. Exposed as breakable. As finite. As fragile. Also exposed is how I take for granted the grace of the body, how I inhabit my mind and ignore my bones and blood and tissue. Until bone breaks, or tissue tears, or blood spills. As I sit here now, trying to put words to my own experience of body, words about trying to capture body in writing, I find in my imagination a little hermit crab, just deprived of its borrowed shell-home. It is so fragile, so *naked* as it scuttles about without a shell of its own, in search of an abandoned shell to move into—it is a tenant, a beggar. Then—*now*—I am reminded of how important after all is the body, the dwelling-place, the home of spirit. Or perhaps it may *be* spirit itself—spirit expressed as body.

* * *

It was December 13, a Thursday, the day of the week when usually I prepare for and then lead my Thursday evening writing workshop in my home, a group of twelve women, some of whom have written with me for many years, some of whom have been with us for only a few weeks or months. We were expecting a huge snowstorm, so large, that by mid-morning the University of Massachusetts had closed, which automatically closes my workshop, since I follow its lead on "snow days."

Those of us who live in snow country—at least those of us who love living here—know the elation that always comes with a snow day. Freedom! Everything canceled that possibly can be canceled. Beauty all around us, and quiet, intimate time with family or alone in a warm house. I turned to a couple of projects that I was wanting to complete for Christmas and realized that I needed a special kind of marker—a *Marvy Marker!*—that my good friend and crafts expert, Katie George, said would write on cloth and not wash out. I needed it for a project I wanted to make with a child whom I have claimed as a sort of adopted grandchild.

The snow had not yet started to fall, although the sky hung low and heavy with it. I thought, *If I hurry I can walk uptown, buy the marker, and get back before the snow has covered the ground, and I'll get my daily walk in, too!* Wrong! I had walked less than a block when the snow began, and it came down as if it was being poured out of a huge celestial bucket, so thick and heavy you could not see far ahead. But so beautiful, and myself so full of joy—I did not turn back.

On the way home, my Marvy Marker tucked safely into my pocket, I could no longer see the ground at all, and about a half-block from my home, I stepped on hidden ice, both feet went up in the air, and I landed squarely on my left hip. A broken bone doesn't hurt instantly if you don't try to stand on it, and so I lay there saying over and over, *Oh, please! Not a broken hip! Please, please, not a broken hip. I promise I won't ever be stupid again. I PROMISE I will never, ever, be stupid again!*

I knew I couldn't stand up. Visibility was poor, and I was on the sidewalk behind a couple of trees and a snow bank. Bargaining with God gave way quickly to wondering how long it would take for someone to find me. I looked around and saw with relief that our postman, Glen, had parked his Post Office vehicle about one car's length away. *Great*, I thought, *he parks, delivers mail to a few houses, comes back, gets in his vehicle and moves a way up the street. He will soon find me.*

A couple of cars passed by. I rested back on the ice and waited. *Well,* I thought, *if you have a broken hip, I suppose it's not a bad idea to keep it on ice!* Thinking that was pretty funny, I realized that my face was being bombarded by snowflakes. I looked up through the few spaces still left on my glasses, into the down-falling snow and thought, *I've never seen snow from this perspective before*—the perspective of lying flat, looking up into the downpour of flakes, and something inarticulate about the perspective of being helpless there. I took off my glasses, quickly thick with snow, and tucked them into my pocket.

The snow simply amounted to glory. No other word will do. It was an absolute overwhelm of beauty, falling gently upon me, as if forever, as if I, too, were falling, as if I, too, were part of the glory. At the time, I didn't have words for this. I still don't. The experience itself was so far beyond articulation, I simply felt, saw, and was enveloped. Perhaps ten minutes after my fall, some passing students found me, sheltered me from the snow with a coat, called Peter, called an ambulance (all four of our town's ambulances were out helping people like me) and set in motion the great machinery of healing.

Three days later words for the experience in the snow began to stir, but it was deep night—my first night in a rehab ward, and I had no paper or pencil. The telephone on my bedside table had not yet been connected. I had no access to home. The night nurse had been curt and brief with me when I asked for pain medicine; I didn't want to disturb him or my roommates for a pencil. Suddenly I felt utterly alone and afraid. The words were coming, though; they would not stop, and I knew they would disappear by morning. A line from Franz Kafka came first, "Even night is not solitude enough…"

Kafka was talking about writing—what the writer needs is a solitude deeper even than night. It was night, and I was in a terrifying and total solitude. In my mind, the snow was coming down, and my own words were pushing to take form. I pressed the buzzer for the nurse, and asked for a pencil or a pen and a bit of paper. He came back with a red ballpoint pen, whispering that it was all he could find. I tore a blank page out of my small address book. I wrote as fast as I could, tearing out more pages and holding the paper so a bit of light from the distant door would tell me if I was actually getting words down. I didn't have my reading glasses, so I could see only a red blur in the dim light, and besides, more light might waken the motor-mouth who was one of my four roommates. I needed solitude, the dark, and the scraps of paper. One by one I filled six little blank pages:

Even night is not
night enough,—
the I have touched

ecstatic—snow
coming downing
down alone
myself and the Dance
the unutterable
dance—the dance
itself—music
& to see and
to Be the dance—
and the writer gets
now and then to
touch the wild
fur of that
the soft fur—of
that beast, life

—the young…
nurse
glances in—stops

                        (page two)
backs up—
tries to see into
the dark what
I cannot see—
a crazy old
woman with a
broken hip
writing in the
dark on a
fragment torn
from her—
she doesn't see
in the dim dark
the strange color
of the [words overwritten, illegible]
rose given [by my]

beautiful friend
... [or the] white bear
how its fur
merges with the
swirling down
snow in "that
rough beast
slouching toward
Bethlehem"
and everything you
have ever lost
is given back to you

                    (page three)
will I fall
onto the ice
of your disregard
if I ask my
question wonder
will you
see me lying
on my back
before your
feet snow
falling into my
face, my eyes

                    (page four)
I had to get
lost out here
lost in this
particularity
this Marvy
Marker – this
<u>this</u> small
storm of falling
snow

If you look
carefully you will
see the

This is as far
as I should
go
    [words overwritten, illegible]
To the extent
that it works it
is a goodbye

                    (page five)
It took a fall
a flight
    [words overwritten, illegible]
The danger is not
so much that we
will lose our
footing, but
that we will
miss the fact of
our flight.
I was a crying,
blubbering mess
& the dark,—deep
dark skin color of
the—of the young
orderly [pushing my
gurney on the elevator]
daring flight to
the silence of race,
the silence of age,
the silence of
class—my
daring to say

<u>your skin is</u>
<u>so beautiful</u>

        (page six)
as the elevator
door opened
"Just a Closer
[walk]…"

It comes in an
instant of <u>being</u>
there—Anne
Dellenbaugh [says]
"Everything is so
transient—
Everything is so [precious]"

You will make
that fragment
into a villanelle
& you will never
capture the
whole feast—
just by your fingertips
brush the white
snow around me
and I have the
final pages of
a new chapter…

          *   *   *

But it isn't the final pages of a new chapter. It is a jumble of lines and images. It is a map back to where I was on a certain important night in my life. In the middle of a medicated fog, I was trying not to lose something beautiful, something ecstatic, something that happened to me after my left foot slid on hidden ice, and the weight of my body fell exactly onto my left hip, breaking it. Something ecstatic. Something too precious to lose. But into my attempt to catch that ecstasy comes the complication of impersonal nurses and a moment of triumph on a gurney, alone in an elevator with a young male orderly: I say to him what I want to say, across race, across age, across silence, across being strangers to one another, across the terror of fracture, across helplessness. Never mind what it was to him (*a crazy old woman with a broken hip?*). Never mind.

As I have said, my own writing that matters most to me are those pieces that have taken me out the to the very edge of what I know and do not know I know. That fine point, that intense moment of *seeing*, of *discovering*—that is the writing that matters most. Not craft, although craft can be the tightrope that gets me over the chasm of silence to what I need to say.

*   *   *

This is my body, broken. The local surgeon who repaired my hip did not leave me with a good repair. Almost two years have passed now since that day when I fell in the snow. I have gone to Boston, I have swallowed something that put nuclear substance into my body so technicians could read the state of my bones. *For thou didst form my inward parts*, the Psalmist says, the original Hebrew translated here into lovely King James English, *thou didst knit me together in my mother's womb. . . . Thou knowest me right well; my frame was not hidden from thee, when I was being made in secret, intricately wrought in the depths of the earth. Thy eyes beheld my unformed substance . . .*"

Technicians at Brigham and Women's Hospital read the frame of my body that was "made in secret" and also read what I did to it when I fell and the further damage done to it by my local surgeon. I will soon go back to Boston to have a full hip replacement.

*   *   *

Yesterday a body worker used acupressure, Feldenkrais exercises, cranial/sacral massage, and only she knows what else. As she worked on my hip, easing tight muscles now that I have had my hip replacement, she told me that people who are survivors of emotional trauma take a lot longer to heal than people who have not experienced trauma. Because trauma survivors have trouble *being in* their bodies. "In fact," she said, "they have trouble *finding* their bodies."

Well, two years of limping around on one leg that is almost two inches shorter than the other (now corrected by Dr. Estok, in Boston) has given me time to find my body, whether or not I'm yet an expert at being in it. The question recurs, though—if my spirit is body, and my body spirit—what script is it that is written on me and within me? What about the stories we are afraid to tell? What about the secrets we keep from ourselves?

"Body my house" has rooms that are comfortable and familiar, but "Body my hound" is wounded; there is a place on my upper back where massage cannot go because it triggers deep weeping without any mental images to explain why it is happening. "Body my horse" has been mostly asked to work, and is comforted by work. A workhorse, not born to privilege or to the pursuit of pleasure, it goes from the field exhausted, eats, sleeps, gets up to work.

By writing the stories of my childhood I have come close enough to my body's secrets to know that I was abused. Some of the details I know, some I may never recover. Most often I think about these things using the metaphor of cave and dragon and treasure and the hero's journey into danger to find treasure.

Writing has allowed me to move from dislike of my own body and my own child-self, to a late-come love for "my house, my horse, my hound" and a deep admiration for the child-self who survived poverty, orphanage, abandonment, and abuse. Good friends have helped; one three-month series of sessions with a good therapist helped; but what brought me home to my own body and to peace with the tyrant child in me who was perpetually afraid that those who loved her would leave her—was writing. Especially writing in the company of other writers in my workshops and retreats who were on their own hero's journey in their own dragon-caves, in search of their own treasures.

I am in awe of the courage and passion with which women have written about the female body and female sexuality in my lifetime. One of the bravest and boldest of those is Rebecca Schneider's intensively researched book, *The Explicit Body in Performance*.[3] In different modes and genres, Audre Lorde, Joy Harjo, bell hooks, and many other contemporary women writers have explored and continue to explore the ways the body is used, misused, and portrayed in relation to gender, race, and sexuality. Sharon Olds's poem "I Go Back to May, 1937" speaks to me of the courage needed for that task, especially when it is embedded in the ordinary intimacy of daily life. It begins with an image of the narrator's parents standing young at the gates of their college: ". . . they are kids, they are dumb, all they know is they are/ innocent, they would never hurt anybody." But the poem ends "I say/ Do what you are going to do, and I will tell about it."[4]

That courage, evident in women's writing about the body, takes my breath away: first, to do the dangerous task of *seeing* what we ourselves and others "perform," to use Rebecca's word, and second, to commit ourselves, dare, force, tease, bribe, beg, beat, harass, and love ourselves enough to "tell about it" even when—perhaps especially when—it involves the *explicit* body.

* * *

Body my house
my horse my hound
what will I do
when you are fallen

When I was young, and pregnant, and the time drew near to give birth, my body practiced contractions. Warmed up. Got ready. Already I have broken a wrist, a coccyx, several ribs, and four vertebrae. Now a hip. My body is practicing. Warming up. Getting ready.

That is all right, the cool, analytical part of me says. But the not so analytical me who lives in this house, the body, is not at all ready to be evicted. I wonder if babies resist being born? And I wonder if I will be born into some other life when this body, my house, falls for the last time. None of the answers friends and preachers and teachers have offered me (reincarnation, heaven, simple returning to the soil, being a drop in the great ocean that is God) satisfy me half as much as standing in the mystery. Sometimes the mystery draws near in what I swear is the presence of someone I have lost. Sometimes it draws near as animal, as fossil, as words on a page— unexpectedly the moment becoming alive. I have watched two whom I loved more than my own life leave their bodies. Where did they go?

We were each one *made in secret, intricately wrought in the depths of the earth.* Our bodies return to the sea and the land. But when "body, my house" is no longer my dwelling place...

I expect to be surprised.

GOING HOME THE LONGEST WAY AROUND,

we tell stories, build
from fragments of our lives
maps to guide us to each other.
We make collages of the way
it might have been
had it been as we remembered,
as we think perhaps it was,
tallying in our middle age
diminishing returns.

Last night the lake was still;
all along the shoreline
bright pencil marks of light, and
children in the dark canoe pleading
"Tell us scary stories."
Fingers trailing in the water,
I said someone I loved who died
told me in a dream
not to be lonely, told me
not to ever be afraid.

And they were silent, the children,
listening to the water
lick the sides of the canoe.

It's what we love the most
can make us most afraid, can make us
for the first time understand
how we are rocking in a dark boat on the water,
taking the long way home.

—P.S.

CHAPTER **13**

Death

What have I ever lost by dying?
—RUMI

Write as if you were dying.
—ANNIE DILLARD

WHEN MY HUSBAND CALLED from California to say that his father had died from a fall suffered while he was inspecting an irrigation pump on his farm, I waited until our three children were in bed before I went to each one to tell them. We had three children, ages eight, nine, and eleven, and although we lived a continent away from Peter's parents, all of them had reason to love the gentle farmer we had lost. I went to each child separately, knelt beside the bed, put my hand on a shoulder, and spoke quietly. "Daddy called, and said that Grandpa has died."

The first child I told waited for a moment, and then began to sob, and rolled into my arms, sobbing.

The second child thought about it and then said, "Grandpa is in a better place." The tone was half question, half seeming to want to reassure me as well as himself.

The third child I told held my words for moment in silence, and then whispered, "Don't ever talk about this again!" The tone was not anger; it was quiet defense against an unbearable fact.

* * *

If I write as a spiritual practice, I will at some point stumble upon the subject of death. My own, or the death of someone I have loved.

196 | HOW THE LIGHT GETS IN

In the writing of this book I have come close to it writing about age and the body. I will visit it again in a chapter I have not yet written. It may be called "On Strangeness"—on what it means to meet someone I think I have lost, suddenly present in the room on an ordinary morning as I am busy washing dishes. That, too: the ecstatic surprise, rather than the stumble.

* * *

Death is a private matter, ultimately. The old song affirms this: *You gotta walk that lonesome valley,/ You gotta walk it by yourself./ Ain't nobody else can walk it for you. You gotta walk it by yourself.* If we live long enough, there will be those we love who take that walk— away from us. And we are left in our own "lonesome valleys" trying to understand who we are, without them.

Writing about death and dying in the context of a spiritual practice requires the kind of courage that Jacob has in the ancient Genesis story, wrestling all night with the angel, wrestling until his hip is thrown out of joint and he has won the blessing for which he is fighting. Maybe it takes a certain hubris, or a certain humility, or a paradoxical mix of both, to wrestle with what William Butler Yeats called "death-in-life and life-in-death."[1] In their last books, Sylvia Plath, Robert Lowell, Elizabeth Bishop, James Merrill, Wallace Stevens, and many other writers have wrestled with the subjects of death and our human response, grief. Mary Oliver, near the end of her beautiful poem "Starlings in Winter," takes a sudden turn to her real subject: *I am thinking now/ of grief, and of getting past it...*"[2] The poet Helen Vendler wrote, "It used to be easier to deal with, when you had heaven to believe in, when there was another place to go at the end of your poem." Death without heaven, she says, "produces more stylistic problems."[3]

* * *

I have twice stood beside the bed of someone I loved with my whole heart, and have said—once by speaking, once by singing— *you can go now.* That, too, is an act of courage, giving permission for what you most dread, what you think you cannot bear. "Lie-d, lie-d, lie," Gillian Welch sings, "I'm not afraid to die." I—unless I am lying to myself—am not afraid of my own death. But I am very afraid of the death of others whom I love.

You can go now, I said. And they did go. I watched them draw in a last breath and release it, and I stood in the unimaginable silence of the breath not taken in. One was my brother, Sam, my only sibling, who was with me in infancy and in the orphanage and (at least in my heart and mind) in the army and in prison and in his alcoholism and in his recovery and in his caring for lost street kids and in his wearing an oxygen mask and always in the knowledge that he loved me without any judgment.

He died of emphysema from cigarettes and from the ravages to his body of alcoholism until his last completely dry twenty-three years. As he lay dying, the nurses on the floor of the intensive care ward laid down a law to us that only one person could visit him each hour, and for only five minutes. This was impossible, since there were close to thirty of us waiting to see him—and only three were blood relatives. All the rest, except his wife, were young people who loved him because he had helped them. Fixed their cars, lent them money, and with his wife, let them sleep on the couch, listened to their stories, and adopted one, rescuing her from an impossible situation.

When the doctor began to talk to us about taking away the machinery that was keeping Sam alive and I realized that some of those young people were not going to see him alive at all, I called Robin Therrien, a social worker in my workshop who worked with young people in trouble and knew my brother. She said, "I'll be right there." She drove through the several towns, met us in the intensive care unit, looked at the crowd of young people, and said, "I'll be right back."

Fifteen minutes later, the hospital social worker from downstairs, the floor nurse, and Robin came back to us. The nurse was warm and apologetic, assuring us that we could have extra chairs in his room, and all of us could go in as often as we wished. When they removed the tubes, he awoke and saw around his bed a halo of young people who loved him. He lived for about thirty minutes. I began singing "Amazing Grace," and a chorus of utterly untrained voices joined me on each chorus.

* * *

Not long after Sam died, I received an invitation to go to a private writing retreat in Arkansas. It was a gift from Shannon Chamberlin, who had attended a workshop that I had led. I admit that my first thought was, "Why would I want to go to Arkansas for a retreat?" In the bruising aftermath of Sam's death, Arkansas seemed half a world away, foreign and uninviting. I thought I just needed to get back to work and as my young daughter had said about her grandfather's death, "never talk about that again."

Wrong. I looked up "Eureka Springs, Arkansas" on the map. It was less than 100 miles from the backwoods hill where Sam and I were born, over the state line in Missouri. I sat with the map in my hands, realizing, *This is not an "invitation." This is a summons.*

I accepted the gift. In the three weeks I spent there, dogwood in bloom in the woods, little box turtles on the move as they were every springtime of my childhood, I wrote only one poem. I sorted, revised, put together my first "New and Selected" collection of poems, *Another River*. Only much later did I connect Sam's death with the title I chose for the collection. It comes from an old spiritual about death: "One more river,/ And that's the River of Jordan./ One more river,/ There's one more river to cross." The final poem in the book is the one new poem I wrote on that retreat. It's about Sam's death, and the death I knew was coming soon, the death of my lifetime friend and mentor, Elizabeth Berryhill. I began trying to write journal entries about Sam. Every effort only disturbed deep waters and left me feeling that I might drown. As I described earlier, in the chapter on the dark night of the soul, his relationship to me had elements of two kids clinging to a life preserver somewhere out on a stormy ocean. Losing him in childhood, and no less in mid-life, shook the foundation of my own survival.

I have learned that when a subject is simply too huge to get the filaments of prose sentences around it—too big, that is, to catch in a usual web of words—sometimes it helps me to rock back into nursery-rhyme rhythm. Old country-music song rhythm. Hymn rhythm. The music, the rhythm of my own earliest language. Something that can hold a primal cry, I suppose. Emily Dickinson's poems scan to hymn patterns, ballad patterns, the rhythms of song in her childhood. Many of Dickinson's poems can be sung to the tune of either "Praise God, from Whom all Blessings Flow," or "The Yellow Rose of Texas."

In the years since that retreat, I have written many pieces about Sam—most of them in a circle of my workshop members—for example, about the day just before his final illness when he parked his truck on the edge of my lawn and came in the door and instead of eating my brownies and drinking my coffee, said, "C'mon, Pat. Get in the truck. I'll buy you a burger." It was such a shock—and only in writing it out much later did I find out why. Had he ever fed me? Had he ever bought me anything? It had always been my role to care for him, my younger brother, my broken brother. I climbed into the cab of his truck, feeling like a kid under a Christmas tree. He handed me a grungy old tape of songs by Willie Nelson and said, "Here, you can have this." I love Willie Nelson. He is for me childhood, Ozark, box turtle, dogwood, home. We drove to McDonald's. Sam ordered two Big Macs, two large diet cokes, and three bags of fries. He parked near the Dumpsters. As he unpacked our food, I asked, "Why three bags of fries?"

"For those little guys."

"What little guys?"

He rolled down his truck window and said, "Those little guys. I always buy an extra bag for them." He threw a fry out the window, and a dozen sparrows left the Dumpsters in a cloud, and settled on the tarmac near his truck.

Then he fed me.

* * *

In the Arkansas retreat, prose knocked a hole in more than I could bear. Prose opened up volumes. As in writing "Letting Go," described earlier, I needed to pull myself in close, go deep, and for that, instinctively I needed *form*. Some containment that could help me hold my grief, pull my grief in toward center, find the song that could sing it. And so I began playing with rhyme and meter, thinking of Sam's death and Elizabeth's pending death. Death and I were face-to-face. My own death seemed preferable to looking at the deaths of two who had made it possible for me to live. At the end of three weeks I came home with a book manuscript that took its title from a song about death and ended with this sonnet:

ENDING

> *The beginning of the end is a beginning.*
> *The end of anything can be an art.*
> *Giving up the greed, the lust for winning*
> *Is the hardest part.*
>
> *To be an artist of the end requires praising*
> *Not just what went before, but what's to come.*
> *The fact of ending is itself amazing;*
> *The lines that will define it, never plumb.*
>
> *Beginning is a gift that comes unbidden,*
> *But ending can be crafted like an art.*
> *What lies beyond is mystery, and hidden.*
> *Ending can be wholeness of the heart.*
>
> *Summon heart, and its companion, breath,*
> *To make an art of what we know as death.*

* * *

Speaking of writing sonnets, Edna St. Vincent Millay wrote (in her sonnet about writing a sonnet) "I will put Chaos into fourteen lines/ And keep him there...."[4] That is exactly what I am talking about—the chaos of overwhelming experience is sometimes made expressible by the safety of a form. Every one of us has an original tongue, and the music, the cadence, of that tongue is our greatest repository of genius. Sadly—even tragically—the traditional ways we have taught writing, both in the Western and the Eastern world, have tended to destroy our connection to our own most valuable asset as writers.

I didn't begin that poem by trying to write a sonnet. I began writing in a sort of childhood voice. I was writing about my first love, my brother. For that I needed my first language of music, the nursery rhyme. As I struggled to say more, it developed into something near a ballad (think country western music, deep in the roots of a Missouri childhood) and so I kept the four-line stanza instead of more-common sonnet forms.

Only the last crafting came from what I know out of formal education—that there is something called "sonnet" and it has fourteen lines. I didn't have to have the sonnet form to make that poem stronger. It could have been sixteen lines in ballad form, four lines to a stanza.

There is a lovely thing that happens when you have learned some traditional forms. The poem itself will sometimes tell you what it wants to become. Trying now to remember my process, I imagine that it was the elegance of the sonnet that called me. Emily Dickinson wrote, "After great pain a formal feeling comes...." The death of my brother, the impending death of my mentor—a formal feeling comes. A desire very deep to move slowly, truly, in the form of a dance or a song. Requiem.

The sonnet is based on an old folk stanza, formalized into the Italian sonnet form by a lawyer in twelfth-century Italy. William Shakespeare adapted it into the "Shakespearean sonnet," Edmund Spenser into the "Spenserian sonnet," and a host of other writers into adaptations. It has developed into many forms that call themselves "sonnet," so many that about the only thing all of them have in common is their length: fourteen lines. If you doubt this, look at Millar Williams's classic book on forms. He includes a sonnet that has only one word on each of the fourteen lines.

Annie Finch has an excellent chapter on the sonnet in her book *A Poet's Craft*. I didn't know until yesterday, when I read her chapter, that what I had written is called an "English sonnet." Since I broke the first twelve lines into four stanzas, however (which I like and will not change to make it a perfect "English sonnet"), perhaps it is a sonnet-ballad. Who cares? I don't. The only thing that really matters is that writing in verse and in meter, first in my own childhood language, then into the formal and elegant form of the sonnet, made a "containment" that I absolutely needed in order to grieve the death of my brother and the other death that was about to happen.

* * *

My mentor, Elizabeth Berryhill, was often called "Bye." Tall, straight as the sequoia tree she planted in her back yard, she was a woman of fierce dignity. She was called a genius in the San Francisco Bay Area newspapers for her astounding work in theater. She was funny—only once in my life have I laughed so hard I wet my pants, and that was in watching a satirical sketch she wrote and directed. It was about a local amateur Shakespeare play-reading group. They were seated in a circle on a bare stage, reading *Macbeth* and bungling it marvelously. Two spotlights from opposite sides of the stage lit the area where they sat. When the line came for Lady Macbeth to speak, she emerged from under the bleachers, stalking straight ahead toward the circle with a lighted candle in her hand. Before she reached the circle, she stopped, glared up into one spotlight and cried out, "Out, damnéd spot!" It went out. Then she glared into the other, and cried, "Out! Out, I say!!" It went out; the stage was completely dark, and we in the audience were undone.

But she was also on fire for social justice. Her production of Maxwell Anderson's *Lost in the Stars* shook the Bay Area before the civil rights movement shook America. It is a musical based on Alan

Paton's novel about South African apartheid (and therefore also about American racism): *Cry, the Beloved Country.* Elizabeth went, a white woman in the mid-1950s, to all of the African American churches in the Bay Area and called for singers to come to try out for the production. It was like nothing any of us had seen—a full, live production in which the cast, half black, half white, struggled, suffered, sang: *Little stars, big stars,/ Falling through the night— / And we're lost out here in the stars.*

I could so easily have been lost out in the stars. Not because of racism—because of poverty. Sidney Poitier, speaking in an interview of his father, once said, *The poverty syndrome nails itself into your being.* The child, the teenager, who grows up desperately poor and gains privilege, wears it always as an outer garment over the "rags where all distinctions start," as I wrote in my poem, "Letting Go."

I met Elizabeth when I was in graduate school in California. I was twenty-two; she was thirty-seven. For the next forty-seven years she mentored me—taught me, listened to me, loved me. Although there were times when I was in danger of losing myself, she never lost me.

I was in awe of her, amazed that she had time for me, and in time, that she loved me. Clearly she was the mother-in-the-world that my poor, trapped blood-mother could not be. Bye was therapist; she was teacher; she was friend. But most miraculously she was an artist who related to me as if I, too, were an artist. Where I could never have dared to fly, her belief in me was wing and wind. On the strength of her belief in me I was able to make my way from the ugly shame of the tenement to a home within myself that I swear, without her, I would have gone to my grave without ever even imagining.

When she received her first diagnosis of cancer, I knew that I wanted to be with her in the journey that lay before her, if she wanted me. I said it: "Bye, I will be here, if you want me to be here. I swear it. No matter what is going on, I will be here." I knew that there were others who loved her deeply, even fiercely, and I lived a continent away in Massachusetts. I was not a relative by blood. My

heart, that engine of my blood, cries out as I write those words—
yes, oh yes, I am!—but the blood lines between us were invisible to
those who gathered to care for her.

Toward the end, because we both loved the old hymns of our
childhoods and knew the antique words by heart, I called her at
her home in California every evening before I went to bed and
sang to her. I have a voice that is fit only for lullabies and for driving alone on long road trips, but that didn't matter. I always sang
her favorite:

> *Be Thou my vision,*
> *O Lord of my heart.*
> *Naught be all else to me,*
> *Save that Thou art...*

and one or two of my own favorites:

> *Day is dying in the West,*
> *Heaven is touching earth with rest.*
> *Wait and worship while the night*
> *Sets her evening lamps alight*
> *Through all the sky...*

or "Just a Closer Walk with Thee," or "Amazing Grace."

Finally I received a call—if I wanted to see her before she died,
it was time to go. I was scheduled to lead a workshop in Ireland. It
was fully registered. I canceled it and flew across the country. She
lived for about a week after I arrived. Members of her family, nieces
and others, were by her side. They knew me only slightly.

*   *   *

I name in my writing what has not been fully nameable in any
other way. In forty-seven years, Elizabeth came to know all of my
secrets, except perhaps those I kept from myself. And if I did not
know all, surely I came to know many of hers. I do not name her
secrets onto my pages. It is myself I am after, and that Presence that

hovers invisible to the outer eye, but is sensed sometimes hovering, surprising, delicate as a lightning bug in summer evening air, but undeniable. Flannery O'Connor's image of Jesus as a ragged figure glimpsed behind a tree. Maybe like that. Or maybe in the face of someone who loves me, when I sit across from her in her living room as the sun goes down over Marin hills, and I see in her eyes that I am seen, in her listening that I am heard—and in that attention, I see and hear myself.

*　　*　　*

They knew me only slightly, her relatives, and as the days drew near for her dying, one of them came to me and said gently, "Maybe it is time for you to go home now."

I was stunned. I understood their need. They were keeping watch around her bed. I was mostly by the fireplace in the living room, honoring their primacy in her life. There was nothing I could say. She was dying. I couldn't tell her, "Your relatives want me to go." But to go would surely break my promise to her: "I will be here if you want me." I knew in my heart that she wanted me.

I sat watching the embers of a fire that I myself had been tending. I had to go. I said that I would go.

Her relatives went home for the night. A woman from one of the Caribbean islands was her hired caretaker. A big woman, her wisdom was as large as her physical presence. Elizabeth trusted her. When the family was gone, I went into the bedroom, bent close, and said, "Bye, I have to go home." I gave no reason.

She whispered, "All right." We were silent then, and I stood in a sense of overwhelming betrayal.

I went back to the fire, sick enough to throw up. In a short while, the island woman came to me.

"You are going home?"

"They told me it is time for me to go."

"They told you that?"

"Yes."

"Elizabeth is very upset that you are leaving."

I said nothing. I think I wanted to die, myself.

Her voice was quiet, almost a whisper, but powerful with incredulity and command. "You should do what *Elizabeth* wants!"

I stood up and walked across the room to the telephone, and called the family member who had told me to leave. I said, "Elizabeth is upset that I am going home."

She thought a moment, and said wearily, "Then you'd better stay."

The next morning, as everyone was busy in the kitchen and in Elizabeth's room, someone in the yard began to scream. The family cat had been killed in the night by some other animal. Pieces of fur and entrails were strewn around the back yard, and the family member who most loved the cat was hysterical. I gathered the remnants of the cat, prepared it for burial, dug a grave under the sequoia tree that Elizabeth had planted, and had a little ceremony of interment with the family member who needed that closure.

When I returned to the kitchen, the person who had asked me to leave met my eyes and said quietly, but deeply, "Thank you."

The next day, Elizabeth died. At the very end, as she was struggling to breathe, I asked if I could sing, and the same woman said, "Please." I began to sing an old hymn that I had often sung to Bye over the phone. It has many verses, more than I remember, but I had brought a small antique hymnal with me, so I had the words. The first two or three verses I knew by heart, and I sang slowly:

> *Abide with me, fast falls the eventide.*
> *The darkness deepens, Lord, with me abide.*
> *When other helpers fail and comforts flee,*
> *help of the helpless, oh abide with me.*

As I began the second verse, Elizabeth took a deep breath and slowly let it out. And did not breathe again. My voice quavered only once, and when it did, the island woman, without looking at the words, joined me in the singing, and we sang together all of the verses, into the vast silence of the breath not taken.

*   *   *

It is not given to me to see what is on the other side of that silence. Sam and Elizabeth walked each their own lonesome valley into the mystery. That I know. They allowed me to go with them as far as I could go.

Where have they gone? I don't know. Are they still here with me? Sometimes I think so. Sam many times has seemed to me to be sitting at my kitchen table where he often sat, after pulling his veterinary supply truck up on the edge of my lawn, leaving the motor running while he ate a brownie left over from my workshop and drank a cup of strong, black coffee before he took off again for his route in the Berkshires or New York state. Only once before today has Elizabeth seemed to be with me—one day when I was worried about something, suddenly her voice said clearly, with all the dignity and power she forever put into speech, "Pat!" And I felt myself suffused with her power. I felt taller, stronger, more whole, as I always felt in her presence.

Today I brought her picture down from upstairs—a black and white snapshot. She is perhaps forty-five years old in the picture, at the height of her work in The Festival Theater that she founded and directed in San Anselmo. Her left foot is up on the low stage, her right foot solidly on the floor of the theater. She is dressed in her perpetual blue jeans and lightweight denim shirt. Her long hair is pulled into its ponytail at the back of her neck. Her right hand is in her pocket, her left elbow rests on her left knee and her left hand is gently on her chin. Behind her, in the shadows, is the architecture of the theater, bare wooden supports. She is thinking. Her gaze is on the stage. She is intent. Intense. She is at her work, and I can see that although she is not smiling, she is happy. She is creating a world. I am part of the world that she created.

*   *   *

I write my way. This day I have written things I have never before put into words. Rainier Maria Rilke wrote:

> have patience with everything unresolved in your heart and try to love the questions themselves as if they were locked rooms or books written in a very foreign language. Don't search for the answers, which could not be given you now, because you would not be able to live them. And the point is to live everything. Live the questions now. Perhaps then, someday far in the future, you will gradually, without even noticing it, live your way into the answer.[5]

If we are to follow his advice, as I have said earlier, it seems to me that we do not write to find answers; we write as a way to *live into* answers. Ancient scripture says, "Now I see through a glass, darkly, but then face to face." Writing about death—about the breath of a loved person who breathes out and does not breathe back in, brings me no further than what I can see "through a glass, darkly." But writing the experience, the details, does bring me face to face—not with answers, but with those I have loved who have gone before me into mystery.

And so I say this: write. Write out of silence to silence. Write out of mystery to mystery. Write out of not-knowing to not-knowing. Write to summon those you love. If you write them, they will come to you. Face to face.

HUSH

Hush. Slow down. Say the names
of those for whom your candle burns.
Say them into the attentive ear
of memory, or of God.
Oddly, now, either one will do.
You are no longer required to believe.
Receive the gift of listening.
Belief is as hard as a hickory nut
that, cracked, holds many mansions.
The faces that you love are chalices.
Hush. Slow down. Tip the chalice,
sip the wine and say it:
All that I remember now are mine.

BURNING THE TOBACCO

After I set fire to the little pile of tobacco this morning, I left the beach. It was bitterly cold, but David had told me to burn the tobacco. I trust him. It is a valuable kind of trust, because we inhabit such different worlds. He's in his twenties, with long hair that falls gracefully over his shoulder when he bends at the waist, his hands folded together as if in prayer to tell me goodbye. He has recently been adopted by a Native American medicine man.

David knows an Indian high in the California mountains who conducts a sweat lodge every Sunday, and he took me there, his little car winding between redwoods, oaks, and fields of golden grass. Sure enough, there was a circle of stones and an arc of branches above it—but no Indian. We walked around for an hour, telling stories. Finally David disappeared into a little house at the edge of the clearing and came back with the news: "He went into town to watch the Super Bowl—it's the Redskins vs. Buffalo."

"Don't be disappointed," I said. The hawk we saw circling above us was mystery enough. I told him that my father's mother—the Native American grandmother I never knew— had spoken to me in a dream. He nodded. He has become wise, and wisdom sits in silence before it speaks. Then he told me to welcome her into my life. "Go to a private place, a special place, and burn this tobacco. Tell your grandmother you welcome her into your life."

Today I walked alone on the beach in a cold wind, and I found lying among the rocks a massive old tree that had ridden the waves and come up beached. It rose in a great grey curve and lifted grey limbs to a grey sky. It could have been a fallen grandmother. I sat under the arch of its trunk and made a little pile of the tobacco. I struck five paper matches before a tiny coal appeared between the palms of my hands held against the wind. I could smell the thin wisp of smoke that rose from the rock. I welcomed my grandmother into my life.

Any moment now, she may come.

—P.S.

CHAPTER 14

Strangeness

There can be no great art...
without a certain strangeness.
—JOHN GARDNER, quoting Samuel Coleridge

"Sir, do you believe in miracles?"
"Is there anything else?"
—WALT WHITMAN

My own suspicion is that the universe is not only
queerer than we suppose, but queerer than we
can suppose.
—J.B.S. HALDANE

WRITING AS A SPIRITUAL PRACTICE approaches strangeness, dances toward it, even dares to reach out, address it, welcome it, invite it to stay a while. Now and then strangeness does stay, but only in the way a dream stays: fadingly, escapingly, teasingly.

Writing about writing, I have been exploring what I think I already know. But writing about *mystery*, I have tried neither to teach nor to preach. I have tried to constantly veer away from that which is familiar and known, toward that which is just beyond my grasp. In writing, this is most commonly done in story and in metaphor. I have met strangeness again and again as I have been writing this book. Trying to describe strangeness is—forgive me!—strange. It requires story. It requires metaphor.

* * *

When Halley's comet appeared in 1910, its tail passing through the earth's orbit, my great-grandmother believed what was being predicted in the news: The world was coming to an end. She repeated many times the story of Mark Twain, who was born as the comet passed over in 1835, and who predicted his own death when it passed over again in 1910. It was first sighted on April 9, 1910, and reached perihelion on April 20. The next day, Twain died.

My mother, six years old, was marked deeply by the excitement, and passed along to me the expectation that the comet would be utterly amazing when it appeared again approximately seventy-six years after 1910. She wanted desperately to live long enough to see the comet again. She was eighty-two. When it finally reappeared in 1986, she had suffered thirty fractures from osteoporosis, was extremely fragile, and had glaucoma in both eyes.

But she was alive, and the comet was anticipated in our neighborhood by students at the observatory at Amherst College with excitement somewhat akin to her own. I called the astronomy department for information and was told that this time Halley's was not coming very close to the earth, but the best viewing would be near midnight on a high point on Route 2 near Amherst, overlooking the Quabbin Reservoir.

It was cold but clear that day, and we planned the trip carefully. She would need her warmest coat, a scarf, mittens, a cap, and sturdy walking shoes. When we arrived at the scenic overlook, there was a line of cars from one end to the other. People in small groups stood clustered, looking out over the reservoir to the eastern sky. Absolutely nothing appeared to the naked eye but the usual overarching symphony of stars.

I left my mother in the warmth of the car and went to speak to someone in a group clustered around the biggest telescope. I was told that it was possible to see the comet, but only if we gazed at a certain star through the telescope until a tiny blur of light appeared slightly to the left of the star.

I turned from what seemed to be students to the man I presumed was their professor. I told him that I had my eighty-two-year-old mother in the car, and that she had been waiting all her life to see Halley's comet. Would he allow her to look through his telescope? He said, "Of course," and I helped her out of the car. The students parted and Mama walked through.

The professor told her to find a certain star and she said, "I've found it!" He told her to gaze at that star until she saw a hazy bit of light to its left. There was a moment of silence, then she cried out, "I see it! I see it!" and stepped back from the telescope.

He offered it to me, then, and I tried. I really tried. Maybe I saw a tiny hazy dot. I told Mama I did. But I'm not sure.

One thing I am sure of, though. Glaucoma or not, I am certain that my mother saw Halley's comet.

Here is my question: What do we see, and what do we see only because we want so badly to see? And what perhaps are we allowed to actually see against all odds of chance and circumstance, logic and prevailing wisdom? To help me with this question, I have read every word of *The Beautiful Invisible* by Giovanni Vignale. He is a theoretical physicist with a list of credits as long as my arm or longer. I was a child who failed fourth grade math and never recovered from what long division did to my scrambled brain. I absolutely cannot understand most of what he tries to teach me, but I look at the tapestry of his arguments, and I do see in the spaces between the threads, filaments of gold, the majesty of scarlet, and the absolute strangeness of the beautiful invisible.

When he describes Newton's and Kepler's discovery and development of the concept of gravity—"the force that holds together the solar system, powers the stars, sweeps the ocean with majestic tides, and yet does not disdain pulling little apples to the ground"— he comments (italics mine):

> This and other results would have probably remained hidden from sight if people like Kepler, Galileo, and Newton had not had the intellectual courage to abandon a point of view that was bolstered by common sense and by authority, *go to the limit*, and embrace a more abstract and, to some extent, fantastical view of the universe. In the case of Newton's theory of gravity this went so far as to contemplate the almost mystical notion of a force acting across empty space, without the mediation of

matter. We know that Newton himself found this idea "inconceivable" (as if he had not already conceived it!) and yet did not shrink away from it, nor tried [*sic*] to propose a more plausible alternative. Perhaps, like Feynman, he thought that it is better "*to live not knowing*, than to have answers that might be wrong."[1]

Embracing strangeness requires a certain willingness to "go to the limit" and at the same time, "to live not knowing." Writing as a spiritual practice, in the sense that I mean it (which is not preaching what we already believe or teaching what we already know, but is exploration), requires this willingness. Often I am told by someone, "I want to write. I *really* want to write." Usually that statement comes from a person who is already writing occasionally, but wishes for a more consistent practice. And I understand. Writing, when it is deepest and truest, pulls us out to the edge. It wants all, not just a small now-and-then commitment. At the edge of what we know and understand, there is sometimes strangeness. I experience that most often in these five ways:

First, as an inner voice, as I described in the chapter on prayer—the experience that Jane Kenyon calls "being broken in upon";[2]

Second, as a comical or playful synchronicity;

Third, as a deeply serious synchronicity that may include fear and awe;

Fourth, as a message given by another person who is gifted with a certain kind of sight;

Last, as a sequence of events that calls into relationship many factors over time and distance that seemingly could not have been connected randomly.

All five of these have occurred during the process of this writing, the comical ones many times.

* * *

First: Mystery sometimes reveals itself as an inner voice.

On an ordinary day years ago, I stood beside my mother's sewing machine in the basement of the parsonage where I lived. I had in my hand fragments of cloth I had chosen carefully, deliciously, to make into a sample block for a quilt. I had never made a quilt, but my mother had, beautiful ones: Log Cabin, Wedding Ring, Texas Star, and others, all burned in Aunt Nellie's fire.

I stood with the finished quilt block in my hand. It was perfect—a square the size of the palms of my two hands, made of smaller pieces stitched together, a light blue flowered print, a dark blue and a white cotton in a pattern that swirled like a child's whirligig—clean and perfect. I was ready to go back to the fabric store and buy enough material for the entire quilt. But as I held it in my hand, I heard words: *You have to choose. Either you will make a quilt, or you will write. You have four children. You have a husband. You have his congregation in the church next door. You cannot have it all. You will either write or you will dabble in a lot of other things.*

I chose writing, and writing alone. I would have no other art form. That day was forty years ago, but only recently have I come to understand that it was a spiritual decision I made that day. I don't know whether the voice was simply my mind talking to my hands, or one part of my mind talking to another part, or the voice of an ancestor, a spirit, or what at that time I called "God." But I do know that I heard the words, *you have to choose,* and I made an answering decision that set the course for the rest of my life as a spiritual pilgrim. I use words to find my way home; I use words to make sense of the complicated, beautiful, inner and outer invisible landscape that surrounds us. After all, writing is making another kind of quilt.

* * *

Second: Strangeness sometimes is funny—especially the sudden in-break of synchronicity.

I have written here and in *Wake Up Laughing* about my suspicion that there is a comic element in the cosmos—that when we are attentive to the mystery, we are delighted in, sometimes even played with. That playful synchronicity is not itself the strangeness I am talking about. Rather, it is the *evidence* of strangeness, the *evidence* of mystery—as lightning is the evidence of electricity striking down—an explosion of the not-at-all-ordinary into the ordinary. Synchronicity sometimes is so comical it's silly—a kind of cosmic slapstick humor that sets you laughing along with—*whom*?

Take, for instance, what happened today.

I've been writing today about my lost grandmother, Elzina. I was thinking of her father's name, "Lakey," how her children in the Ozarks say she was Cherokee, how she lived her entire life along the Trail of Tears. How the name is found nowhere among the Cherokee, but appears briefly among the Creek people. And I was thinking how when she was only sixteen, she married an older, divorced man, the father of a child. How she never learned to write—even her own name. I was not thinking at all of my grandfather. His name was Harv Vogt. Suddenly the computer dinged with an incoming email. It is here before me—Ted Kooser's *American Life in Poetry,* which regularly sends a poem. This one is "Column 247." The title of today's poem is, *Grandpa Vogt's—1959.*

My fingers froze on the computer keys: I had been writing to my Grandma Vogt, figuring out that she died in 1958. Whatever else one might say, that's strange. These kinds of random experiences, as fleeting as a touch on the shoulder, a wink of an eye, the most delicate sort of synchronous information coming at exactly the right moment in my writing, have occurred over and over again through the years of writing this book. I have come to expect these experiences, to laugh with them, to accept them gratefully as a kind of dialogue. Not dialogue with "Grandpa," although come to think of it, I've been told he made life pretty miserable for Grandma, so his interrupting her here might be evidence to substantiate his presence. Rather, this sort of playful synchronicity seems to me to be dialogue with mystery—a nudge, an affirmation, a comical sort of *Pay Attention!* and an undeniable *Yes.* Yes, you are on the right track. Yes, you are in relationship. You are seen and understood and loved. My reaction is internal laughter and delicious joy.

The poem from Ted Kooser, of course, is not about *my* Grandpa Vogt. It is by Ben Vogt of Nebraska. It's about a Christmas dinner in which everyone waits impatiently for pictures to be taken before they can touch the feast. I write these words a few days before Christmas. The last sentence of Ben Vogt's poem is: "They'll hold the image/ as long as need be, seconds away from grace."

I do. I hold the image of my Grandpa Vogt, and I am laughing—seconds away from grace.

* * *

Third: Sometimes the quality of strangeness in synchronicity is serious, not at all amusing.

The last time I saw my mother, she was a grey fox on a hill in Wildwood Cemetery. I had not gone to her grave for two years because I was afraid to go. Before she died, she had given her body to the medical school of the University of Massachusetts, and I understood the rightness of that decision. She had wanted to be a nurse when she was young, but she had no money for the required uniform. She had loved and read about medical science all her life. In fact, she had been happy to go to a nursing home at the end of her life; she liked being among nurses.

Mama was fierce. She was, all my life, a force of nature. I believe she was brilliant, and that if she had been born into another economic class and into a later time she might have been an inventor, artist, or scientist. Anything but "mama." She could bless and curse in lightning sequence.

Only a handful of ashes came back from the medical school. It seemed to me to be all right (I did not ask permission) to scatter them just under the surface of the ground on her gravesite. Two of my daughters went with me at dusk on the evening of my birthday to bury her ashes. I have told the story more fully in *Wake Up Laughing*—it is enough here to say that as we finished, there was an explosion of noise in the branches that were a canopy above us. Some animal, invisible to us in the fading light, was simply screaming.

A year later on my birthday I went to the grave. As I knelt beside it reciting a poem that my mother loved, a huge, lean, black dog ran toward me and stood on the other side of the grave, the hair on his back a ridge of bristles, the growl in his throat terrifying. I felt in the very marrow of my bones the words, *Don't come here. This is mine.* The voice was my mother's.

The dog's owner came running, grabbed him by the collar and pulled him away, saying, "He would never hurt anyone."

It was two years later when I asked Peter to go with me on my birthday. Again it was dusk. He waited in the car while I approached the grave. Again I recited the poem that she had recited to me each year on the first day of June, my birthday: James Russell Lowell's lines, "What is so rare as a day in June?/ Then, if ever, come perfect days…"

Everything was still—no animal appeared. When I was done, we drove slowly around the curve of gravel road toward the back entrance of the cemetery, and there, only a few feet away, was a grey fox. It did not move. I asked Peter to stop and turn off the motor. The fox didn't move. It kept eye contact with me. I slowly rolled down the window. It sat down and continued to gaze at me. After a bit it stood, turned, and walked slowly away into the trees.

The fox was my mother, or a messenger from my mother, and the message was neither warm nor cold—neither blessing nor curse. It was rather, a farewell. I saw clearly that she was wild. She was beautiful. And she was on her own journey.

She gave me what she could: poetry, an intimate love of the natural world, laughter when I am in a good mood, ferocity when I am faced with what I understand as injustice. On the first day of June every year since then, if I am in town, I recite the poem beside her grave. She is no longer there.

The day before she died was like the days before. I visited her in the nursing home, walked with her down the hallway and back, sat by her bed joking with her, talking, remembering. As I turned to go, she said matter-of-factly, "You are the best thing that ever happened to me."

The next day, she died. Strange—and wonderful, that blessing.

*   *   *

Fourth: Mystery now and then meets us through the strangeness of a message given to us by another person with a certain kind of gifted sight.

Near the end of writing this book, I look back. For seven years I have had no other writing project. There have been poems, of course, journal, of course, and short prose pieces written in workshops and retreats. But this book has been my only writing project for fully seven years. It was not until I was well into the writing that I realized the moment that was its origin. The experience was strange.

I had led my annual two consecutive weeks of workshop at Pacific School of Religion; a writer named Wendy Simpson participated in both sessions. I worked intensively with a total of thirty writers, fifteen in each week-long session, giving them four hours of group work each morning and private consultations with manuscript responses in the afternoons. At the end, I was exhausted.

And so, when Wendy wanted to take me to a special restaurant that overlooked the Bay, I hesitated. But she was a delightful presence in the workshop, and in the second week showed us a short film she made for television that won a national award. It was stunning. I said yes.

In that dinner conversation she told me that she was a psychic. She had been working privately with a few families and law enforcement to help find missing and abducted children. The work was sometimes grim, and it was dangerous. When I wrote to ask her permission to tell her story and to use her name, she replied that I could do so and wrote, "It is okay to share my feelings—that it was more difficult to do than I thought—the visions, finding remains, seeing and experiencing all the pain of the families, that I really wanted to use my sight without having to encounter such personal terror and to help those who really wanted to find their own path."

She didn't want to do that work any more, and she enrolled at Pacific School of Religion to do graduate study. She continued:

The truth is that I was searching for a more meaningful use of my gifts, not that helping people find closure in the most difficult of experiences wasn't meaningful. I just "saw" more than I wanted to—felt more than I could handle—was really uncomfortable most of the time in my own skin. I hoped that I could be a better person and contributor to living dreams if I could find a better way, a better fit—you know, a way that is quietly full of mystery and the sense that all is as it should be. I didn't feel that way working on cases....In seminary I found living waters—a way to share my gift that did not drain me, that brought insight and joy to my life as well as the receiver, and it also brought new and deep friendships in spirit for me. I learn every time I read for someone—and my faith in the world of spirit/afterlife/endless love grows and grows. I am clearly shown the value and importance of each life that I read—the potential, the cry for healing and wholeness, the very essence of the soul's deepest longings. What could mean more? God/The Mystery/Divine Love—whatever we each name it—It is. And it loves and cares for each of us in form and beyond what we know of life in bodies, more than we could ever embrace. I have learned this.

I was astonished by her story, and moved by her integrity, her earnest desire to figure out the spiritual and the practical meaning of her gift. At the same time, I had lived for a long time with a fairly solid agnosticism about psychic phenomena, despite a few experiences of my own that I have privately considered evidence of a strangeness in which much more is possible than meets the physical eye.

A few years after that dinner, Wendy and her husband came to a writing retreat in my home in Massachusetts. After the retreat she offered to give me a psychic reading, something I had never sought, although I had experienced one once, as I recounted in *Wake Up Laughing*. She sat on one end of our long couch, and I sat at the other end. She told me she had no need to close her eyes or to engage in any behavior that was not completely usual—she would not go into a trance, or anything like that. She would simply listen—to me, in my silence, and to the spirits that she said would gather around me. For a time, she prayed out loud, gently, quietly, thanking a long list of people—my ancestors, her own ancestors, God, Jesus, and any unknown spirits who might be with us. During the course of her silences and her speaking she laughed gently, telling me that I was surrounded by a great number of spirits who love me. "Sam," she said, "is right here." I asked her about Elizabeth. She paused and then said slowly, "Elizabeth is busy. She has a lot of work to do—she is not so near right now."

Strange, I thought. I have often felt the presence of my brother. I see him in the last twenty years of his life, dry, a recovering alcoholic, happy among the crowd of runaway and castaway teenaged children that he and his wife Eve welcomed into their home. I see him fixing old cars for them, fixing broken hearts for them. I see them crowded around his bed—twenty or more young adults he had loved and helped, so many some had to stand on the other side of the glass wall—as he lay dying. And most often I see him sitting at my kitchen table. He is always grinning at me, another bad-taste ethnic joke or wild story about his cat, "Go-Home" (named because he haunted their back door and would not go home), about to be told. But Elizabeth has not felt close, except in that moment of my waking to the sound of her voice saying my name once. Nothing more.

Wendy spoke gently about various people whom I had known—but there was nothing that surprised me. It felt as if a friend from where I had lived before had come and was giving me news of people I love but whom I don't see any more. Everything she said was common, ordinary, and felt true. She was ending the session when suddenly she said, "Oh, there's something important I haven't told you. When I started the reading, the very first image I saw was a large tree. A really big tree, and one branch—a huge branch, almost as big as the trunk of the tree itself, is still attached to the tree, but lying on the ground. That branch is your spirituality."

At the time, I thought, How can she say that? I'm working so hard—I'm crossing the river to Chicopee every week, working with women in the project, reading their manuscripts, relating to them around the edges of the workshop. That's my spiritual practice now. That, and my workshops for the general population—there's not a word of theological or religious language in my teaching, but nevertheless, isn't it my spiritual practice? What more is required of me?

But under my question was uneasiness. Only much later, halfway through this writing, did I see that, in fact, I was out on a limb, lonely for a more direct and conscious life of my spirit. I had been too busy to even know that the loneliness was there. Wendy saw, and she had the courage to name it: "You need to pay attention to your own spiritual life," she said.

Brave woman. Truthful woman. Gifted woman. Willing to go forward all the way into what she saw, even into strangeness. I saw the tree and knew that she saw me. But I wasn't ready to do anything about it. Slowly, though—in fact over several years—the invitation grew into the question, *What is my spiritual practice now—is it possible that now, at this time in my life, writing itself is already my spiritual practice?*

*   *   *

Fifth and last, mystery sometimes reveals itself to us in an amazing shower of synchronicity involving events, people, circumstances that come into relationship across time and move into a configuration that suggests to me the explosive glory of a fireworks finale. Awe and love and beauty all at once that simply amounts to revelation, and a sense of *how could I have doubted that I am loved?*

What I will write now was an experience like that—with roots far back in my life, and a very recent fullness of flowering.

Everything I needed in college was paid for by the church that sent me there: tuition, clothing, books. They even refused to allow me to have a part-time job; they wanted me to be free to study. And I did study. I felt the weight of the miracle that I was living—I knew only too well what I was being rescued from. Occasionally, my English professor, Thomas Perry, for whom I did some babysitting, would slip me an extra five dollars, saying it was from "an anonymous donor." A loaf of bread cost ten cents then; five dollars was a considerable sum of money.

In the second half of my senior year, my mother called and told me that Sam had disappeared from the Army, and she was going to California to find him. She said I had to drop out of college immediately and go with her, to help her. Sam was nineteen, stationed in Barstow, California. He had been in the stockade for returning late from a leave. Another soldier, a twenty-one-year-old who had a criminal record of stealing guns from the fort and selling them, was also there. Sam had no criminal record.

Because the heat was merciless, the two were told they could go outside and sit on a bench in the shade of the stockade. The older boy said to Sam, "Let's jump in that truck and get out of here." They did. The key was in the ignition; they drove to the edge of camp property and left the truck there, hitchhiking to San Francisco where they disappeared.

Sam was absent without leave, and would soon be considered a deserter—a potentially life-destroying event at that time. Mama demanded that I drop out of college and join her. I adored Sam; I began to pack.

My roommate, without my knowledge, went to Dr. Perry, and he called me into his office. When I arrived, three of my professors sat in the small room, and none of them were smiling. Dr. Perry did all the talking; I remember clearly and exactly what he said; "Don't be a fool. You are a poor girl, here on a scholarship. If you leave, you will never come back. You can help your family more if you finish your education—they will still be in trouble when you graduate."

He was right, of course, and I knew he was right. It was only a few more months until graduation. I called my mother and told her what they said, and for the first time in my life I refused to do what my mother demanded.

She was mentally ill—I know that now. But I didn't know it then. She screamed, "You little whore! You would walk over anybody to get to the top." And hung up on me.

When I graduated, I went immediately to California. Mama was in a small apartment in San Francisco. Sam was in prison. He had turned himself into the Army only days before being named a deserter. A chaplain told my mother not to go to the court-martial. "It will only upset you," he said. "He has committed no criminal offense other than walking away from the Army, so the most they will do is give him a bad conduct discharge, and he's not Army material anyway." The chaplain promised to be there. After the court-martial he told my mother that the other boy's father was a career military man, so they gave that boy for his defense the man who usually was the prosecutor. That boy, with a criminal record, was given a bad conduct discharge and six months in the stockade. Sam, who was blamed for the entire event, was given a dishonorable discharge and a full year in the maximum security prison at Lompoc, California.

I took a bus to Lompoc, stood in the line of women and children waiting outside the high fences with the barbed wire at the top. No one spoke. The sun was cruel, but not so cruel as the high towers, the guards in the towers, their long rifles. Sam was allowed to talk to me: his hair yellow as a child's, his blue eyes. "I wish you hadn't come, Pat," he said. "I didn't want you to see me like this." He was nineteen. I was twenty-one.

Mama had secured a job for me in San Francisco, packing Bibles for mailing at the American Bible Society. After I had been there for a few weeks, she wanted me to meet her pastor, the minister at the huge Glide Memorial Methodist Church. I imagine that she expected him to tell me what a good girl I was to be helping my family. I'm fairly certain she had bragged about me to him, told him I graduated with honors from college—that sort of thing.

What he said was, "What are you doing here?"

I said, "I'm trying to help my family."

He said, "You should be in graduate school," then immediately picked up the phone and called Georgia Harkness at Pacific School of Religion. "I have a young woman here who should be a student at PSR," he said.

They didn't discuss me. He reported that she said, "Send her over."

Georgia Harkness was the first woman to obtain full professorship in an American theological seminary. She was instrumental in gaining ordination for women and became a leading figure in the modern ecumenical movement. After we talked for a half hour, she said, "We want you for a student."

I responded, "I don't have one red cent, my brother is in prison, and my mother is falling apart."

She said, "Never mind. We'll find you a job and a place to live. We'll make it work." And she did.

* * *

It is fifty-five years later. One of our daughters[3] has been invited to give a lecture at Pacific School of Religion—the second annual Georgia Harkness lecture. She has invited Peter and me to attend, and we sit in the PSR library (now the Bade Museum) where at age twenty-one I sat across from him at a library table, watched his fingers push a pencil across a page, and loved his hands before I loved the rest of him.

Along with one hundred twenty other people, we listen as our daughter gives the lecture named for the woman who said to me, fifty-five years before, "We want you for a student," and "We will make it work." Past time and present time collide. I am here and I am there, and I am held, I am loved, and the mystery that holds me holds all of creation in an inexhaustible joy.

Our daughter's speech was on October 13, 2011, seven years after I began writing this book. Days later I received my contract from Oxford: It was official; they would publish it. And I sat down to write how it happened that I was able to get a graduate education.

* * *

Something out of the ordinary happens: a *confluence* (Vignale's term—more about that later) of events happens, events intricately interrelated in ways that seem too ordered to be accidental.

How in the world—how out-of-the-world—is this sort of thing possible? I have played with a lot of possibilities, including that I have slipped off some edge of sanity. But there is Vignale's *The Beautiful Invisible,* in which he lifts up strangeness as a component of invention. And there is Madeleine L'Engle's *A Wrinkle in Time,* used by NASA to describe to nonscientific visitors something about the nature of time, that time is folded, or "wrinkled"—the folds touching one another—one time touching another time, and at least for L'Engle, suggesting possible interaction between one time and another.

Whatever one may think of L'Engle's suggestion, we all know that times do touch one another in the human mind. Writing together with others, when story, metaphor, and intuition are welcomed, can be a setting where mystery moves. I have experienced many times over the years that something strange—something mysterious, something very beautiful—happens when people write together in an atmosphere that is held absolutely sacred from any bullying, any intimidation, any ridicule, any "put-down." New work, like a newborn human infant, should be greeted with welcome and with honest mention of what is beautiful, healthy, alive.

The strange, the beautiful thing that happens is this: Every person has a rich language that is unique to him or her. Before we can learn and incorporate "craft" in writing, we must first learn to recognize and value the strengths and the beauty in our languages of origin, and in our ability to tell our own stories in our own voices. In safety and in practice, a beloved community can evoke, strengthen, and celebrate the strange mystery of human genius that is in every one of us.

As a workshop leader, as a teacher, I hold writers in a safe place, and they hold me as a writer. On a recent evening I offered a prompt in workshop: *Go back in your memory or imagination and find yourself or your character walking on a road or street that is very familiar. Begin to write something that your eye sees, then continue writing with that image or depart from it. Write anything that comes.*

In the twenty minutes of silence, as we wrote together, I tried to follow my own suggestion, and wrote an experience that I had never written before. It happened soon after I returned from the orphanage to the tenement. I was twelve years old:

There is a tough bunch of prairie grass between the cracked pieces of concrete, and the girl who is walking home from seventh grade sees it. She thinks about prairie. She thinks about cracked cement on top of prairie. She sees that the dark green blades of grass are claiming the earth for their own. She imagines grass as far as the eye can see. She imagines horizon and clouds and wind in her face. She imagines the rich loam below the concrete and asphalt, and she sees in her mind the fossils that she knows lie embedded in limestone under the loam. She knows they are there because she has walked in creeks where curled snails and crinoid stems are laced through stones when she goes to the camp for kids in her part of the city. All year long she dreams of that camp. But on this day, walking home from school, she understands for the first time that fossils—little prehistoric shells and snails are here, too, in her city, under the broken concrete. She is suddenly filled with joy knowing that under her feet there is prairie and under the prairie there is bedrock and in the bedrock there are fossils three hundred million years old. She does not have that number yet, but she does know that the fossils are her ancestors and the tough, green, solitary bunch of grass is triumphant. She, too, is triumphant, because she, too, will survive. She, too, will grow up through cracks in the concrete. She belongs to the rock. She belongs to the fossils. They are hers and she is theirs. She turns, then, having reached the tall, grey tenement where she lives. She walks up the six dirty concrete steps, opens the heavy brown door with its broken lock and climbs the wooden stairs to third floor. I leave her there because I am that girl. I am that tough bunch of prairie grass. That dark apartment cannot hold me any more.

I didn't consciously realize that I was writing about a *crack*. In concrete. As the writers in the circle quietly named what they thought was strong in my first-draft writing, one of them pointed it out to me, gently laughing as he quoted Leonard Cohen's lines that give this book its title: *there is a crack in everything. That's how the light gets in.*

That strangeness, the way the delicate touch of an image can evoke something in metaphor that is central to your work, something you never would have found by left-brain analytical planning, is for me a kind of holy process. It requires waiting and listening and trusting whatever image the unconscious gives. It requires attention to what is given, no matter how common and unremarkable it may seem. That attention, that trusting, cracks open something inside, and lets in the light.

*   *   *

Writing as a spiritual practice is a hero's journey, a journey that in some way every human being must make. Each of us has his or her own bag of tricks, a personal mythology made up of certain moments that we carry with us, consciously and unconsciously, understood or not at all understood. I didn't want to write a book about tenement and slum and orphanage. I have written those images in poems, translated them into fiction and nonfiction, into songs and oratorios and plays and novels and memoir. I didn't want once again to visit my own central images and metaphors. I wanted to figure out what Jesus means to me now, long-time outside the church and uncomfortable with any formal "affiliation." I wanted to write about spirit, about religion—its greatness and its failures—about how writing can be one way to find our own spiritual paths. But like every other human wanderer, I couldn't lay down my own ragbag of memory, my own backpack of burden. Those things I carry are my artist's palette, my musical scale, the dance that I alone can dance.

William Shakespeare wrote perhaps the best definition of writing toward strangeness into mystery:

> *So we'll live,*
> *And pray and sing, and tell old tales, and laugh…*

And take upon's the mystery of things,
As if we were God's spies...[4]

What better counsel could be given us as writers? Not that we must understand, not that we must have all knowledge of craft, design, history of literary theory, but that "The weight of this sad time we must obey,/ Speak what we feel, not what we ought to say."

King Lear is near the end of his life, about to be imprisoned with his daughter, Cordelia, when he says those words to her: "We two alone will...pray and sing, and tell old tales, and laugh.../ And take upon's the mystery of things..."

Edmund, deciding to kill them, replies in disgust, "Take them away."

But Edmund failed, didn't he? He couldn't kill them—Lear and Cordelia are still here. I have seen them twice, once on the stage of the Royal Shakespeare Company, and once when King Lear was clothed in a bathrobe on a high school stage in a small New England town.

Strange, but true.

* * *

John Gardner says there are five qualities of good fiction, and the most important is the last one on his list: *a quality of strangeness.*[5] Here in this place where I write, wind moves after days and nights of steady rain. It is a west wind this morning; it is October, and the last yellow leaves blow east toward the morning sun. The wind is the cleaning woman of the earth. She dries things up after rain; she bids the leaves to let go, tumble to the soft brown below.

The experience of visitation after death is in every culture on earth. It is in me. I can no more say there are no invisible presences than I can say I have no children, or I had no parents. I have been surprised into attentive awareness of them, I have felt them. Once or twice I have seen them in dreams that are more real than waking. I have been told what I did not know, could not have known, in dreams that turned out to be true. I don't know how this works, or why—I simply experience it. When I am writing—deeply writing, lost in the home of my soul that is writing, I catch glimpses in synchronicities, as if I am being gently played with or joyfully accompanied by someone otherwise lost to me. In this long effort to write this book, there have been moments when I felt the presence of a long dead author on whose words I was intensely focused. If I am a little crazy, I am in good company, for most families have stories of someone knowing something in strange ways: knowing someone has died without having been told; knowing ahead of time some occurrence that later happens, with no way to know how the knowledge could have been given or received.

Trying to write this chapter, I gathered books. I read authors who say there is nothing but randomness. The popular cosmologist Lawrence M. Krauss goes even further: the source of everything that is something is *nothing*.[6] Fred Alan Wolf asserts that everything is dream, but he does raise the question of who is the "Big Dreamer" who dreams the dream in which we lesser dreamers participate.[7] Some whom I read saw no meaning in the cosmos, nothing more than comfort to ideas of afterlife. Other authors saw meaning, design, experienced healing that is mysterious and relationship beyond the physical body to something we can neither control nor understand. They did not regard the mystery as malevolent, no matter how violent or cruel or tenuous our lives may be. I read Michael Talbot's *The Holographic Universe*,[8] and read critiques and reviews of it that both praised and condemned it. I read authors who say we live many lives that overlap, the memories from one life breaking through into the here-and-now of this life. And I made forays into reading about the wild and fantastical lengths to which some people have gone to make a religion out of "strangeness" itself.[9]

None of that reading turned me to my own work. In fact, the more I read, the further I seemed to be from my own writing. But this morning, in some despair about how to say what I felt I need to say, I felt myself addressed, not by a ghost, not by a god, but by the *New York Times*. It was one of those moments that holds strangeness—when you have been wanting help but not asking for it, needing intervention but not even admitting it to yourself. It was synchronicity. I read in the *Book Review* that Alfred Kazin was "God haunted." Really? Kazin? That ultimately sophisticated reviewer and writer? In the next-to-last sentence of his memoir, *New York Jew,* Kazin says, "I want my God back."

Well, I thought, *me too.* I want my god back, but not wrapped in Sistine Chapel clouds and trailing a long white beard. Not male, not female, not Warrior, not King, not Goddess. Not a god who curses enemies or begets only one son and if he has even one daughter she is not mentioned as such in the scripture of my tradition. Not a god who blesses one people above all others. Not a god who sends any begotten son or daughter to hell. Or to war.

I want the Presence that cannot be named, the mystery of what lies under the name. I want Jesus back, too, but not the white, blond-haired Jesus of the Sunday school pictures of my childhood. I want the utterly human, historical, Semitic, desert Jesus behind and underneath the layers of doctrine—the Jesus who loved outcasts, who welcomed women, treated them as equals, and generally made himself so obnoxious to the current establishment that they had to get rid of him. I want that strangeness. That crossing of taboos. That breaking down of tradition and ritual. I want the less-assumed Jesus, the more complicated, more human Jesus who clearly enjoyed the defensive, argumentative, bitchy woman at the well who refused him a drink. And later, at the end of the story, after the disciples are amazed that he is talking to a woman, after they take up his attention (and the reader's), she sets her water pitcher down, leaving it behind and therefore giving them all a way to get a drink. The disciples offer him food, and he replies that he has food they know nothing about. What food? I don't believe it is some heavenly, invisible food. I think his food is nothing other than the words of a woman with real, important, honest questions.[10]

That is the Jesus who was not afraid of the woman with a flow of blood,[11] the taboo of her touch. That is the Jesus who was rude to a foreign woman who asked him to heal her daughter, and got reprimanded by her for his rudeness.[12] I want the Jesus of the oldest stories, before Paul and the writers of the four gospels had their ways with him—the man who spoke Aramaic, called his god "Abba," the intimate form of the word "father." I want to—and I do—find him at a table in a women's prison, on the sidewalk in a housing project, in those places where I think he mostly abides, as in Rabindranath Tagore's words, "among the least, the lowliest, and the lost."[13] It was for one of those that he accepted the touch of a woman who was considered untouchable because she had an unremitting flow of blood.

I have been untouchable. I have been bloody and ashamed and needy and ugly and poor. But a handful of people, at different times, saw me. Touched me. Let me know I was worth saving.

I don't want any of the painful harnesses of dogma, the corsets of ritual, the torture racks of discipline, the boredom of institutional requirements, the punishment by guilt or by reprisal with which organized religion often snares the "God haunted."

I don't know what separated Kazin from his God. But in that moment of reading, my own came close. A mystery, knowing what mental muddle I was mucking through, addressed me about it. The message was, *Stop reading, and write. Write what you know and what you don't know. Trust your own voice.* Hmmm. That's what I say to writers in all my workshops and retreats. *Write what you know and what you don't know. Trust your own voice.* If hearing it said to myself is a miracle, it is an everyday one—the kind that Walt Whitman suggested when he was asked, "Sir, do you believe in miracles?" and answered, "Is there anything else?"

What I want back is the common everyday walk in awareness of the presence of mystery. Mystery isn't always strange. What is strange is how seldom we *see it,* how seldom we *hear it.* Mystery is as common as the gravel road and the blackberry hanging ripe on a vine in August heat in my childhood; it does not have to be paid for by any particular belief. It doesn't go away. I'm the one who goes away. Walks away. Runs away. Crashes away. The mystery is as common as the beam of light, spruce-filtered, falling on the fifth step of the stair this morning in my house in Amherst, Massachusetts. *It is the common, seen uncommonly.* When we see, when we hear, when we intuit how much we are loved, it is the common that is uncommon. It is the ordinary that is the body of spirit, the physical presence of mystery. I think I was reaching for this understanding when I wrote this poem:

THE PATIENCE OF ORDINARY THINGS

It is a kind of love, is it not?
How the cup holds the tea,
How the chair stands sturdy and foursquare,
How the floor receives the bottoms of shoes
Or toes. How soles of feet know
Where they're supposed to be.
I've been thinking about the patience
Of ordinary things, how clothes
Wait respectfully in closets
And soap dries quietly in the dish,
And towels drink the wet
From the skin of the back.
And the lovely repetition of stairs.
And what is more generous than a window?

THE FISH

for Natty

Boy. So small, the world
is only five years old.
In his father's hands, a fish
gasps alien air.
Daddy, he says, It can be yours
while it's swimming in the water.
His father opens his hands.
There! they call to one another,
There!—as the silver body
disappears, a shadow in the sea.
Their voices are full of gladness.
Their hands are holy.

                                        —P.S.

CHAPTER 15

Beloved Community

Truth can appear as disaster in a land
of things unspoken.
—JOY HARJO

Be with those who help your being.
—RUMI

"IN A LAND OF THINGS UNSPOKEN," Joy Harjo says, "truth can appear as disaster." She is a member of the Creek (Muskogee) nation, a poet who tells the truth "in a land of things unspoken."[1] As writers, as spiritual seekers, we all live in that land. It is the landscape of the human heart. But Harjo speaks to her own history, and native children on reservations and off-reservation cities in America are still among the least likely in our nation to be adults who enjoy a full education, a well-paying job, the security of good health care. The truth of how native peoples live often is—disaster. And those of us who enjoy the better fruits of American life simply don't have to see how it is across the river, across the boundary line of the reservation, across the proverbial tracks. Racialized poverty in all of its forms is a disastrous truth in the land of things unspoken. Writing as a spiritual practice must be about seeing rather than not seeing, speaking rather than not speaking.

* * *

When I was asked to be a guest leader in a workshop for janitors, secretaries, and other staff members at the University of

Massachusetts, I looked forward to it with pleasure. The group had been meeting for a year or more, using my workshop method. As I prepared for the event, I chose my writing prompts carefully: I would have time for two writing times and two response times, as the group told each other what was strong in the new, first-draft work. For the first write, I would offer the random objects I use with all my workshop participants—about fifty familiar objects. Each writer would choose one object and freely write for about fifteen minutes.

For the second prompt, because the group had been meeting for some time and was already bonded—a safe place, I thought, to write about anything—I would offer a prompt that might call up an emotional memory that could be used for a fictional character or as a bit of memoir. The prompt was this: "Take a moment to center, then find in your memory or imagination a photo or snapshot of someone important to you, or to your character." I repeated that a couple of times, giving a beat of time to find an image. Then I said, "When you have the picture, begin writing with these words, *In this one, you are...,* so you are writing to the person in the picture."

When it was time to read, several writers read aloud, and the work, as is usual in this prompt, was focused, clear, and beautiful. It calls up someone of importance to the writer, and so the material matters. It asks the writer to address the person in the picture; that invites the writer's intimate voice. In fact, this prompt evokes such intimacy, I never use it until a group has already achieved safety.

Finally a woman speaking in a strong Asian accent offered to read, but in several tries, she could say only two or three words before being overcome with weeping. In thirty-two years of leading workshops, I have never experienced such an outpouring of anguished crying. I asked her to wait until her breath returned. She did that several times, but could not read. I offered to read for her; she refused. Instead, she laid her paper down in her lap and spoke barely above a whisper. Because of our practice of confidentiality in workshops, I can't specify which genocide she had escaped, but she said she could not tell anyone the details—it was too terrible.

When we are teaching, we are ourselves learning—or should be. That was surely true in this case. For a moment I was terrified—then I heard myself speaking to the group: *You are her community. She has dared to let you know that she has stories that need to be told. You must hold her. I have to go, but you must continue to be here for her and help her to write what she cannot yet speak.*

I saw then in a deeper sense than I had ever understood before that a community of nonjudgmental support is more crucial to a developing writer than a teacher can ever be. I was not the important person in the picture. The woman wrote what she wrote because she was writing in community. She couldn't speak her truth yet, but it was all right that I had invited it, and it was all right that she tried. Now she knew she could at least write it.

* * *

If we who write and we who seek to be in relation to mystery do not speak the things unspoken, who will speak them? And if we are to speak, to continue speaking, how are we to be supported? What do we need in order to sustain us in that work?

Rumi said, "Be with those who help your being."

Of course some spiritual seekers choose a hermit-like solitude, and some writers, by choice or by inability to do otherwise, lead lives marked by destructive loneliness. I believe with Rumi, however, that most of us need to be with those who help our being. Although there is a need for necessary solitude in order to do the very private listening that both writing and spiritual search require, there is also a need for companionship, both in our writing and in our spiritual seeking. The form that necessary solitude and necessary companionship take, of course, must be found, tried, tested, and honored by each individual.

For the first half of my life there was the church.

And for the last thirty-two years there have been my communities of writers.

*   *   *

The words "Beloved Community" were frequently on the lips of Martin Luther King Jr. It was the end for which he worked, about which he dreamed, and for which he died. He was a child of the church, and for all of its complexity, for all of its failures throughout the two thousand years of its existence, it cannot be denied that the church has created people like King, in whose lives we have glimpsed the mystery.

Personally, I may never again be able to be a part of that "Beloved Community," but I do bow to it. I do, with all my heart, thank it for saving me from the two-room tenement on Olive Street in St. Louis, for sending me to college and for giving me a graduate school education.

Until my mid-forties, the church was my beloved community. It was never perfect. The very minister in St. Louis who persuaded his congregation to establish for me the scholarship warned me not to bring an African American girl with me to church again, because "I'm afraid they won't give you the scholarship if you do." I wrestled with that dilemma and invited her to go again the next Sunday. But she couldn't go. Her grandmother was Catholic, and she said it was a sin to go to a Protestant church.

I had no way to understand what I would be missing if the church decided not to give me the scholarship, and I had no glimmer of realizing the politics Reverend Harris must have been dealing with in persuading a small congregation to use money for me that it wanted to use to move to the suburbs and be more middle class.

I lived a long time before I had any inkling of how difficult it is to build and maintain a beloved community. In fact, I had to try doing it myself alongside my husband in a church in Amherst, Massachusetts, in the 1970s. It was a complicated time for churches, and this story would be different if Peter were telling it. He would begin with the ways we were not wise enough, not able enough. When I tell it, I want to brag about him, tell about the hard choices he made in a divided land, his insistence upon inclusiveness and his stand against the war. Our congregation was divided over the war in Vietnam. When the Baptist student minister burned himself to death in protest two blocks from us on the campus of the University of Massachusetts, ten thousand students marched past the church to the town center to protest the war, and someone came into our (always) unlocked sanctuary, tore the American flag into pieces and left them on the altar. When Richard Nixon ordered the bombing of Cambodia on Christmas Eve, Peter called from the pulpit for his impeachment.

There are things I am proud of in those years: the busload of our high school kids headed for a work camp in Appalachia; the entire busload standing up in a Southern restaurant and walking out when their teacher, Sam Turner, was refused service because he is a black man; other busloads of kids on work camps in Puerto Rico and urban Washington, D.C. I am proud of our efforts to help them see, and of our hope that they would never forget what they saw.

In all of this Martin Luther King Jr., and those who marched and witnessed with him, gave us a sense of a community that included churches like ours, but was much greater than any particular organization. It felt like a community of like-minded people who could affirm each other across all kinds of difference—a community that actually could make a new world. He said so many times:

But the end is reconciliation; the end is redemption; the end is the creation of the beloved community. It is this type of spirit and this type of love that can transform opposers into friends. It is this type of understanding goodwill that will transform the deep gloom of the old age into the exuberant gladness of the new age. It is this love which will bring about miracles in the hearts of men.[2]

*   *   *

Now, and for many years past, my own beloved community has become the writers who write with me, those who read my words and respond to me, those in workshops and retreats, and those with whom I meet informally to share our work.

Often it is not easy—it can actually be quite dangerous—to try to find "those who help your being." For writers and for spiritual seekers alike there are groups, classes, workshops that promise community and instead destroy freedom and tear down confidence. I have written in *Writing Alone and with Others* that there is one acid test for the health of any group, class, or workshop one might try: *When I leave, do I feel more like writing, or less like writing?*

A similar test would be useful in considering a spiritual community: Do I feel more open to mystery, more able to personally be in relationship with mystery, or do I feel that I am outside unless I meet their requirements?

If the answer in either case is not one that is freeing and enabling, be careful. You may need to get out. It may be poison. Even if it is wonderful for someone else; even if the leader is famous—what matters is whether they are, and are among, "those who help your being." And that does not mean after they change you. It means as you are right now.

Knowing what helps your being requires deep listening to your own self, and honoring that listening, believing yourself, even if it means altering some relationships in your life that may resist your changes.

My book *Writing Alone and with Others* is largely about the writer's need for support, and ways to create and protect a community of writers that will sustain growth in craft and create safety for experimentation. Any prompt or exercise can be a trigger for spiritual search: comedy or tragedy, fiction or nonfiction, poems or plays. All manner of ways of writing can be doorways to apprehending mystery. The seeker himself or herself brings to the writing a longing for spiritual connection, and when we are committed to a desire to touch the mystery, as Goethe promises, the mystery touches us.

* * *

"Be with those who help your being." That may be no more than one other person who, when you share your words, your own "truth in a land of things unspoken," listens and hears, significantly enough that you come away more able to write, more able to seek, more empowered for having risked being openly who you truly are.

For most of us, writing is already in some sense a spiritual practice. When we try not to write, it burns, glows, within us like a fire that wants air. And so we do what we must do. We line up words, one after the other. We write.

Emily Dickinson hand-wrote her poems into little booklets called "fascicles" and stitched them together with needle and thread. Although Garrison Keillor has read my poems seventeen times on *The Writer's Almanac*, and more than a hundred have been published in literary magazines and anthologies, my books of poems have been rejected by every press I sent them to. I admit I didn't sent them to many; I published them all myself. We can do this. The Internet has opened the world to itself, to see and write and publish. Art is not about the marketplace. It is about courage and honesty. It is about telling the truth and believing in our own voices, our own images, our own sounds and move-ments. If Dickinson could make her books with a needle and thread, we can honor our own words, make them into books or their cyber equivalents, give them to readers who love us. It is what artists have always done—singers, dancers, quilt-makers, carvers of limbs cut from cherry trees. We make our art "to find and illuminate the shape of the human heart"[3] and we give it most deeply, I believe, to warm the hearts of people who care about us, and about whom we care. People who help our being. That is be-loved community.

It may be that no one will ever read our words except our-selves—and the mystery—attentive, listening even before the words come, breathing "Yes" into our inner ear. It may be that we will be read only by those who are related to us, those nieces, nephews, sons, daughters, cousins who may carry the genes of our ancestors into another generation. What can be more important than that? What immortality can be more important than the passing on of story? Of course, it may be that our words will find a home beyond our own families, but either way, what we know, what we intuit, what we think we see (or in fact do see), can give us a lasting place in the wisdom of the world, even if it is received by only one listener/reader, in our time or after our time, for whom it makes a difference.

When I was mothering four small children, Peter and I were living in a parsonage and most of the time caring for some ad-ditional person or persons. No doubt some one of our children will write about those days, their crazy parents. There were seven refugees from Saigon for three months during the Vietnam War, ten Hare Krishna monks who used our basement for a few weeks as a place to chant, any number of overnight guests who needed to sober up—all just folks who needed a place to be safe for a while. It doesn't need to be said that I was not doing much writing.

At that time my closest friend, "Casey" (Marjorie Casebier), three thousand miles away, was dying of a brain tumor. The last words she wrote to me were on a postcard—only ten words. It was a quote from the Book of Revelation:

What you see, write it in a book.

She signed it, *Love, Casey.*

This is that book.

THAT ONE

Fugitive now,
I cannot run fast enough.

More than half a lifetime spent
and still I don't know who God is—
that One whose breath is on my neck,
hot sometimes like love at fever pitch
then gone like love seems gone
when the lover sleeps, satisfied,
and I lie wide awake with the galaxy
open, beckoning,
and I cannot go.

That One erases
every system I was taught to trust,
breathes Yes
on the short hairs
at the back of my neck,
breathes into the chamber of my ear
until there is no galaxy, open or closed,
until there is only breath: my own
and that Other Breather's breath.
Never breathing Come.
Never breathing Go.
All afternoon,
in every sort of weather,
breathing

—*P.S.*

CHAPTER 16

Freedom

Now that I'm free to be myself, who am I?
—MARY OLIVER

What is God's will for a wing?
Every bird knows that.
—ST. TERESA OF AVILA

I sit at my kitchen table, writing by hand, by lantern and candle-light. A heavy snowstorm has broken huge branches off of trees and left much of the northeast without electricity. We have been without it for 24 hours—no furnace, no refrigerator, no light. No telephone, no computer.

Later, typing these handwritten words, I know that the blackout had only begun—we were "without power" for five days and four nights. Because our kitchen stove is gas burning, we lit the burners on top of the stove and hung a blanket across the doorway that has no door. It made a warm cave inside the house. Several neighbors who have no gas came to our door with thermoses for hot water; eight of us spent one lovely evening talking around our kitchen table by candle and lantern light after a dinner of stew made on the stovetop.

Back to the words written by hand:

Tonight I have been reading Joy Harjo's *The Woman Who Fell from the Sky*. It seems entirely appropriate to read her poems by the light of a candle. She says, "I believe in the power of words to create the world…" And she does. Create the world in this book of mourning, this song of creating.

Today an estranged friend came and shoveled our driveway. It is heavy, wet snow—everywhere branches fallen and still falling, electric lines down in the street. And then she came in, wet and cold. I had not seen her for perhaps two years, but I had known that one day she would come. We didn't know she was here until she appeared at the back door after all the shoveling.

Her coming, the warmth and gladness of it, closes the last crack, break, fissure, in the part of my heart that was torn when I made a large change in myself—and therefore, as is often the case, in some of my relationships. There have been several huge changes in my life: from poverty to the privilege of education and a stable marriage; from being a minister's wife to being someone outside of organized religion; from thirty-two years of leading weekly writing workshops in my home to ending that part of my work completely; from involvement in unwise relationships that had to end, causing pain to all involved.

Sometimes people you care about can't bear the changes you make in yourself—even the changes you have to make for survival. At one point in my life my mother asked me to visit her therapist, and I did. He counseled me never to expect that she could forgive me for not dropping out of college in the last half of my senior year to try to help her and my brother. Even though I went to them as soon as I graduated. "She can't do it," the therapist said, "because she dropped out of nursing school to help her sister, and that decision determined all the rest of her life."

But sometimes people can—and do—accept your changes. It may just take a while. Tonight I am still warmed by the memory of this morning. It was lovely to wrap my arms around the cold, wet, snow-soaked coat of my friend and welcome her into this kitchen, watch her warm her hands over the gas burner, both of us laughing, warming ourselves.

Now see how Harjo is right? How words create worlds? How my words have created this little world—barely, imperfectly— the candles burning down. I will blow them out, turn off the burners, extinguish the lantern light. I'll find my way by memory and by touch upstairs to our bed, warmed by Peter's sweet body.

* * *

Is there any writer anywhere who has not asked himself or herself "Who do I think I am?" How dare I take up my pencil and try to form words onto paper? How dare I think that my story, my poem, my thoughts are worthy of putting into words? And even if they were, how dare I think I have the skill to do it? Who do I think I am?

Unfortunately, that question can't be answered by any of the personas a writer may have lived under: *I am my father's, my mother's child*—(Oh, no—they don't want me to write family secrets!); *I am a Christian, a Muslim, a Buddhist, a Wiccan*—(Oh, no—I don't want to preach) or (Oh, no—I don't believe everything I'm supposed to believe!); *I am a B.D., a Ph.D., an M.A., an M.D., an M.F.A. I am a Pulitzer Prize winner, a runner-up in the local newspaper contest*—(Oh, no—now that I've won a prize I have to prove that I deserve it!) or (Oh, no! That was an accident! I can't ever do it again!)

In short, *Who do I think I am?* Now that I am no longer the person I used to be, who do I think I am? Now that I want to write, how dare I? Who do I think I am, trying to write toward understanding the mystery in which I live and move and have my being—how dare I? Who in the world do I think I am?

* * *

Both a spiritual practice and a writing practice—for that matter, *any* serious practice undertaken for the purpose of creation or discovery, any practice that involves creative thinking—depends upon freedom. But freedom in spiritual practice is easily lost into dogma, and freedom in writing is easily lost into the demands of a job or the pressures that can come from others as well as from the writer's own self.

In *The Beautiful Invisible,* Vignale is writing about the creation and development of scientific theories, but he might as well be talking about writing as a spiritual practice. "Discard too much," he says, "and you are left with a soulless abstraction. Discard too little and you are trapped in a labyrinth of complexity."[1] He suggests that creative thinking "grows at the *confluence* of fantasy and truth." He means by "fantasy" theory, or abstraction—and by "truth" he means that which is held to be true, or acceptable "form." Something here feels exactly right to me, and I want to explore it more.

Confluence. What a beautiful word.

* * *

Once I was one of ten women chosen to accompany a dear friend, Anne Dellenbaugh, and her sister, Meg, on what I believed might well be Anne's last wilderness trip. She was a wilderness guide by trade—a student of feminist theology and a practicing Buddhist by passion. She had battled cancer until chemo wasn't working any more and chose not to have a radical surgery that was as likely to end her life as to save it.

Anne and I had led several wilderness trips together on the west branch of the Penobscot River in Maine—I led times of writing, and she taught me to paddle a canoe and far, far more about this beautiful earth. This time, for several days we paddled down the Green River of Utah to its confluence with the Colorado. She waked us before daylight voicing a Native American chant, and when we had gathered each morning before daylight, she led us in a walking meditation on top of one spectacular cliff after another. Above us the Big Dipper hung like diamonds in an ebony sky. We moved beneath it slowly in a circle as she repeated softly the words from her Buddhist practice: *Everything is transient. Everything is precious. Be here, now.*

The tradition out of which she spoke was not my own. It felt ancient and formal to me. So did the shape of the dipper, tipped in the sky as if to pour out mystery and miracle on our heads.

Far below us in the dark, the Green River hurried on toward the Colorado. Beneath our feet were the red rocks of Utah and occasional fossils, ringed sticks of stone the size and shape of my little finger, crinoid stems 300 million years old. The cliffs held the river in a form carved through immeasurable time, a form we would follow after the sun rose. We were creating ourselves, hoping to create wholeness in the wilderness guide we loved so much. The freedom of the river carrying us within the ancient form of the cliffs was a context perfect for our purpose.

Writing as a spiritual practice requires that kind of confluence. We can't reach the explosion of new, creative thought without both form and freedom. Relating this to spiritual journey and writing is a complicated matter, but it is very important. To say what I mean, I need four stories: two about spiritual practice, and two about writing practice. They are all about the need for freedom.

* * *

Story Number One, about spiritual practice: a bishop's wife, Jesus, and me.

Forty years ago when I was a minister's wife, I was asked to lead a retreat for wives of ministers in our denomination. I led the retreat using writing, painting, and a technique I learned in theater called "family sculpture." The wife of our bishop attended the retreat as a participant. She was a lovely, warm, older woman; I was glad she was there.

I closed the retreat by having all twenty or so of us sit in a circle on the floor. In the center on a cloth I placed a loaf of homemade bread that I had baked the day before the retreat. I broke it in half and placed beside it a pitcher of grape juice and some small paper cups. I quoted Jesus's words at the last supper, "Do this in remembrance of me." I invited us to break the bread and give to one another morsels of bread and a bit of juice, in no particular order, just if we felt moved to do so.

It seemed beautiful to me, but when it was over the bishop's wife drew me aside. Her voice trembled as she said, "Who do you think you are? You can't serve the sacrament! You're not ordained!"

Even then I understood that this beautiful woman had sat graciously through what to her was a scandalous soiling of something that to her was sacred. She had generously waited to speak about it to me privately. But her question, "Who do you think you are?" was, in fact, the central question for me. My answer then was a shocked silence. I had known that I was pushing the boundaries, but I didn't know how grievously, or how my act that day predicted my move out of the very church that had rescued me from poverty and provided me with a college education.

My answer now is that to me Jesus's words, "do this in remembrance of me" refer to whenever I break bread, not to whenever I participate in an ecclesiastical sacrament. To me, every meal, every bite of bread, every sip of wine—if I am only attentive to it—is holy. As I said earlier, Máire O'Donohoe, my nun friend, replied when I asked her to explain holy water, "Pat, all water is holy."

*   *   *

Story Number Two, about spiritual practice: a Buddhist monk, a robe, and a decision.

Anne, the wilderness guide, long before she became so ill, told me late one night beside a river in Maine, after all the other canoeists had gone to their tents, that she wanted more than anything to be a Buddhist monk. "Not a nun," she said. "A monk." And years later, recovered from the cancer that had threatened to take her, clad in a robe she had made by hand from pieces of cloth given her by her closest friends, she was ordained a Zen monk. Within a year, however, she told me that she could not continue as a monk. Here, in her own words, is the rest of this story:

> I want to tell you something about why I "gave back my vows."
>
> I've always followed my own inner compass, my own intuition. I think it's an avenue of creativity for me—that my own life is my canvas and experimenting and exploring through my work has always been a big part of how I explore my relationship

to others and to the world. When I became a Zen monk (actually more a novice priest, but the ordination is the same, and as you know I wanted to be a monk, not a nun, and not a priest!), I put myself onto a path that required that I locate myself in a hierarchy and submit to its authority. Zen is both formal and hierarchical in the extreme, which I don't necessarily think is a "bad" thing, but it certainly didn't work for me (and truthfully, given the unprecedented times we are living in and our desperate need for new models and designs for nearly every part of society and culture, I think all such rigidly self-perpetuating hierarchical structures must be carefully scrutinized). So, as far as my preceptor was concerned, I had not yet "earned" the right to teach, or to make decisions about liturgy, etc., even though I had, in fact, been doing all that for many years! So, by mutual agreement, I "gave back my vows."

Of course, I didn't give back the vows. They are in me, mine for life. Rather, I chose to live them differently, in a different context. In fact, as I reflect on it now, a decade later, I see both the ordination and the subsequent revocation of the ordination as equally important. Had I not been ordained, I might have spent many more years thinking I had missed something, perhaps even that I had lost my way. My brief period of monkhood freed me to pick up my own path again, and to be both comfortable with and delight in a nearly formless and, though guided by a teacher, a much freer path of practice.[2]

* * *

Story Number Three, about writing practice: a man, his writing, and his wife.

Once I had as a participant in my workshop a man who was a successful publisher of fine art books. He was writing a novel; his descriptions of the workplace were stunning. The presses, the designers, the varieties of inks, and the interactions between the men in his business were handled brilliantly. But every time a woman walked onto his page, the craft collapsed. The woman had "raven hair" or was a "ravishing blond." She spoke in hackneyed caricature of a real female voice, and the men in the scene suddenly were made of cardboard.

I am extremely careful with a new writer; most problems in the writing correct themselves as tension lessens in the writer and learning happens in everyone in the workshop. But this man had been with me for a good long time, and he was a superb writer so long as no woman appeared in the scene. I asked him for a private conference and told him as kindly as I could that I just could not believe in his female characters. I had specific examples to show him, and I compared those passages to similar passages of description or dialogue done completely convincingly for male characters.

He listened carefully, and finally said, "Pat, you are asking me to write honestly out of my experience of women. If I were to write as you want me to, I would write my way right out of my marriage."

I understood what he meant. Once as a young writer I confessed to author Elizabeth O'Connor my own fear of telling the stories of my mother, my brother, and others whose life stories were embedded in my own. What if my mother felt hurt? How could I tell some of the hard things about my brother's life? What about Peter and my children? She listened patiently and then responded, "Pat, you have so many absentee landlords of your soul!" I understood that if I was ever to write my own truths, I would have to free myself and yet take great care to do no harm. I published nothing about my husband, my brother, or my children without asking their permission. For others, sometimes I just claimed my own freedom, omitted names, or changed details. To tell the truth and do no harm sometimes means telling stories that others do not want told, even when it would do no harm, even when names and details are changed. Then the bottom line for the writer is courage.

*   *   *

Story Number Four, about writing practice: Maureen Buchanan Jones needed fiction ("fantasy," to use Vignale's term) to write the truth of her life.

When I first entered Pat Schneider's writing workshop, I heard people reading from their writing, and I heard some of them use a first-person autobiographical style. It took my breath away. How brave they were! I wrote in third person, creating a character that was me but also not me. I thought I was cheating. I thought I was being chicken.

One night, after I read a short piece about a me character that wasn't me, using a third-person She, the people in the group responded to the writing. They commented on my use of images, rhythms, metaphor, and interior atmosphere. And then one woman said, "I can see this young woman. I'm afraid for her, but I believe in her. I think she's going to make it."

No therapy has ever come close to touching what that woman and the other people in the room accomplished that night. By using the third person, I was able to see this version of me, my seventeen-year-old self, as outside myself. I saw that frightened, brave girl as the people in the room saw her. It was as if they went back with me to that cataclysmic moment and whispered in my ear: "You're strong. You're going to be all right." I felt a healing I had never imagined.

From that experience, I am able to tell the members of my writing workshops and retreats that writing in the third person allows us to walk around ourselves, examine ourselves from many perspectives. The third person gives enough distance to see ourselves as whole beings. It allows recognition, acceptance, celebration and forgiveness. It allows us to re-create ourselves. Putting our memories into a third-person character opens up our ability to tell our story as if we are complete. Because we are.

I am still that seventeen-year-old. Now I carry her with pride and tenderness. She became one of my heroes that night in Pat Schneider's living room.[3]

*   *   *

Writing as a spiritual practice necessitates freedom. Freedom in the spiritual realm, and freedom in the writing realm. Freedom to change, to become new, even if some whom we love can't go with us into that freedom. Freedom to grow spiritually, even if it means outgrowing some of the forms of spirituality we have loved, aspects of which we may still love. Any of these changes come at the cost of some anxiety. Søren Kierkegaard famously said, "Anxiety is the dizziness of freedom."

Anne Dellenbaugh says that her formal giving back of the vows of monkhood was not really giving them back, because they live within her, but she practices them differently. That has been true for Peter and me also, after we left the church. The men in charge of our part of the Methodist church in the 1970s required that if Peter left the ministry, he "return his ordination." At the time, I was simply scalded by that requirement, but Peter is a far more gracious person than I. He said to me, "Pat, they can take the piece of paper, but they cannot take back the ordination. They said themselves ordination is from God." Because Peter at age fifty was brave enough to lose all of his professional credentials and begin again, I was given the opportunity to teach, to write, and to create along with him and others the network that is Amherst Writers & Artists.

I have learned that everything we lose opens us to more than we could ever have imagined if we can only open the clenched fists of our own fear, to receive what the mystery will offer. It offers freedom to grow, to change, to become, and also freedom to fall on our faces, make stupid, perhaps even cruel, mistakes. Freedom to be silly, childish, confessional, emotional, boring, exhausted. For if we don't have those freedoms, neither will we have the freedom necessary to achieve great breakthroughs at the confluence of fantasy and truth, abstraction and form, the past and the present, today and tomorrow.

* * *

But am I free? A long time ago I figured out that the mystery is not like a cruel father whose "love" damns his children to burn forever in fire—or abandons them as my father abandoned me. *But if the mystery demands anything of me at all*—whether it be "the death of the autonomous ego" as the priest suggested near the beginning of this book, or "merging into the all," or baptism, or declaring certain beliefs, or practicing certain habits or rituals—then it seems to me the mystery is like a needy mother who demands that I prove my love by some act, as my mother demanded over and over again of me. If I am not free, is the mystery itself free? Free to be in a relationship to freedom, to a free creation? To me? Does my freedom depend upon the freedom of the mystery itself—free to change form, free to initiate and respond in relationship? Theologian Laurel Schneider has written:

> Divinity in the multiplicity of incarnation occurs with the freedom to come and to go: to fold into the Deep, a brooding implication; to unroll a surface of explicit presence; to strain out of the womb into a homeless, starry night; to weave gravitational complexities that we call communities or worlds.... "Divinity is, if nothing else, free. And this means that it is also free of theology and doctrine." The stories we tell of it, however, form the fabric of imagination about what is possible for us...[4]

What wonderful news! This turns out to be the heart of the matter I have been moving toward in my entire exploration. Is it possible for me to be free? Free in my spirit regardless of what happens to my body? Can I hope to become as free as I imagine Nelson Mandela was when he was in prison, as I imagine Dietrich Bonhoeffer was as he stood on the scaffold awaiting his imminent hanging by the Nazis? In "Canary," a marvelous poem about Billie Holiday, Rita Dove says, "Fact is, the invention of women under siege/ has been to sharpen love in the service of myth.// If you can't be free, be a mystery." Isn't she talking about a deep personal freedom that lies under bondage?

Am I truly free if anything at all is demanded of me in order to be in right relationship with mystery? In my experience, the mystery does not demand—it offers. What is offered is relationship, and relationship that is open and free needs attention given by both parties. Even knowing that relationship is offered requires attention. The mystery offers and we, if and when we can be attentive, respond. In an earlier chapter I wrote how Hugh Vernon White taught me that "God's love is God's attention." I think he would agree that my *own* love is *my* attention. In a good relationship, attention works both ways. Both parties offer, listen, see, respond. That interaction—a free relationship with mystery—is the source of the deepest joy a human being can experience.

At the absolute moment of wrestling this question into articulation I see how it was there from the beginning, how it has been a great whale, now and then surfacing for a moment in the ongoing narrative of my unconscious. I am not alone in this struggle. My generation of seekers is torn between the idea of the "autonomous ego" and the idea of the interconnectedness of all things that culminates in a final merging with "the all." In addition to Laurel Schneider's book, the most helpful book I have found about this issue is Catherine Keller's *From a Broken Web*,[5] in which freedom does not necessitate separation. She proposes "four non-polar conceptual dyads: being one/being many, being public/being private, being body/being soul, and being here/being now." Put into poetry, there are Czeslaw Milosz's beautiful lines: "The purpose of poetry is to remind us/ how difficult it is to remain just one person,/ for our house is open, there are no keys in the doors,/ and invisible guests come in and out at will."[6]

The issues are complex, and the roots of the complexity go far back into the history of human thought. I am neither a philosopher nor a theologian. I am a writer. To answer my questions it was necessary to write my way through my own dark night, through my own aborted attempts to "do good," through my forgiving and confronting my own need for forgiveness. I am stunned to see how my understanding of mystery is tied into the details, the everydayness of my life. My story. How writing my story in poems and in this book makes it possible for me, in words from T. S. Eliot's *Four Quartets*, "to arrive where [I] started / And know the place for the first time." In some sense, to know myself for the first time.

And yet, strangely, all that I know now of the mystery through study and a long life's experience, I held in my heart as a five-year-old in a worn-out orchard in Missouri when I first opened myself to mystery and felt the presence move toward me and claim me. All that I have learned brings me back to all that I experienced in my first conscious encounter with mystery. Emilie Townes, past president of the American Academy of Religion, used as the theme of her 2008 presidential address a phrase from *Jonah's Gourd Vine* by anthropologist, folklorist, and novelist Zora Neale Hurston. Townes wrote:

> Walking across the rim bones of nothingness as scholars of religion means we take all that we have learned, all that we hope to say, research, and teach, and place it in a space of the ultimate unknown where the immensity of our world drops from our scholarly teeth into a global creation where we recognize that our scholarship, our form of the conversion vision, can be put to good use in the fiercely mundane as well as in the fastidiously erudite.[7]

Yes, I am free. I am more than free—I am *assisted in my freedom* by mystery. In fact, it is our very freedom and a function of our interconnectedness as human community that results in our having to "walk across the rim bones of nothingness," having to traverse the dark night of our own souls. But whatever my own form of the conversion vision (the "changed world" inside me, and all around me) may be, it "can be put to use." To me, that means spiritual orientation is inseparable from ability to change the world toward justice, compassion, and sanity. My spiritual practice "can be put to use in the fiercely mundane as well as in the fastidiously erudite."

My spiritual practice is to write. And where I can, to help others to write.

* * *

It amazes me that what I struggled to figure out about freedom now was already there in the poem that precedes this chapter—a poem of my own, written, filed away and forgotten for many years. I knew the answer then in metaphor, but not in language I could write out in prose. If we don't allow ourselves to write in metaphor, there are doors inside ourselves that we may never be able to open.

My poem says the mystery is something like a lover who invites, but does not demand. And the narrator is something like a beloved who maintains a certain solitude within intimacy. Neither lover nor beloved turns away. The mystery (the lover) loves and offers the star-spangled galaxy of ecstasy, and the beloved, the narrator, rests in the loving. The lover (the mystery), satisfied by the closeness of loving, falls into dreaming, but does not go away. The lover breathes on the neck of the beloved. There is the undeniable, ever-present "Yes" of Presence.

"That One erases / every system I was taught to trust…," the poem says. In a real relationship of love, it seems to me that all theories, systems, dogmas, requirements, rules, can fall away until "there is no galaxy, open or closed, / until there is only breath: my own / and the Other Breather's breath." Both breathers are free if love is real.

Freedom means that the one (the One) who loves never breathes "Come" or "Go" or any other imperative. It never coaxes. Never manipulates. And although "love seems gone" as in the poem, actually the lover never goes away. It is the breath that reassures—the lover is "Closer…than breathing, and nearer than hands and feet."[8]

* * *

In the heat of physical love there is often a desire to "merge" with the other, as a drop of water might merge with an ocean. But in the poem "I cannot go." I cannot *be fully* in ecstatic union with mystery for more than a fleeting, delicious experience. I can be in relationship with mystery, but it is a relationship in which I remain human. I remain myself. I touch, and am touched, but I remain free, because isn't the only love relationship worth having, one that is between free agents? Anything else, it seems to me is not a relationship of *love.*

In my experience, I am not controlled by mystery. I am loved by mystery. Following an ecstatic experience or a *vision* of ecstasy (in the poem, "galaxy"), I am a woman who has to get up, fix breakfast, pay bills, live my human life. The beloved breathes, holds me in loving attention.

The mystery, strangely, protects my freedom by a certain distance. Even though I am loved ecstatically by mystery, the mystery holds me but does not consume me, just as a lover, satisfied, holds the beloved who lies awake, awed by the vision of galaxies, by "the bath of all the stars."[9]

*   *   *

It was my mother—so unable in many ways to love me wisely—who protected me from the harsh aspects of her fundamentalist tradition and at the same time, in the warm heart of that tradition, guided me to turn my face toward mystery and ask for a personal relationship. I asked, and the mystery turned toward me and welcomed me, as I described in the chapter titled "Ransom." From that day until this, as I sit writing these words, I have continued now and then to ask. Not in a sense of begging, but in a sense of turning again and again toward a beloved. Writing this book has been that kind of asking. In all the ways that love happens—in the asking, in the offering, in the resting, in the occasional flying (not falling, *flying*)—that relationship has continued: the breath, "on the short hairs at the back of my neck"—the utter intimacy.

The relationship is real. It is alive. And it is complex. My experience, and my own lifetime of thinking about these things, convinces me that my relationship with mystery does not place me in a "kingdom" of "the chosen." It does not give me answers that I can impart to others. It does not give me a "How To…" book on spiritual practice. Who do I think I am? I understand myself to be only one among countless sentient beings and non-sentient creations (I will not leave out the rocks)—every one of us beloved beyond our ability to comprehend. Beloved, and free.

CONFESSION

Apprehended on the slant
of air between two trees
crow-fractured morning
after morning, I would
name you if I knew how.
I don't. Know. How
you leap over naming,
sidle under, squeeze around,
you lilac, thistle, burr,
belonging to no species,
you chipmunk-sudden,
slug-utterly unaccommodating—
you rainfall prism beautiful,
earthquake terrifying,
still of night-deep darkness
comforting,
you rock, you rock,
you unnamable, unknowable known
how you scamper/swim
creep/crawl soar/sink
stride/fly—you mountain, you
desert, delicious, delirious
madness-making laughter
you ocean, you faucet, you ripple,
erupt! Spray! Spout, you silence,
you suggestion, you
impossible, unbelievable
god

—*P.S.*

CHAPTER 17

Joy

. . . there is an angle of experience where the dark is distilled into light: either here or hereafter, in or out of time: where our tragic fate finds itself with perfect pitch, and goes straight to the key which creation was composed in. And comedy senses and reaches out to this experience. It says, in effect, that, groaning as we may be, we move in the figure of a dance, and, so moving, we trace the outline of the mystery.[1]

—CHRISTOPHER FRY

THIS QUOTATION GAVE ME the word, "mystery." And it helped me to frame my intention in writing this book: I would try to "trace the outline of the mystery."

Once upon a time there was a woman who fell from the sky. I can believe that, because a poet told me so, and I love the story. A woman fell from the sky, and the earth was created to give her a landing place.

Once upon a time there was a goddess with a thousand hands and in each hand an eye. I can believe that, because a friend I love told me so, and I love the story. If you have an eye in each hand, I am told, you will know how to practice true nonviolence.

Once upon a time there was a prince, and he was sheltered from ever seeing pain or suffering. But one day he saw an old man, and he gave up his crown and took up a mendicant's bowl. I can believe that, because I have heard the chanting of men in orange robes, and I love the story.

Once upon a time there was a man who bent down in the dust and wrote with his finger to prevent a crowd from throwing stones at a woman. I can believe that, because I was told it by my mother, and I love the story.

Once upon a time there was a child who looked far down into a well to see stars reflected there. Stars far down in the water, far down in the earth. I do believe that, because I was that child, and I love the story. I told it to myself. I tell it to myself again when I have need of stars in deep, dark places.

Once upon a time, once upon a time, once upon a time—there was story. There *is* story. Story can be the clothing that makes the mystery visible. Story kept us alive when food failed, when water dried up, when the body itself began to fall.

I have told my stories. The last story I will tell is about joy.

Joy is different from happiness. Joy doesn't make any sense. Happiness makes sense—there are predictable happy moments having to do with love, with success, with the arrival of babies, with funny behavior of dogs, cats, gerbils, and people—but joy most often comes unannounced and utterly unexpected.

After Peter and I left the church, I was in some part of me bereft. One Sunday morning in early June after we moved to our new home only a couple of blocks away, I sat on the back steps and listened to the bells ringing from the church Peter had served for so long. There were mourning doves under the spruce tree in our yard, their melancholy mating songs blending with the sounds of the bells.

I did not know who I was in this new world.

Then I received a telephone call from a social worker named Deb Burwell in a mill town across the Connecticut River. Would I come and lead a workshop for low-income women?

The thought was enormous. I had come out of poverty. I had escaped it. Now I was being asked to go back into it, be face to face with people caught in a place that I knew only too well. I hedged, asked her to come visit my weekly workshop for writers in Amherst, to see if what I was doing was what she wanted.

She came and visited, and during the break she talked with Peter. In the course of the conversation she told him that her father was a clergyman.

"Oh?" Peter said. "Where did he go to school?"

"At Pacific School of Religion," she said.

She had been a baby in my arms before we left that school for Peter's graduate work at Boston University. Before she left our house that evening, she said yes, that she did want what I was doing in the workshop, and I began going every Sunday evening to Chicopee to lead a workshop for women living in a housing project near the river.

All day each Sunday, I worked on their manuscripts, typing their handwritten words, first with all the errors intact, then on a separate page with my handwritten praise and suggestions, then on a third page a clean, corrected, typed copy with several extra copies, in formal manuscript form. In the years that followed, when they joined me as trainers to train others to lead similar workshops, they would tell trainees that seeing their own words in print for the first time simply changed their lives.

But it took me all day every Sunday. And after a while, as I drove the thirty-minute drive across the river, I would say to myself, "I've got to stop this! It takes me all day! I'm going to stop!"

Then I would write with them for two hours. One night I laid a dozen ordinary potatoes on the table around which we sat, and one of the women wrote the funniest erotic prose poem I had ever heard. On another night the same woman wrote for the first time about being sexually abused by her grandfather, and sat shaking as I had shaken after reading on the radio my story about the dirty milk bottles. On Father's Day we all wrote to our fathers or to some man who had functioned for us as father. I wrote for the first time to my father, and saw him for the first time as he must have been when I was born, twenty-one years old, younger than my own son, too young to know the implications of marrying a woman nine years older than he was, too young to guess how complicated, how wounded she was.

On the way home, driving back across the river, every Sunday night I sang at the top of my lungs.

It was ecstatic joy.

Earlier in this book I wrote about "the dark night of the soul," and poet W. H. Auden's invitation: "Follow, poet, follow right/ To the bottom of the night," and after that writing I expected ecstasy, because wasn't it always darkest right before the dawn?

Well, not necessarily. Ecstatic poets, prophets, saints seem to flower in the midst of trouble. Auden himself says it:

> *With the farming of a verse*
> *Make a vineyard of the curse,*
> *Sing of human unsuccess*
> *In a rapture of distress;*
>
> *In the deserts of the heart*
> *Let the healing fountain start,*
> *In the prison of his days*
> *Teach the free man how to praise.*[2]

Being with those women, writing our stories to one another, was healing me. As I was with them in a crowded office above a bank and beneath a karate studio, they were with me in the interior rooms of my childhood. All of us writing out of our own secret rooms in "the land of the unspoken."

Elizabeth O'Connor[3] has written that we are not called to our own soul work by "ought" or "should." Rather, we are called by joy. She says that if we are working out of ought or should, we are not only in the wrong place ourselves; we are blocking someone else whose joy it might be to be where we are. She taught me to judge my work by its quality of joy.

Joy is not pleasure. It is not fun. Pleasure and fun pale in the light of joy.

Different traditions have different words for it. Joseph Campbell calls it "bliss." Roman Catholics speak about "vocation." Protestants refer to one's "calling." Perhaps it is part of what is meant by "enlightenment."

I have felt that kind of joy now and then in writing. Certainly in the poem that precedes this chapter, where every word flew onto the page almost faster than I could shape its letters. I have experienced it in writing, in work that moves me outside of myself, and in turning my attention toward mystery.

* * *

Robert Burns wrote, "Grow old along with me! The best is yet to be,/ The last of life for which the first was made." Is that true? Can it be true? When I was young, I doubted it. When I was middle aged, going through my mid-life crisis and experiencing my belly's mid-section spread, I flat out disbelieved it, even with some disgust. "The last of life for which the first is made?" Impossible.

But now I am beginning my seventy-eighth year, and I am ending this book, and last night, as if all at once (although I know it has been dawning on me for at least the second half of this writing), I fully realized that he is right.

I have once again written myself into a new place. Why don't we hear about this more often? This incredible sweetness that can come, this lovely letting go? Why don't we hear more often what it means to have lived long enough to let go of holding on so tightly? Why haven't our poets, artists, novelists, given us more images of the relief that can come when we open our hands and our hearts, when we accept our own story and tell it, at least to ourselves, honor it so that we can let it go?

Everything is transient. Everything is precious. Be here, now. To be here now when you are forty-five is often to be exhausted from the day's work and from the thought of tomorrow's work. To be here now near the end of life, here with love or with the memory of love—along with the memory of stars and galaxies and the intimate roads of home—is to know how transient, how precious, the now is. And that knowing becomes more intense, more suffused with joy, every day.

Joy is our own selves, moving "in the figure of a dance" that we neither choreograph nor understand—a dance that traces "the outline of the mystery." Maybe my soul is, in fact, my joy. Maybe my joy is my soul—or a glimpse of it. That uncontrollable, unexplainable experience that is the heart's own Ferris wheel, lifting us up, allowing us to rock there under the sky, and then setting us gently back down on our feet again. Joy does not ask to be believed in—it is "beyond belief."

"Follow your bliss," Campbell says.

Be led by your joy, I say.

Joy is evidence that there is, in fact, such a thing as soul. The soul is the window, the door, the aperture, the opening, the crack where the light gets in, and we ourselves, souls that we are, joy that we are, turn toward the mystery at the heart of the universe. That is a movement in the figure of a dance. So moving, we trace the outline of the mystery.

BLESSING FOR A WRITER

May you hear in your own stories
the moan of wind around the corners
of half-forgotten houses
and the silence in rooms you remember.

May you hear in your own poems
the rhythms of the cosmos,
the sun, the moon and the stars
rising out of the sea and returning to it.

May you, too, pull darkness out of light
and light out of darkness.
May you hear in your own voice
the laughter of water falling over stones.

May you hear in your own writing
the strangeness, the surprise of mystery,
the presence of ancestors, spirits,
voices buried in the cells of your body.

May you have the courage to honor
your own first language, the music of those
whose lives inhabit your own.
May you tell the truth and do no harm.

May you dare in your own words to touch
the broken heart of the world.
May your passion for peace and justice be wise:
remember—No one can argue with story.

May you study your craft as you would study
a new friend or a long time, much loved lover.
And all the while, lost though you may be in the forest,
drop your own words on the path like pebbles

and write your way home.

—P.S.

NOTES

Introduction

1. "A Postcolonial Tale," *The Woman Who Fell from the Sky* (New York: W.W. Norton, 1994), p. 7.
2. Rabia al 'Adawiyya, "It Works," *Love Poems from God: Twelve Sacred Voices from the East and West,* tr. Daniel Ladinsky (New York: Penguin Compass, 2002), p. 12.
3. 1 Corinthians 13:12, King James Version.

Chapter 1

1. Stephen Nachmanovitch, *Free Play: Improvisation in Life and Art* (New York: Tarcher, 1991).
2. Stanley Moss, "Psalm," *New and Selected Poems 2006* (New York: Seven Stories Press, 2006), p. 22.
3. Emily Dickinson, *The Poems of Emily Dickinson*, ed. R.W. Franklin (Cambridge, MA: Belknap Press of Harvard University Press, 1998), p. 33.
4. Ira Progoff, *At a Journal Workshop* (New York: Dialogue House Library, 1975).
5. Louise Erdrich, *The Last Report on the Miracles at Little No Horse* (New York: Perennial, Harper Collins, 2001), p. 227.
6. Catherine Keller, *The Face of the Deep: A Theology of Becoming* (London: Routledge, 2003). Also Genesis 1:2.

7. Emily Dickinson, *The Poems of Emily Dickinson,* #598, p. 269.
8. Meister Eckhart, *Meister Eckhart's Sermons,* Sermon IV, "True Hearing," translated into English by Claud Field, Christian Classics Ethereal Library, 1909.
9. Exodus 33: 18–23, Revised Standard Version.
10. Anonymous (14th c. English), *The Cloud of Unknowing,* Christian Classics Ethereal Library.

Chapter 2

1. Alfred Tennyson, "The Higher Pantheism," *The Holy Grail and Other Poems* (London: Strahan, 1870).
2. Pat Schneider, *Wake Up Laughing: A Spiritual Autobiography* (Amherst, MA: Amherst Writers & Artists Press, 1997).
3. Matthew 6:6, Revised Standard Version.
4. Stanley Moss, "The Bathers," *New and Selected Poems 2006* (New York: Seven Stories Press, 2006), p. 44.
5. Yorifumi Yaguchi, "The One I Wanted to Call," from *The Banquet in Heaven* (Tokyo: Eihosha Press, 1994). English translation by the author. Nancy Lee, who has taught for many years in China and Japan, gave me this information on the word *kamisama*: "A look at the definition of Shintoism, Japan's national religion, explains the presence of many shrines in Japan, where people venerate many objects in nature and great ancestors. I remember a young Japanese Christian woman, studying here, explaining to a group of American young people that in her home in Japan there were two shrines: one to the family's ancestors and one to Buddha. While Buddha is not technically considered a god, images of him are everywhere and people pray to him. Thus the word *kami* is plural, *gods*. And thus the search by Christians for a word for the one true God, as Yaguchi's poem illustrates, can be difficult."
6. Nepo, "God's Wounds," *Essential Sufism*, ed. James Fadiman and Robert Frager (San Francisco: HarperSanFrancisco, 1997), pp. 207–208.
7. Mary Oliver, "Yes! No!" *Owls and Other Fantasies; Poems and Essays* (Boston: Beacon Press, 2003), p. 27. Writing about our relationship to the natural world, Oliver says this: "To pay attention, this is our endless and proper work." I hold that it is the heart, also, of spiritual practice, whatever form that practice may take.

Chapter 3

1. For a study of "Freewriting," see Peter Elbow's books, Oxford University Press.
2. Christopher Fry, *A Sleep of Prisoners* (New York: Oxford University Press, 1951).
3. Emily Dickinson's family embraced the fundamentalist revival movement that was current in her lifetime and in the Congregational Church across the street from the Dickinson home, where they worshipped. Emily was one of only two students at Mount Holyoke Female Seminary who refused to publicly confess Jesus as her savior, after which her name was listed as one to whom they had failed to give hope of salvation. In the revivalist theology of Dickinson's day, as in fundamentalist Christian belief today, the word "ransom" is common. It appears in hymns and in sermons. It means that Jesus "ransoms," or pays, or "atones" with his blood for sin, and "buys" the salvation of the sinner. The word "ransom" is often used interchangeably with "salvation." Theologically this doctrine is called the "substitutionary doctrine of atonement," in which God accepts the blood of His only begotten Son as substitute for the sinner's punishment. Sinners who accept Jesus, in this view, are "ransomed" by his sacrifice.

   This makes Dickinson's statement appear to be heretical. Rather than the fires of hell, she says, "Silence is all we dread," and "There's ransom [salvation] in a voice." Yet according to Dickinson scholar Dorothy Huff Oberhaus, "whatever else one may say about Emily Dickinson, her données, her forms, and many of her most arresting tropes place her within the tradition of Christian devotion." Oberhaus's revolutionary and brilliant work makes clear that Dickinson redefined the theology of her parents and her time, and that she understood her own writing to be her spiritual practice. (Dorothy Oberhaus, *Emily Dickinson's Fascicles: Method and Meaning* [University Park: Pennsylvania State University Press, 1951], p. 3).
4. Ecclesiastes 3:1, King James Version.
5. Calvin Luther Martin, *The Way of the Human Being* (New Haven, CT: Yale University Press, 1999). (*Note*: while the name "Eskimo" was preferred among the people with whom Martin lived, it is in other places now considered a derogatory term, and "Inuit" is preferred.)

6. Theresa Vincent's collection of poems is unpublished at the time of this printing.
7. This belief is still held in some conservative Christian circles. It is clearly stated in the traditional American gospel song, "Ain't Gonna Let Nobody Turn Me 'Round." Many versions of the song exist, performed by Joan Baez, Rachel Tucker, the Freedom Singers, and Sweet Honey in the Rock. The version I refer to is titled "Freedom Road," sung by the Black Boys of Alabama, including this verse: "God knows I got good religion/ I got it when I was young./ I'm sanctified and filled with the Holy Ghost,/ The devil can't do me no harm."
8. Pat Schneider, *Writing Alone and with Others* (New York: Oxford University Press, 2003).
9. Madeleine L'Engle, *A Circle of Quiet* (New York: Farrar, Straus and Giroux, 1972).
10. www.christianarmor.net/GoingHigherSomeday.htm.
11. Emily Dickinson, *The Poems of Emily Dickinson,* #39, p. 33.
12. Mary Oliver, "The Journey," *New and Selected Poems* (Boston: Beacon Press, 1992), p. 114.
13. Ben Shahn, *The Shape of Content* (Cambridge, MA: Harvard University Press, 1957).
14. Janet Burroway, *Writing Fiction: A Guide to Narrative Craft* (New York: Harper Collins, 1987).

Chapter 4

1. Genevieve E. Chandler and Pat Schneider, "Creation and Response: Wellspring to Evaluation," in *The Psychology of Creative Writing,* ed. Scott Barry Kaufman and James C. Kaufman (New York: Cambridge University Press, 2009), pp. 316–331.
2. Peter Elbow is the informal "dean" of the Writing Process Movement, a revolution in the teaching of creative writing in the United States that emerged in the 1970s as a groundswell of dissatisfaction with traditional methods of teaching writing. Its basic assumptions were first articulated by Dorothea Brand in her 1934 classic book, *Becoming a Writer,* and by Brenda Ueland in *If You Want to Write,* 1938. Peter Elbow's *Writing without Teachers,* 1973, and his continuing lifetime of publishing has developed the

theoretical foundations and sustained the work of both writers and teachers of writing like myself.

3. Hans Christian Andersen, "The Tinder Box," in *The Classic Fairy Tales,* ed. Iona and Peter Opie (New York: Oxford University Press, 1974).

4. Jan Haag, whom I quoted earlier, also helped me here. I had written, "the soul wanders, homeless, until it can take up residence in the new self, no longer defined by the old pain." Jan responded, "So true—but to grow, to move forward, we have to let ourselves burn to ash and then see what rises from those ashes—otherwise, we are like hollowed out trees barely standing after the fire has eaten their insides clean away—like lava that takes the shape of trees it has consumed. What remains or rises anew still contains our essence; we are still there but transformed." And that is what I do come to, writing on.

5. Joy Ladin, *Transmigration: Poems* (Riverdale, NY: Sheep Meadow Press, 2009).

6. Frances Balter, *Zeal* (Amherst, MA: Amherst Writers & Artists Press, 2010), pp. 20, 40.

Chapter 5

1. Mother Teresa, *Come Be My Light: The Private Writings of the "Saint of Calcutta,"* ed. B. Kolodiejchuck (New York: Doubleday, 2007), p. 214.

2. *New York Times*, January 14, 2007.

3. "Ray Bradbury," interview by Frank Filosa. In *On Being a Writer,* ed. Bill Strickland (Cincinnati: Writer's Digest Books, 1989), pp. 52–57.

4. Philip Levine, *Don't Ask* (Ann Arbor: University of Michigan Press, 1928), pp. 71–72.

5. D. H. Lawrence, "Benjamin Franklin," in *Studies in Classic American Literature* (New York: Thomas Seltzer, 1923), p. 13.

6. Sy Safransky, "Bitter Medicine," *Four in the Morning* (Chapel Hill, NC: Sun Publishing, 1993), p. 1.

7. Psalm 139:7–12, King James Version.

8. Pat Conroy, *Beach Music* (New York: Doubleday Dell, 1995), p. 208.

9. Margaret Robison, *The Naked Bear* (Amherst, MA: Lynx House Press/Panache Books, 1977).

10. Deborah Gerlach Klaus, "Sins of the Flesh," *Hayden's Ferry Review* 38 (Spring/Summer 2006). Virginia G. Piper Center for Creative Writing, Arizona State University, Tempe, Arizona.

11. John McGahern, "A Private World." DVD of McGahern reading from *Memoir* at the Town Hall Theatre, Galway, on September 22, 2005. A Hummingbird/Harvest Films Production for RTÉ.

12. John Gardner, *On Becoming a Novelist* (New York: Harper & Row, 1983), pp. 5, 17, 39, 81, 84, 115–129.

13. Pat Schneider, *Wake Up Laughing*.

14. Hans Christian Andersen, "The Tinder Box."

15. Matthew 6: 23, Revised Standard Version.

16. There is a fascinating exploration of Dante's vision of hell and its profound effect on historical Christian theology in Laurel Schneider, "When Hell Freezes Over," chapter 7 of *Beyond Monotheism: A Theology of Multiplicity* (New York: Routledge, 2008).

17. W. H. Auden, "In Memory of W. B. Yeats," "*W. H. Auden*" (New York: The Modern Library, Random House, 1958), p. 54.

Chapter 6

1. The reference in the second stanza is to Jacob, the Jabbok is the river where he stopped to sleep, and the ladder is "Jacob's Ladder." Published in *Another River* and read by Garrison Keillor on National Public Radio's *The Writer's Almanac*.

2. Madison Smartt Bell, *New York Times*, January 17, 2010.

3. John A.T. Robinson, *Redating the New Testament* (Philadelphia: Westminster Press, 1976).

4. Oliver Wendell Holmes, *The Deacon's Masterpiece or the Wonderful One-Hoss-Shay: A Logical Story* (New York: Houghton Mifflin, 1858).

5. http://dharma.ncf.ca/introduction/precepts/precept-1.html (accessed June 4, 2012).

Chapter 7

1. T. S. Eliot, *The Sacred Wood: Essays on Poetry and Criticism* (London: Methuen, 1920).

2. William Wordsworth, with Samuel Taylor Coleridge, helped to launch the Romantic Age in English literature with the 1798 joint publication, *Lyrical Ballads*.

3. In the 1950s the brave new world of Randall Jarrell's and Lionel Trilling's "New Criticism" was dismantling Romanticism. Ezra

Pound introduced the bodhisattvas of Buddhist poetry to theoretical and critical thinking and stressed "Imagism," by which he meant images of "real things." According to Allen Ginsberg, Pound "was calling for direct perception, direct contact without intervening conceptualization, a clear seeing attentiveness…one of the marks of Zen masters, as in their practice of gardening, tea ceremony, flower arranging, or archery." William Carlos Williams's "Modernist" dictum, "No ideas but in things," was a welcome corrective to those who were tired of the Romantics.

It remained for the next generation, the "Postmodernists," to shatter a too-convenient access to "the real." They taught that there is no such thing as "objectivity." Norman Mailer has said, "We observe the observer." (Mailer quoted by Lee Siegel, "Maestro of the Human Ego," *New York Times Book Review,* January 21, 2007.)

4. Allen Ginsberg and Bill Morgan, *Deliberate Prose: Selected Essays 1952–1995* (New York: HarperCollins, 2000), p. 264

5. Variously attributed to Picasso, Mark Twain, and others.

6. For more on this subject, see the essay by Hayden White in the collection *On Narrative* (W. J. Thomas Mitchell, ed. [Chicago: University of Chicago Press, 1981]). The classic narrative form taught in mid-nineteenth-century classrooms in America may be more born of the Renaissance and Enlightenment, born with "perspective," and carried by the colonial drive forward (always forward) into so-called progress.

Chapter 8

1. Janet Elsea, *First Impression Best Impression: Learn the Secret of Making a Lasting Impression in the Four Minutes that Can Make or Break You* (New York: Simon and Schuster, 1984).

Chapter 9

1. Antonio Machado, "Last night, as I lay sleeping," *Times Alone: Selected Poems of Antonio Machado,* tr. Robert Bly (Middletown, CT: Wesleyan University Press, 1983), pp. 42–43.

Chapter 10

1. Pat Schneider, *Writing Alone and with Others*. For more on the Amherst Writers & Artists (AWA) method, trainings in workshop leadership, and AWA workshops and retreats, visit www.am herstwriters.com and www.patschneider.com.
2. Florentine Films DVD, companion to *Writing Alone and with Others,* contains *Tell Me Something I Can't Forget,* the international prize-winning film of Pat Schneider's workshop for low-income women, as well as interviews with Pat Schneider and AWA workshop leaders. Available from www.amherstwriters.com.

Chapter 11

1. Our four children are: Rebecca Schneider, who at the time of this writing is completing her second term as Chair, Department of Theatre Arts and Performance Studies at Brown University. Her latest book is *Performing Remains* (Routledge); Laurel Schneider, who has just accepted a position as Professor of Religious Studies at Vanderbilt University and whose latest book is *Beyond Mono-theism: A Theology of Multiplicity* (Routledge); Paul Schneider, whose fifth book from Henry Holt, a history of the Mississippi River titled *Old Man River,* will be released in fall 2013; and Bethany Schneider, who is a professor of English at Bryn Mawr. Her first novel, *The River of No Return,* will be released in the spring by Penguin/Dutton under the pseudonym Bee Ridgway.
2. "I am distressed for you, my brother Jonathan; very pleasant have you been to me; your love to me was extraordinary, surpassing the love of women." (2 Samuel 1:26, English Standard Version)
3. T. S. Eliot, "The Hollow Men," *The Complete Poems and Plays 1909–1950* (New York: Harcourt, Brace, 1930), p. 58.
4. For more information on Amherst Writers & Artists, visit www.amherstwriters.com.
5. Muriel Rukeyser, "Käthe Kollwitz," part 3, lines 25–26, written in 1968, *The Collected Poems of Muriel Rukeyser,* ed. Janet E. Kaufman and Anne F. Herzog (Pittsburgh, PA: University of Pittsburgh Press, 2005).
6. Philip Levine, "The Simple Truth," *The Simple Truth: Poems* (New York: Random House, 1994).

7. For more on this topic see *Opening Up: The Healing Power of Expressing Emotions* by James W. Pennebaker, published by the Guilford Press (New York, 1990) and *Writing and Healing: Toward an Informed Practice* by Charles Anderson and Marian MacCurdy, published by the National Council of Teachers of English (Urbana, IL, 2000).

8. Peter Elbow writes in "What's Good about Writing," *Vernacular Eloquence: What Speech Can Bring to Writing* (New York: Oxford University Press, 2012): "This potentiality for resisting the culture shows itself vividly in literature. Consider people like Walt Whitman, Emily Dickinson, e e cummings, Virginia Woolf, James Joyce, Mallarme, 'concrete' poets, and L=A=N=G=U=A=G=E poets. (See Roy Harris on French writers exploiting spatial potentialities in writing that are unavailable in oral language.) They were all drenched in their cultures, but they used writing to push back against expectations and linguistic conventions. This 'cult of originality' in writing might be peculiar to our culture; some even call it decadent or dead-end. Yet it reveals a *potentiality* in writing that is there to be tapped."

9. Fred Alan Wolf, *The Dreaming Universe: A Mind-Expanding Journey into the Realm Where Psyche and Physics Meet* (New York: Simon and Schuster, 1994).

10. Mohandas Gandhi, no contemporaneous citations. Widespread attribution to Gandhi begins in post-1990 inspirational books.

Chapter 12

1. For more on the importance and function of private writing, see Peter Elbow, "In Defense of Private Writing: Consequences for Theory and Research," *Everyone Can Write: Essays Toward a Hopeful Theory of Writing and Teaching Writing* (New York: Oxford University Press, 2000).

2. May Swenson, "Question," *Nature Poems Old and New* (New York: Houghton Mifflin, 1994), p. 45.

3. Rebecca Schneider, *The Explicit Body in Performance* (New York: Routledge, 1997).

4. Sharon Olds, "I Go Back to May, 1937," *The Gold Cell* (New York: Knopf, 1987).

Chapter 13

1. Quoted in Rachel Donadio, "The Closest Reader," *New York Times Sunday Book Review*, December 10, 2006.
2. Mary Oliver, "Starlings in Winter," *Owls and Other Fantasies: Poems and Essays* (Boston: Beacon Press, 2003).
3. Quoted in Donadio, "The Closest Reader."
4. Edna St. Vincent Millay, *Mine the Harvest (Poems)*, Part X (New York: Harper's, 1954).
5. Rainer Maria Rilke, *Letters to a Young Poet* (New York: Random House, 1984), p. 34.

Chapter 14

1. Giovanni *Vignale, The Beautiful Invisible: Creativity, Imagination, and Theoretical Physics* (Oxford: Oxford University Press, 2011), p. 50.
2. Jane Kenyon, *A Hundred White Daffodils: Essays, Interviews, the Akhmatova Translations, Newspaper Columns, and One Poem* (Saint Paul, MN: Graywolf Press, 1999), p. 165. Kenyon, like many other writers, describes an experience of being "given" a poem. She calls the giver, "The muse, the Holy Ghost." I have not had that experience, if what she means is a kind of dictation in which she feels herself to be only the scribe—an experience some writers claim. I suspect from the wider context of her work that she does not mean that, however. Rather, I think she means the experience I, too, have had of a poem: "...this just fell out" (p. 171).
3. Laurel Schneider, *Beyond Monotheism: A Theology of Multiplicity* (New York: Routledge, 2008).
4. William Shakespeare, *King Lear*, Act V, Scene 1.
5. John Gardner, *On Becoming a Novelist* (New York: Harper and Row, 1983).
6. Lawrence M. Krauss, *A Universe from Nothing: Why There Is Something Rather than Nothing* (New York: Free Press, 2012).
7. Fred Alan Wolf, *The Dreaming Universe*.
8. Michael Talbot, *The Holographic Universe* (New York: HarperCollins, 1991).
9. Michael Largo, *God's Lunatics: Lost Souls, False Prophets, Martyred Saints, Murderous Cults, Demonic Nuns, and Other Victims of*

Man's Eternal Search for the Divine (New York: HarperCollins, 2010).
10. John 4, Revised Standard Version.
11. Luke 8, Revised Standard Version.
12. Mark 7, Revised Standard Version.
13. Rabindranath Tagore, *Gitanjali* (Radford, VA: A & D Publishing, 2008).

Chapter 15

1. Joy Harjo, "A Postcolonial Tale," *The Woman Who Fell from the Sky* (New York: W. W. Norton, 1944), p. 7.
2. Martin Luther King Jr., "Facing the Challenge of a New Age," address delivered at the First Annual Institute on Nonviolence and Social Change, Montgomery, Alabama, December 3, 1956.
3. Novelist, workshop leader, and good friend, Lane Goddard, wrote this to me in a note.

Chapter 16

1. Vignale, *The Beautiful Invisible*, pp. 14–15.
2. Anne Dellenbaugh wrote this in response to my request for the story in her own words.
3. Maureen Buchanan Jones is at the time of this writing the executive director of Amherst Writers & Artists. Poet and novelist, she is author of young adult novels and of *Blessed Are the Menial Chores*, her first collection of poems, published by Amherst Writers & Artists Press, 2012. I heard her speak about this experience and asked her to write it for this book.
4. Laurel C. Schneider, *Beyond Monotheism*, pp. 167–168 and 207.
5. Catherine Keller, *From a Broken Web: Separation, Sexism, and Self* (Boston: Beacon Press, 1988), p. 5.
6. Czeslaw Milosz, "Ars Poetica," tr. Czeslaw Milosz and Lillian Vallee, http://info-poland.buffalo.edu/classroom/milosz/ars.html.
7. Emilie M. Townes, "Walking on the Rim Bones of Nothingness: Scholarship and Activism," *Journal of the American Academy of Religion* 77.1 (2009): 1–15.
8. Alfred Tennyson, "The Higher Pantheism," *The Holy Grail and Other Poems* (London: Strahan, 1870).

9. Alfred Tennyson, "Ulysses," *A Victorian Anthology, 1837–1895* (Cambridge: Riverside Press, 1895).

Chapter 17

1. Christopher Fry, "Comedy," a short essay included in a book titled *The American Realist Playwrights*, pages 68–70. I have not been able to locate a copy of this book or information about it. Northrup Frye's essay titled "The Structure of Comedy" follows on pages 70–80.
2. W. H. Auden, "In Memory of W. B. Yeats," *Selected Poems* (New York: Random House/Vintage, 2007), p. 88.
3. Elizabeth O'Connor has written a number of books about the practices of community life and pioneering missions in the inner city as practiced in the Church of the Saviour and the Potter's House, a remarkable faith community in Washington, DC. Her books include *Journey Inward, Journey Outward.*

NOTES FOR TEACHERS,

WORKSHOP/RETREAT/GROUP LEADERS,

COUNSELORS, AND

SPIRITUAL DIRECTORS

This is not a "How To" book. Rather, it is an invitation to a reader to look over my shoulder as I do the thing itself: write as a spiritual practice. In that way I hope it can act as a guide for individual writers, an example of using one's own life story to trace the presence of mystery and the outlines of grace. However, I would like it to be useful also to those who teach and lead classes, workshops, or writing groups, or are counselors and spiritual directors.

Guidelines on how to create and maintain a healthy writing group, workshop, or class, along with suggested prompts for writing, are covered fully in my earlier book, *Writing Alone and with Others* (New York: Oxford University Press, 2003) and the book's companion DVD that includes the international prize-winning film about my work across lines of class and difference, *Tell Me Something I Can't Forget*, (Florentine Films/ Hott Productions).

Concerning writing as a spiritual practice, here are a few suggestions that may be helpful:

1. Writing as a spiritual practice is, in my definition, simply a desire on the part of the writer to explore his or her own life experience and imagination as a lens through which to glimpse, and sometimes even to be deeply touched by, mystery. It is my experience that we are held in personal, loving, indescribable attention by a presence we have, as humans, given many names. Whether we

call that presence "God" or some other name, everything we have ever seen or heard, experienced or dreamed, can be found through writing to be an avenue to healing and a doorway to revelation. When we write about our own lived experience, moments come of reflection, of wonder, of grief, of pain, of praise, of petition, of ecstasy. But if we write truly, those come not by manipulation or demand, but as the gift of our honesty, our humility, and our search. That means writing will not always feel like "a spiritual practice." But if we don't maintain the practice (the intention, the desire), gifted moments are much less likely to arrive.

2. In encouraging others to write as a spiritual practice, do not limit your suggestions and prompts to subjects or images that are closely identified with "the spiritual." That which works as a symbol for divinity to one person will likely distance another. Even if your group is a fairly homogeneous collection of people within one religious tradition, I have found it best not to use traditional devotional images (candles, lotus blossoms, rosaries, etc.) unless they are grouped with images from differing traditions used as a prompt. Our religious origins may be very different from the tradition or lack of tradition that we currently embrace.

3. Any prompt can trigger in the writer a sense of mystery, if the writer has an intention or a desire in that direction. Any of the 150 prompts in *Writing Alone and with Others* can be useful for a group centered on writing as a spiritual practice. An old, much-used wooden spoon will feel like love to one writer remembering a good grandmother, while another will remember being beaten with a wooden spoon. Either memory can lead a writer to reflect on love or its absence. Choose or create prompts that welcome humor as well as serious reflection, imagination as well as memoir.

4. Try to surprise your writers with your prompt. Some of your people may have been thinking about what they want to write on their way to the meeting. I find it distracting and unhelpful, therefore, to begin a session with a meditation or any other stimulation. As soon as the session begins, remind the group that your prompt is offered for use only if there is not something more important that they want to write about. The surprise of the prompt is important in stirring the unconscious to find a significant visual image. Keep your

prompt simple, without discussion or analysis. One clear, simple prompt like a group of objects, a collection of photographs, or a provocative line of poetry or prose, given gently, will send your writers off into complex and tangled imagery of their own.

5. Help your writers to understand that we often begin and abandon that beginning several times before we get our true subject. Encourage them to write at first as if they are painters with words, describing whatever their mind "sees," and be ready to abandon that as soon as something else appears in their mind's eye. This may happen several times before they begin to forget that they are writing and actually experience action or image as they write. The deep writing state is close to a dream state, and that is where we want to be in first-draft writing. Encourage them to experiment with a variety of forms: fiction, poetry, etc.

6. Never require that a writer come to some "spiritual" conclusion at the end of writing time. Even subtle pressure from a leader or from other participants can cause a writer to accept premature conclusions about what they have uncovered in their writing. Encourage them to see an unfinished piece or a partial memory as part of a process, the meanings of which they may not discern until some later time.

7. Fiercely protect the privacy of your writers. Do not allow group members to ask questions about what has just been written, or to refer to characters in the writing as the writer him- or herself. Train them to use "the narrator," and to treat everything as fiction, even when they know it is not. See guidelines in *Writing Alone and with Others* for more ways to keep your group healthy.

8. Writing as a spiritual practice should be simply writing, exploring our own story and our own questions. The spiritual practice part is simply being open to the presence of mystery in our practice. In a dependable, neutral setting, with some good comfort snack food and drink on the side, our own personal images of past experience and present questioning will be most likely to find expression in our writing as a spiritual presence.

9. Make room for playful and courageous experimentation, including a variety of forms: fiction, poetry, monologue, dialogue, as well as memoir. (See page 253 on the value of using a "fictional" voice.) Encourage your writers to be free of expectations for what

will come as they write. I find the analogy of making a quilt help-ful. Each writing piece is just one part of a much larger pattern that will someday be our journal, or our book of collected pieces. Let each quilt block have its own integrity, tell its own story. An-other block will tell another part of the story. Things will be whole, our telling will be fair, only when all of the pieces are together. Rilke says, "Be patient with all that is resolved in your heart." Allow yourself to write, one block, one story, one poem, one frag-ment, at a time.

10. If all else fails, contact me. Perhaps we can find solutions together.

Pat Schneider
Amherst, Massachusetts
January, 2013

ACKNOWLEDGMENTS

Behind this book is another book on which it rests. This book takes the method described in my first Oxford book, *Writing Alone and with Others,* uses its prompts to jump-start writing, heeds its counsel in times of insecurity or fear, and on that foundation, explores writing as a spiritual practice. The learning and the tools I have gained from my "village," my community of writers, my own circle of *"those who help my being,"* are what made both books possible.

Over the past thirty-two years, thousands of writers have used my workshop method as described in *Writing Alone and with Others,* and in the film that is a companion DVD to the book. We have used it in classrooms, living rooms, prisons, shelters, hospitals, and countless other venues across America and in Ireland, Canada, Malawi, Liberia, the border of Kenya and Somalia, India, Scotland, Mexico, and France. Although it has been my task to write it onto pages, the method and the practice grew among us.

In addition to my workshops for the general population, for fifteen years I led a workshop in a housing project in Chicopee, Massachusetts, and also wrote with writers in a jail and in a workshop for pregnant and mothering teens. Among the co-creators of the Amherst Writers & Artists (AWA) workshop method in its outreach form, for empowerment and/or healing across class and other difference, are the following: Julie Benard, Mary Ann Blanchard, Karen Buchinsky, Anthia Elliot, Evelyn Fitzpatrick, Lynn Goodspeed, Diane Mercier, Teresa Pfeifer, Corinna Spenard, Robin Therrien, Enid Santiago Welch, Dorothy Zimmek, Deb Burwell, Sarah Browning, Diane Gary, Larry Hott, Cindy Davenport, and Peter Schneider. A few among many who have taken our work into new areas are Máire O'Donohoe in Ireland; Celia Jeffries, Bisi Iderabdulla and Mary Tuchscherer in Africa; Patricia Lee Lewis in Mexico, Scotland, and other retreat sites; Sue Reynolds and James Dewar in Canada; Aaron Zimmerman among the homeless in New York City; Lawrence Spann, Janice Haag, and John Crandall in Sacramento, where medical professionals, caretakers, and those with life-threatening illness write together; Carolyn Benson and Sara Weinberger with the incarcerated in Massachusetts. Profound gratitude to Maureen Buchanan Jones, Patricia Bender, and Kate Hymes, who took the helm of AWA when it listed, and righted it, and to Elise Rymer and Valerie Leff, whose faithful support has made all of this work with under-served writers by Amherst Writers and Artists possible.

Special Thanks To

Peter Elbow, whose work has changed writing and the teaching of writing forever, and for whose personal guidance and encouragement I am deeply grateful; Elda Rotor for accepting my first book at Oxford and Oxford editors Brendan O'Neill, Joellyn Ausanka, Rick Stinson, and Patterson Lamb for their patient help on the manuscript; David Hatcher and Marian Calabro for proofreading; and Connie Gabbert for the cover design that so beautifully says it all.

Writers Who Read and Responded to Parts or All of This Book in Manuscript

Mary Jo Balistreri, Carolyn Benson, Patricia Brown, Margie Bucheit, Karen Buchinsky, Margaret Bullitt-Jonas, Maggie Butler, Marian Calabro, Michael Childs, Portia Cornell, Cindy Davenport, Anne Dellenbaugh, Peter Elbow, Susan Flynn, Lane Goddard, Anita Greene, Marty Gwinn, Janis Haag, Madlynn Haber, Kate Hymes, Laurie Isenberg, Janice James, Aprille Janes, Terry Jenoure, Becky Jones, Maureen Buchanan Jones, Sharleen Kapp, Sarah Kavanagh, Cynthia and John Kennison, Dylan Klempner, Lynn Kimmel, Elaine Koerner, Nancy Lee, Valerie Leff, Cindy Littlefield, Joan Mallonee, Al Miller, Kate Murphy, Máire O'Donohoe, Bob Paquette, Carol Paul, Al Perry, Polly Peterson, Leslie Poyner, Peggy Reber, Kari Ridge, Nina Robertson, Elise Rymer, Jane Schneeloch, Lena Sclove, Sharon Senovich, Wendy Simpson, Ellie Skinner, Ellen Summers, George Teter, Robin Therrien, Marybeth Toomey, Georgann Turner, Theresa Vincent, Suzanne Webber, Scott Winger, Laura X, Yorifumi Yaguchi, Aaron Zimmerman.

People Who Allowed Me to Use Their Words or Their Stories

Anne Dellenbaugh, Máire O'Donohoe, Maureen Buchanan Jones, Theresa Vincent, and Wendy Simpson, whom I asked to tell their own stories in their own words; Susan Flynn, who asked me, "What's under that?" Joan Mallonee, who helped me to discover what was under that; Robin Therrien, Joy Policar, Leslie Poyner, Suzanne Webber, Máire O'Donohoe, Bob Paquette, Deborah Gerlach Klaus, Al Miller, and many others who gave me permission to name them on my pages; Lane Goddard, Janis Haag, Jane Schneeloch, and Becky Jones who read the entire manuscript more than once and saved me from myself countless times, and my brother, Sam, who before he died gave me permission to tell the truth.

Companions on the Way

Thanks to every person who has written with me or to me, responding to my words on pages while the ink is still wet, or in letters when the ink is dry and the book is in the world. You have been, and you still are, "*those who help my being.*" Special thanks to Maureen Buchanan

Jones for many late nights of healing talk; Jan Haag, journalist, poet, teacher who read this manuscript three times and still calls me "friend"; Sharleen Kapp for every Diet Dr. Pepper in every diner we could find; Evelyn May for knowing me longest and not giving up on me; Elizabeth Berryhill, Joan Mallonee, and Anne Dellenbaugh for holding my heart when it was broken; Florence Clark, Kate Hymes and Bisi Iderabdullah, all of whom have called me "sister," and Sapphire, Patricia Bell-Scott, and Patricia Romney who treated me as sister acr light gets in."

Finally, My Greatest Teachers

Lelah Ridgway Vought, my mother, who gave me life, poetry, Ozark fossils, and laughter; Elizabeth Berryhill, who mentored me and mothered me where my mother could not; Sharon Senovich, the sister I found in these pages; Sam Vought, our brother, my first best friend; Becca, Laurel, Paul, and Bethany, who ate my breakfasts, endured my "family conferences," sang with me my lullabies, forgave my worst mistakes, grew up into teachers and writers every one and gave me brilliant, tough editing; Sarah Schneider Kavana, and Natty Schneider, Ruthie May Therrien, and Samantha Klein, all of whom call me "Grandma" and will carry my best dreams into a new generation; and Peter Schneider, resident theologian, clarinetist, and poet, who has loved me longest and best. Peter, you have given me what poet Archibald MacLeish called "The greatest and richest good,/ My own life to live in. This you have given me/If giver could."

PERMISSIONS

POEMS BY PAT
SCHNEIDER APPEARING IN
THIS VOLUME

1. "Sometimes Writing," previously unpublished.
2. "Tonight, Words Are Turtles," previously unpublished.
3. "To Break Silence," *Olive Street Transfer* (Amherst: Amherst Writers & Artists Press, 1999), and *Another River* (Amherst: Amherst Writers & Artists Press, 2005).
4. "About, among Other Things, God," *Christianity and the Arts* 7.1 (2000), and *Olive Street Transfer*. Also *Another River*.
5. "Nursery Rhyme," previously unpublished.
6. "Personal Address," *Long Way Home* (Amherst: Amherst Writers & Artists Press, 1993), and *Another River*. Read by Garrison Keillor on Writer's Almanac.
7. "Imagine a Hallway in Childhood," *Long Way Home*.
8. "Instructions for the Journey," *Olive Street Transfer* and *Another River*.
9. "Perhaps," previously unpublished.
10. "This Is a River," *Minnesota Review*, n.s.17 (Fall 1981) (Corvallis: Oregon State University Press). Also *White River Junction* (Amherst: Amherst Writers & Artists Press, 1987) and *Another River*.
11. "Welcoming Angels," *Long Way Home* and *Another River*. Read by Garrison Keillor on *The Writer's Almanac*.
12. "To My Favorite Veterinarian on an Unhappy Morning," previously unpublished.

13. "Letting Go," *Long Way Home* and *Another River.*
14. "Your Boat, Your Words," *White River Junction,* and *Another River.*
15. "Mama," *Excursis Literary Arts Journal* (Knickerbocker Station, NY, 1996). Also *Olive Street Transfer* and *Another River.*
16. "What I Want to Say," *The Patience of Ordinary Things* (Amherst: Amherst Writers & Artists Press, 2003), and *Another River.*
17. "Braided Rug," *Crossing Paths: An Anthology of Poems by Women* (Richmond, MA: Mad River Press, 2002), *White River Junction,* and *Another River.*
18. "The Letter," previously unpublished.
19. "AfterMath," previously unpublished.
20. "The Undertaking" (excerpt from play) *Prize Plays* (Nashville, TN: Abingdon Press, 1961). Awarded first prize, national contest. Produced on national television and toured by theater companies on East and West coasts.
21. "Two Thousand Deaths," previously unpublished.
22. "When I Was Thirteen Years Old . . ." *Wake Up Laughing* (Negative Capability Press, 1997), reissued by Amherst Writers & Artists Press, 1977.
23. "This Flight," *Long Way Home* and *Another River.*
24. "Even Night . . ." previously unpublished.
25. "Going Home the Longest Way Around," *National Storytelling Journal* (Winter 1988) (Jonesborough, TN: NAPPS); also *Long Way Home* and *Another River.*
26. "Ending," *The Patience of Ordinary Things* and *Another River.*
27. "Hush," previously unpublished.
28. "Burning the Tobacco," previously unpublished.
29. "The Patience of Ordinary Things," *The Patience of Ordinary Things* and *Another River.*
30. "The Fish," *Cistercian Studies Quarterly* 35.3 (2000), and *Another River.*
31. "That One," previously unpublished.
32. "Confession," *Cistercian Studies Quarterly* 35.3 (2000), and *Another River.*
33. "Blessing for a Writer," previously unpublished.

INDEX